Praise for *I Don'...*

"Kim Korson must be stopped. M̶...... ..... than me."

—Jon Stewart

"I Don't Have a Happy Place is the book you'll beg your friends to read—for its pitch-perfect humor, scintillating wit, and refreshing depiction of life in all its extraordinary, and ordinary, absurdity. Kim Korson is certainly a new and exciting voice in nonfiction, unafraid to shout out loud the things you and I may only dare to think. I haven't laughed like this since David Sedaris."

—Julia Fierro, author of *Cutting Teeth*

"I love this book. It's like 95 percent cacao chocolate—bitter but delicious."

—A.J. Jacobs, *New York Times* bestselling author of *The Year of Living Biblically*

"In the razor-sharp, acerbic *I Don't Have a Happy Place*, Kim Korson—think: Jewish, female, Canadian David Sedaris—recounts her adventures as a true malcontent."

—Miranda Beverly-Whittemore, *New York Times* bestselling author of *Bittersweet*

"Makeup-wearing dads, squirrel attacks, death, Phil Donahue—there's something for everybody in Kim Korson's great new book. And if not having a happy place is what it takes to make writing so hilarious, smart, and honest, I selfishly hope Kim remains miserable within reason for many years to come."

—Dave Hill, author of *Tasteful Nudes*

"Korson's preoccupations—checking crime blotters for neighborhood stats, being certain that her first child would come out crazy, avoiding chitchat at parties—may keep her firmly in her cranky cave but will strike a funny bone in readers."

—*Publishers Weekly*

I Don't Have a Happy Place

Happy Place

••• *Cheerful Stories of Despondency and Gloom* •••

KIM KORSON

GALLERY BOOKS

NEW YORK   LONDON   TORONTO   SYDNEY   NEW DELHI

Gallery Books
An Imprint of Simon & Schuster, Inc.
1230 Avenue of the Americas
New York, NY 10020

First Gallery Books trade paperback edition April 2015

GALLERY BOOKS and colophon are registered trademarks
of Simon & Schuster, Inc.

For information about special discounts for bulk purchases,
please contact Simon & Schuster Special Sales at 1-866-506-1949
or business@simonandschuster.com.

The Simon & Schuster Speakers Bureau can bring authors
to your live event. For more information or to book an event,
contact the Simon & Schuster Speakers Bureau at 1-866-248-3049
or visit our website at www.simonspeakers.com.

Interior design by Jaime Putorti

Manufactured in the United States of America

10 9 8 7 6 5 4 3 2 1

Library of Congress Cataloging-in-Publication Data

Korson, Kim.
  I don't have a happy place : cheerful stories of despondency and gloom / Kim Korson.
    pages cm
  1. Korson, Kim. I. Title.
  CT275.K8345A3 2014
  920—dc23

                        2014027606

ISBN 978-1-4767-4026-3
ISBN 978-1-4767-4031-7 (ebook)

for rich and ella and oscar

. . . what i've left behind looks trifling.
what's ahead looks black.

—Stephen Schwartz, *Pippin*

Author's Note

this is how i remember it.

Paulette

......

Samantha Narvey had all the good Barbies. They showcased the latest sold-separately fashions, traveled in their Country Camper (with vinyl pop-out tent), and sunned their twisty bodies, naked, on floating orange chairs in the Pool Party pool. Her dolls never lost their plastic heels or tall brown boots or mini hangers. Samantha Narvey knew how to take care of her things—and Samantha Narvey had a lot of things. Like a yellow Sit 'n Spin and a playground for her Weebles; a garden-themed bedroom, with grass green shag carpeting and painted flowers growing up the walls; a bathroom with two sinks in it. She also had a hyperactive brother who got blamed for everything and a greyhound puppy named Gucci. If Samantha Narvey had to use the bathroom, she'd say she had to *make* in this hushed voice that grown-ups seemed to be crazy about. Her well-heeled grandparents spoke with elegant accents, like Count Chocula, and traveled overseas regularly, returning home with offerings of burgundy velvet culottes or sectioned chocolate orange slices. Samantha was darling and poised. When we took ballet together, she didn't look dumb in her elephant headdress, nor did she take the wrong turn during the recital and end up in that line of gazelles. Samantha Narvey was only five years old, and yet she had it all. And just in case the scales weren't completely tipped in her favor, just in case she didn't already have every single thing known to man, in the summer of 1973 it was her babysitter, not mine, who drowned in front of our eyes. I wondered what more the world could bestow upon her.

It was early July, and my family, along with my parents' best friends, the Narveys, were off to the Laurentians, a lake and mountain region an hour away from our home in Montreal. I was gung ho to leave the city—even at five years old I knew it never fit me the way it did others. If Canada was America's pleas-ant yet wishy-washy cardigan-wearing aunt, then Montreal was the aunt's annoying daughter—the one who returned from a summer abroad kissing everyone on both cheeks, wearing a fou-lard, and answering only to the name Sylvie.

My parents had bought a small brown Monopoly house from a ripe old lady eager to wrap things up before she expired. Shortly after the deal was done, the sexy A-frame next door went on the market and the Narveys snatched it. Our house came assembled with the dead lady's old-fangled furniture. Marilyn Narvey hired a decorator to fill their three-storied triangular home with the latest everything. We weren't rich like the Narveys, just solid middle class. My father had a fledgling company in the *shmattah* business, manufacturing inexpensive and unfortunate-looking ladieswear. "What can I tell you?" he would say when my mother turned her nose up at the samples he brought home, "The ugly stuff sells." If we were a TV family, we'd be the token Jews who move in next door to the Cunninghams on *Happy Days*. We'd eat supper at six p.m. but the similarities would end there. Mr. C was a proud lodge member, owned a hardware store, and tucked his short-sleeved button-downs into his sensible pants. My father wore a turquoise Speedo with the words *Designed by Bill Blass* embroidered across his private parts.

"Macaroni and cheese for lunch," Marilyn Narvey said to their live-in housekeeper, Paulette, who traveled with them on weekends. Oversized tortoiseshell sunglasses held back Marilyn's strawberry blond wedge. She smoked a pack of menthols a day but smelled like Chloé perfume. Turning to Carmen, Paulette's sister and my keeper for the next few weeks, Marilyn added, "Popsicles if they behave."

There were ten homes on our side of the lake, with a slice of road connecting them. Our house was separated from the Narveys' by four old pines and a tangle of pricker bushes. We all had lake views out front and a mountainy forest out back. A forest I was convinced, and my brother confirmed, was home to Bigfoot.

"Do we *have* to go to hockey camp?" Neil Narvey said, whacking the hood of my father's car with his Evel Knievel Stunt & Crash vehicle.

My brother—let's call him Ace—was nine and a hockey fanatic. Neil preferred burning things. However, the camp was close to our house, so the grown-ups could wander through the small shops in town or drink wine, plus it would give the frogs Neil liked to mangle with his BB gun a deserved break. Samantha and I were only five, so we stayed back with the hired help.

"In the car, loser," Marv Narvey said to his son, pulling up in his brown Cadillac. He grinned at his own joke and his mustache straightened into a line. Marv Narvey was tall and reedy and could easily be mistaken for Burt Reynolds's Jewish cousin. He was bawdy and relished inappropriate jokes none of us appreciated, but he also had anger problems and could snap like a frozen Charleston Chew without warning, so we all pretended to laugh. In future years, he'd divorce Marilyn, pants me at a Passover seder in front of fifteen people, and die of lung cancer.

"We'll be back after lunch," Marilyn said.

"Don't worry, Mrs. Narvey," Paulette said, hands loose on Samantha's shoulders. "We'll be fine."

My mother didn't offer any parting words or instructions to Carmen, just waited in the idling car, air conditioning blasting, eyes straight ahead out the windshield. My father leaned on the driver's side, raking his hair with the oversized pick he kept in the back pocket of his ironed bell-bottoms. His hair was naturally curly but not curly enough for his liking, so he'd rake and fluff until it mushroomed to satisfaction. Only after it reached optimum height would he slide into the car and wave goodbye with the hand that supported his heavy turquoise ring. The Narvey Cadillac pulled out first, my father's car following. Their wheels crunched into the gravel, leaving a puff of dust hovering, like Pig-Pen's dirt.

"All right, girlies, what do you all want to do?" Paulette said as we walked over to the Narveys' (bigger) yard.

"Popsicles," I said, even though I'd just finished two bowls of Sugar Smacks. Paulette ignored my suggestion, as did Carmen, and I decided then and there that they were lousy at their jobs. I pined for our Swiss au pair from last year, the one I convinced that it was Canadian to put Coke on Fruity Pebbles instead of milk—that was the kind of administration I could get behind. Paulette suggested we go inside and play board games, which was code for *Let us watch the small color set in my room, Carmen, while the children entertain themselves.*

Samantha and I had on matching shorts, as we often did. Marv Narvey manufactured children's clothes and sometimes brought home doubles. I was wearing my number-one pair: the navy polyester knee-lengthers with fake frayed edges and a mother-of-pearl snap that was smooth to the touch and made a satisfying click every time I opened or closed it, which was incessantly. Sam wore the olive ones but didn't use all the functions the way I did.

We were shirtless that day, by choice, but still spent most of the time hugging our torsos so no one would see our *mosquito bites*, as Marv Narvey called them.

Sam wanted to play our hundredth game of Snakes and Ladders but I had other ideas. We had an arsenal of made-up games, and the best ones always happened on her turf due to the thriving toy industry she had going over there. At my house, we had to use our dumb imaginations, enlisting ceramic ashtrays as swimming pools and my jacks and checkers pieces as makeshift swimmers. Homespun games could really flourish with the proper trimmings, and those trimmings were at Samantha's place. I had secret plots to overthrow my mother so I could move into the A-frame and engulf myself in plastic.

Part of me believed my mother had outlawed the good toys so I'd want to be friends with Sam. It would be easier for everyone's weekends and holidays if I got along with her best friend's kid. The good news was, my relationship with my own sibling was relegated to noogies and mental torture, so Samantha Narvey was the sister I didn't have. Which meant not only could I use her stuff whenever I wanted, I could treat her any way I liked and she'd most probably still like me.

Of all the goods in the Narvey household, for my money dolls were tops. My mother was crabby about dolls—my mother was crabby, period—and they were not welcome at our place. All I wanted that morning was to get my hands on Baby Alive. Even with the doll packed up in the box on the shelf at Silverberg's toy store I could smell her plastic face, but I imagined that out in the sun it would be ambrosial. Lucky for me, Sam was a blue-chip sharer and had no problem splitting the tasks of stirring water into the powdery flakes or feeding the baby by jamming the Special Spoon into her O mouth, and she always let me spank the baby when she misbehaved.

However, as good at sharing as Samantha Narvey was, I had no interest in being part-time owner of Baby Alive. I wanted sole custody. Who divvied up a baby? Marilyn Narvey had a rule about not letting toys leave the premises, something about her house not being a library, but every now and again I would squirrel goods up my shirt or in my sleepover bag without anyone seeing. I spent hours in bed at night masterminding ways to kidnap Rub-a-Dub Dolly or smuggle out a sleeve of their Dixie Riddle Cups. Those kinds of rules just begged you to pinch stuff.

We packed a plastic sack with the tackle we'd need for our game, *Babysitters at the Lake.* As it turned out, somewhere between dice rolling and trying to find Baby Alive's diapers, our own real live babysitters had left the house and gone down to the water without telling us. I could see Carmen through the living room's floor-to-ceiling window, sunning herself on the dock with her feet swirling the water. Paulette, who couldn't swim, was loafing on an orange sheet she'd smoothed on the grass to face the sun. I wondered how long they'd been out there relaxing without a care in the world or a job to do, like rescuing us when the house suddenly burst into flames.

"There are eels in there, you know," I told Carmen when we got down to the water.

"Nuh uh," Sam said.

"Yuh huh. I saw them. You weren't even there."

She pretended not to care but I saw Carmen's eyes flick toward Paulette, who gave a quick shake of the head, which was code for *Don't listen to the brunette—she doesn't know what she's talking about.* Sam unloaded our supplies and Carmen continued her aggravating toe plinking, assuring me without words that she was from Trinidad and not bothered by our Canadian eels.

"There are only small fish in the lake," Samantha said, like she was a kindergarten teacher all of a sudden. "Rainbow trouts."

"How's about a nice Hawaiian Punch?" I said under my breath, but Carmen heard and pinched my leg—my mother's signature move, which she probably gave Carmen the A-OK to use on me whenever she felt like it.

"Should we move her to the shade?" said Sam, pointing at the trees. "I think it's too hot for babies."

My polyester shorts were trapping sweat and heat and I was sure one more minute in the incinerating sun would cause them to combust, but I'd already gone through the rigmarole of begging Sam to do our work close to the water so we could make the food and dunk the baby if she got dirty. I'd won that battle, and it had been vigorous work negotiating with Sam because Neil had reported that if you did not take proper care when drying Baby Alive, she would rot, with mold around her face and maggots in her belly.

"Plus we can dump the poo," I said, my final argument to seal the deal.

"*If* she makes."

The lake was small, about three miles long and half a mile across. It wasn't much of a good-time lake. No motors of any kind were permitted, which meant no waves or music or happy people whizzing by waving hello and pretend-toasting us with cans of Fresca. If boating was your leisure activity of choice, you cruised around in a pedal boat, which was basically a raft with bike pedals and didn't even go fast enough to catch a breeze. All the houses on the lake seemed to have one. Ours was white, shaded by a faded red vinyl canopy with teeny yellow-and-orange flowers on its underside and dangly white fringe around the perimeter.

My mother didn't do bathing suits, so my father took me out on the water, sometimes allowing me to drive. My legs were too short to pedal and steer at the same time, forcing me to pick one or the other. I always went with the steering option. I liked push-ing the silver tiller and being in charge of which direction to float, plus it was less taxing. Most of my boating hours, however, were spent splashing out the daddy longlegs that took up residence on board.

I heard Marv Narvey tell Carmen and Paulette they were allowed to take us out on the boat but we all had to wear those orange life jackets that were scratchy and rode up to your neck when you sat in the bucket chair, so we never went. Sometimes we put Sam's dolls in and pushed them out to sea, pulling back hard on the thick white rope that was tethered to the dock, tug-of-war style. We once thought Gucci might enjoy a trip on the high seas, but it turned out greyhounds didn't really like boating, and his sharp nails scrabbled on the fiberglass seats, causing him to fall overboard, and Marv Narvey had to jump in, fully clothed, to rescue him. Once the dog was safe on land, Marv kicked it in the stomach, even though it wasn't Gucci's idea to go for a ride. Gucci remained ashore after that.

"Let's feed her," Sam said, tying the bib around the baby's neck. "You fill up the bottle."

As she ripped open the packet of food, a puff of banana-scented dust took flight. I leaned over on my belly, stretching my arms toward the lake as the sun broiled the backs of my knees. We busied ourselves with the meal preparations and Carmen meandered off the dock, standing ankle deep in water. She pretended to be casual by resting her hands on her hips as the sand swallowed her big feet, but I knew she was really surveying for eels. The lake was cool and clean and clear to the bottom in the shallow end but still it irked me to wade around. I knew creatures took cover under there, most notably the Loch Ness Monster and the child catcher from *Chitty Chitty Bang Bang*.

"Girls, you hungry?" asked Paulette, who, moments before, was snoring, eyes covered by those buggish sun goggles the Narveys kept in a bowl next to the baby oil and sun reflectors. But we were too busy to stop for lunch. The baby took forever to eat. Her O mouth gave her a constant look of surprise but also didn't accommodate the amount of food we were determined to shovel in. Plus, we wanted her to make.

"I'm going in," said Carmen.

Marv Narvey had hired a lake guy to rope off a swimming area, making his section look like a summer camp. There were a series of ropes and buoys letting us know where the water got deep.

"Come, girls." Carmen slapped her hand on the water's surface, trying to entice us. We were pleased to have a babysitter who was seaworthy, but our allegiance was to Baby Alive. We weren't budging until she filled that diaper.

"Maybe she's too tired to make," said Sam. She held the baby by her foot, carrying her over to the grass where Paulette was now sitting up and watching her sister cool off.

"Why are you moving her?" I said. "The sound of the water will make her go."

"Nuh uh."

"How do you even know?" I said, preparing to fight.

"Because."

"Because why?"

"Because I'm the mother," Sam said. "And she's mine."

I wanted to push Samantha Narvey and her stupid baby deep into the water and watch them be swallowed up by eels, but I chewed my thumb instead. I waited for Paulette to "*girls*" us but she was no longer stretched out on the orange sheet. Carmen was lolling around in the deep end, doing some made-up stroke that involved stretching her neck so her head remained above water, like my nana. I made a mental note to tattle on our babysitters, since one was out having a leisure swim and the other had gone missing. Just then, Paulette emerged from the house wearing Marilyn Narvey's best bathing suit, a yellow towel hanging off her shoulder like she was Malibu Barbie. She walked into the shallow end.

"You can't swim," I said.

Paulette balled up her towel and threw it onto the dock. She dug into the sand to steady herself. "Not to worry, girlies. I'm just gonna stay right here in the shallow end."

I knew Paulette couldn't swim, didn't even bring a bathing suit with her on weekends, but she was a grown-up, so if she said she was allowed to stand in the shallow end, we believed her. Sam and I didn't want to be alone on the grass so we moved our operation one more time back to the dock. Paulette watched her sister treading water by the far rope—the one for intermediate and expert swimmers, if this had been a swim test at camp.

"She's making!" Sam said. "She's making!"

We hugged, we squealed, then ripped off the diaper to see if there was a poo. As we checked for evidence, another voice snapped the air.

"I'm swimming!" said Paulette. "Look at me! I'm swimming!"

The babysitter who was not fit for sea, the one who promised to stay ankle-deep, was now loose in the open water.

"I'm swimming!" Paulette kept insisting, but it no longer sounded like an achievement. Her voice was gurgly. Her head popped out of the water like a Whac-A-Mole at the fair. Carmen flutter-kicked herself over at high speed, trying to hold on to her sister while shouting, "Yes! Yes, you are!" But Carmen didn't sound proud or happy about it. Both their heads were dipping, bodies tugged under as if the Loch Ness Monster had them in its clutches. I covered Baby Alive's eyes so she didn't see the wrestling or the splashing. Or when Carmen came up alone.

There was one unruffled second, a tick of calm.

Then Carmen propelled herself out of the lake. Instead of using the dock to get out of the water, like you were supposed to, she hopped up and over the small rock wall that lined the length of the Narveys' property. Her mouth was open but no sound came out and Samantha moved closer to me, linking her fingers into the belt loop of my shorts. I squeezed the baby. Carmen ran in small circles, like Gucci chasing his tail, still not making a sound until she banged into the edge of the picnic table, flicking some sort of internal switch that caused strange animal howls to spew from the deepest part of her guts, weird cries that bounced around our ears and across the lake all the way to the neighbors' houses, the ones we always had to be quiet for.

Halfway up the steep stairs to the house, Carmen changed her mind, darting back toward the lake, along the dock where Samantha and I stood. Not noticing we were still there, she plunged back into the water, only to hoist herself right back out and up the stairs again to the house, leaving us alone by the water that had just swallowed up the babysitter. In her frenzy, Carmen kicked Baby Alive's spoon—the Special Spoon—into the lake and the Bitey Banana packet stuck to her ankle. This is when our parents returned, lazy with wine and hamburgers and laden with hockey gear. This is how they found us.

Marv Narvey and my father jumped into the lake with their jeans on, looking for the body. Samantha, scooped up by Marilyn, was now a rumpled heap on her mom's lap, facing away from the action, being rocked and shushed and *poor-baby*-ed. The boys stood behind me, watching our fathers attempt superhero status, and I heard Neil say "Cool," then Ace's hockey glove thwacking

Neil's stomach, which made Neil say "Whaaat?" I stood alone, gripping the baby, tingly with the thought that a body might pop out of the lake at any moment. I wondered where my mother was.

When our dads came up with nothing, no one spoke. They just holed Sam and me up in the house for the next few hours. We were supposed to be resting in her room but we escaped into her parents', pressing our faces against the wall of triangular windows at the tip-top of the A. There was a flashing blue light and a policeman asking questions of Carmen, who was wrapped in the sheet and shaking her head. I hoped the Mounties would come on horses wearing their tall hats, but it was just a regular old police cruiser like on *The Rockford Files*. I wondered if Marilyn Narvey knew that Paulette was dead in her very best swimsuit. It was orange.

"What do you think she looks like now?" I said, but Sam didn't answer, hadn't made a peep since the incident. Samantha liked to keep herself in a jar with the cap twisted on tight, but I handled my business differently. I wanted to spill my contents all over the floor to see what was in there, but we were at Samantha's house, so it was Samantha's rules. I knew no one would talk about it at my house either. Where was Paulette and what did she look like? All I could come up with was the time my nana made oatmeal cookies and had to soak the raisins in a cup of water for thirty minutes but left them in for two hours. I imagined bulgy, puckered raisins wearing orange bathing suits, floating along the water's edge.

Neil heard me talking, so he opened the door and whipped backgammon pieces at us, then tattled that we were out of Sam's room, so I had to go home and ended up missing the part where our neighbor landed his seaplane on the water to drag Paulette out. We never saw Carmen again. When they shipped Paulette's body back to Trinidad, Carmen sat in first class.

For the next few days, as expected, no one was talking. But I had questions. Why go swimming if you didn't know how? What actually was a "death wish," because no matter how many times Neil offered that up, it never made sense. And would someone just please tell me if they saw the Special Spoon, because I didn't know if the doll even worked without it. What would happen to the baby now that Sam couldn't even look it in the eye? Probably get all crusty and the maggots would come. I'd bet anything that Samantha would just get a new one. She'd probably get a truckful of new stuff. As soon as word got out that her babysitter drowned she'd be special, branded as the one whose babysitter ("who really was part of the family") died.

There was a reserve of attention and sympathy and tokens for victims like Samantha Narvey. There were select head tilts and looks of sorrow, the likes of which I'd never see. Samantha was about to be marked. If your goldfish dies or your cat has leukemia, the general public doesn't really care. If your great-grandmother flatlines in a chair, people might say that she had a long, happy life (even if she didn't), and then they'd carry on with their shopping. But when the real stuff happened, you hit the pity lottery. Conversely, if your babysitter's *sister* drowns, your mom makes you stay in your room a lot, and if by accident you try out shouting the word *fuck* when sequestered in there, you don't get any kind of pass, you just get your mouth washed out with a fresh bar of Irish Spring.

The Narveys left town, went to recuperate at their grandparents' place in Palm Beach. I had nothing to do so I wandered the dirt road a lot, waiting for someone to be outside to offer up a head tilt or sad eyes or even a sorrowful *tsk*. I hung around the Melnicks' driveway for a spell, hoping the grandmother might come out. She liked to walk the road with a giant stick and had crazy green eyes, intricate as marbles. Plus, she always had Kraft Caramels in her pocket.

Her grandson had killed himself, just like his mother before him, and so Mrs. Melnick knew a thing or two about hard times. It hit me that out of the ten houses on the road, tragedy had struck two of them, leaving me wondering if the street was cursed. But as I spent the next few weeks alone, waiting for someone to notice me, I knew full well who was probably cursed.

Some days, I'd end up at the Narveys' front steps, making a snorkel mask of my hands and peering into their vestibule even though I knew they were poolside drinking Anita Bryant's orange juice and getting presents, probably about to go to Disney World. But even though I knew Marilyn wasn't in her walk-in closet selecting today's caftan and Neil wasn't trying to fry a toad with his magnifying glass and Samantha Narvey wasn't at the table waiting for me to play Fuzzy Pumper Barber Shop any more than Paulette was vacuuming, causing Gucci to hide under the couch, I looked in a handful of times anyway, because you never knew. Plus, maybe there were clues or at least a pair of Paulette's shoes. Something.

My father continued to take Ace to hockey camp, while my mother cranked up the window unit and watched the *Today* show, then *The $10,000 Pyramid,* and then *The Young and the Restless*. One night when I was supposed to be sleeping I heard her tell my father that Marv Narvey was making the kids swim every day so they wouldn't be scared of water for the rest of their lives. Ace was already scared of the water, just born that way. Not to mention that the following year he'd almost drown at summer camp during free swim and then, after that, *Jaws* would hit theaters, leaving my brother landlocked for the rest of his life.

I was scared of all kinds of things: my bedroom spontaneously going up in flames, pink strep throat medicine, riding my bike.

I feared seeing people eating dinner alone, Sweetums from the Muppets, saying "I love you," and birds. I was terrified of birds.

For a year after the babysitter sank, Samantha and I added a new game to our repertoire. We'd play it every time I was dropped off, and it would turn out to be my all-time favorite game. It was called *Paulette*. Sam and I would inevitably fight every time to see who'd get to be the star player, but in the end we decided we could each get a turn. On the bright side, if you weren't the dead babysitter, you'd get a chance to be everyone else.

Eventually, we'd mess with the history, adding new characters that never even showed up that day, like Mrs. Melnick. Sometimes, I'd add accents. It all depended on my mood. If we're being honest, my drowning was far superior to Samantha Narvey's. I took my time going under and my gurgles were just that much more believable. If Sam was Paulette first, the game ended faster, leaving me ample time to take the stage and really do the drowning justice. Sometimes, just when you thought I was dead, I'd pop back up.

Sam's bed would be the dock and we'd leap onto the grass green shag, yelling out the requisite *I'm swimming! I'm swimming!* I'd perfected the flailing arms overhead, doing it just like Kermit the Frog cheering. I could milk that scene for an hour. I wanted to be Rich Little when I grew up and this was a great way to hone my craft. Samantha played along, but she didn't do the voices like I did. Her heart wasn't in it.

Whenever we'd play, I'd make sure to include a mention of the Special Spoon in some creative way. Sam would raise her tiny blond eyebrows, but I knew deep down she was as mad about that spoon as I was, no matter what her eyebrows said. She swore her mother threw away Baby Alive after the drowning, but I wasn't convinced. I would bet anything that she was stashed in a dresser somewhere, brown crusty death water sloshing around in her belly every time someone opened a drawer. I should have taken her home that day. Popped her head off and hung her outside to dry properly. I would have loved her even if she were filled with maggots. Sam never said another word about our baby and I never got over it, even when she got the fully poseable Bionic Woman Doll with Special Purse and the Bionic Beauty and Repair Station with Scenic Backdrop.

Months after Paulette died, I'd still see her arms thrashing around in my head before I fell asleep. I wanted to ask Ace if he saw anything in his mind at night, or if he thought Paulette swallowed half the lake water and rounded out like a giant balloon, but then I remembered lying in bed the night it happened, and how when I asked him if he saw the body pulled out by the seaplane, instead of answering me, he launched pellets from Neil's target practice rifle at my head, assuring me that if they made contact, my bed would blow up instantly, and also did I hear that crunching outside, because it sounded an awful lot to him like Bigfoot loping around our window.

The Narveys got themselves a new babysitter from an agency. Elicia was also from Trinidad and had asthma so bad they had to keep an oxygen tank near Sam's Barbie Dreamhouse in the basement, just in case there was an incident while vacuuming. She had a small color set in her room, and on Sunday mornings she'd let us watch church with her on TV. When Neil acted up, she'd pinch his neck skin with a maneuver she called the Clinch. I wondered if she swam.

The following year we got a sitter of our own to live full-time in the basement of our modest three-bedroom Spanish Tudor. Her name was Hortense. She was French-Canadian and wore this complicated hairdo, the likes of which I'd only see a few years later on Mrs. Garrett in *The Facts of Life*. Hortense was not winning any popularity contests with me, not only because she spoke in clipped bossy tones and didn't like me, but also because she made me drink glasses of milk no matter how many times I tried to convince her it was against my religion.

Hortense didn't believe in television and wore a dental-hygienist–blue uniform even though no one asked her to. Eight months into her stay, when the phone rang at three a.m., I bet my mother fumbled for her glasses just before she picked up the receiver to hear the news that Hortense's sister had been murdered, somewhere near St. Joseph's Oratory, a landmark Montrealers called the Shrine. There were no screams or seaplanes or first-class tickets to the Caribbean. Just a starched uniform left on the bed, like a police chalk outline of a housekeeper, and a call to the agency for a new sitter.

Latchkey

......

It was happening all over the neighborhood. Street by street, mothers appeared in kitchens wearing slimming slacks, announcing their news over the crunch and smack of Melba toast and cottage cheese. I like to imagine that the mothers decided upon the changes at hand conspiratorially at an outdoor meeting that took place shortly after *The Joker's Wild*. Weather permitting, they'd each show up wearing special garb, like zip-up jumpsuits or, even better, long black hooded robes. Sadly, we lived in a suburb heavily populated by Jews, not witches. There were no summits or secret convocations, but there was a leader. He spoke in dulcet tones and had a Muppety face. He called them to action and they got off the sofa. If I saw their captain today, I'd look him straight in the eye and say: "Fuck you, Phil Donahue."

I was nine when it went down at my house. Up until then, I thought we were doing just fine with *The Mike Douglas Show*. The theme music was groovy, Mike was avuncular and sang to us daily, plus he didn't boss his viewers around. But Phil Donahue was positioning himself as the latest craze and my mother liked to keep up with the times. Back when it was customary for women to stay home and keep house, you might find my mother perched on the chester-field holding my brother as an infant, wearing a pencil skirt and a whipped-up lacquered beehive. As bras began to go up in flames, she made sure to have bell-bottom denims and long middle-parted hair the color of vanilla Jell-O instant pudding. And when Phil Dona-hue infiltrated our den, she remodeled her look once more. The hair shortened and pantsuits began filling the closet.

Women fought for equal rights and economic justice, and my mother joined NOW to get a lapel pin. Feminism was spreading through every 'ville, town, and hamlet and there was nothing we could do about it. Phil Donahue murmured into his sticklike mic and women all over North America heard him.

Well, my mother mostly heard him. It's quite possible she stepped out for a handful of Bugles during part of his tutorial. But these were the fundamental tenets of feminism, as presented in my house:

1. Wear pants.

2. Do not let a man open the door for you (and if he does, make throaty sounds of outrage and disgust).

3. Veto the kitchen.

4. Have other people watch your children, or—better— have them watch themselves.

5. Barbie: You are not welcome here.

Now, tenets 1 and 2 were my mother's own business. If she wanted to practically knock my father over en route to the door, or dress like a fellow, fine with me. I think it was fine with my father, too. Actually, it was a boon to my father. All this business about my mother's slacks afforded my father undivided freedom to become the Cher of the household.

My father enjoyed a costume change more than any lady I knew, plus he had an outfit for every occasion. I wasn't exactly sure what occasion called for constricting banana-yellow jeans with matching shirt separated by a brown leather Gucci belt, but he had one at the ready, should the need arise. His closet was lined with deluxe cowboy boots he claimed he had to wear— something about high arches, which was in line with those girls at camp who were forced to get nose jobs due to their pesky deviated septums. The ultimate accessory in his wardrobe was a full-length raccoon fur coat he insisted was "really in right now." My father's 1970s look fell somewhere between European porn director and Jewish buckaroo.

Veto the kitchen, tenet 3, worked in my favor. Here, women everywhere relinquished their grandmothers' recipes and jilted the avocado green Amana Radaranges they would have once been pleased to win on *Let's Make a Deal*. This was dynamite news for my mother and, frankly, for the rest of us, seeing as her two specialties were meatloaf with hard-boiled eggs squished inside, and liver.

When my mother vetoed the kitchen, we traded our plates for compartmentalized aluminum trays. Out went homemade gray meats, in came Swanson's Salisbury steak (with the superstar apple cobbler, which was the best dessert they had). If my mother was too tired to heat something up, heaping bowls of Technicolor cereals were served. Suburban nutrition in the seventies was a free-for-all. Health nuts existed, sure, but they were usually to the tune of your great-uncle grinding his own peanut butter or your weirdo art teacher trying to share the squares of carob she brought to school in waxed paper baggies. Most of the homes I went to considered SpaghettiOs to be a respectable dinner as long as you'd had your Flintstones Chewables that morning.

Cooking was not the only thing my mother was tickled to give up; forsaking the supermarket was a golden side effect of feminism as well. Since fresh peas and carrot pieces were lumped together in the TV dinner tray, she didn't see the need to suffer all those aisles and push a cart in the name of fresh produce. Somehow, she found a tiny little deli-style market that delivered. Every Monday, a call would be made. We'd walk by and shout "Fruity Pebbles" at her, then she'd nod and bark it to the grocery guy. "Uch, *no*," she'd say while placing the order, "that's *two* bags of Doritos and *one* box of powdered donuts." And our groceries would show up a few hours later in a small cardboard box.

Things started to go sour for me at tenet 4. Here, mothers threaded keys onto brightly colored lanyards, then scattered out the door like the marbles from Hungry Hungry Hippos. If we're being honest, I didn't know where my mother ran off to in those early days and I didn't ask. No kid did—we were kids—all we cared about were Popsicles and our bikes. (Well, you cared about your bike. I was terrified of mine, convinced I'd fall off and get run over by a speeding truck.) Although most kids spent their free time roaming the hinterlands of suburbia, returning home only at the ding of the dinner bell, the kinds of outdoor pursuits I preferred involved attaching a long string to my oversized plastic yellow Slinky and taking a leisurely walk around the block.

If you loved tag or kickball, if you liked roller skates or Frisbee or fresh air, I imagine it was a pretty breezy time to be a kid. If you preferred watching *Hee Haw*, listening to Bobby Vinton albums, and pretending your Clue pieces were performers in your bedroom's production of *Mame*, well . . . childhood might just have been wasted on you. But no matter what kind of kid you were, chances are you spent a decent portion of your after-school hours with a house key noosed around your neck and a *TV Guide* in your hands.

My mother broke the news about my latchkey status on a Sunday night, during a commercial break of *The Wonderful World of Disney*.

"When you get off the bus tomorrow, you can use the key to let yourself in," she said, the lanyard pinched by her spikey nails.

"Where will you be?" I asked.

"I'll be back by dinner."

My older brother, Ace, apparently would not be home either. I suspect there were batches of nine-year-olds who were fine with this arrangement—thrilled, even. I, on the other hand, had questions. Mostly about fire and emergency appendectomies and robbers and exploding furnaces and *It's coming from inside the house!*

"Uch, don't be crazy," my mother said. "Anyway, bad things don't happen during the day."

"What if I get sick?"

"You won't."

"What if the power goes out?"

"*Pffft*. It's still light out."

"What if the doorbell rings?"

"Then don't answer it," my mother said. "Just stay in your room if you have to."

"What if they keep ringing? What if they look normal?"

"Do not answer the door. Remember," my mother said, handing over her best advice along with the house key, "Ted Bundy was good-looking."

3:15 p.m.

The red Plymouth Duster sat outside my house, a solid four feet from the curb. Wearing his usual navy sport coat and tie, Grandpa Solly sat at the wheel, his eyes focused on nothing ahead. My mother must have made the call the night before, sometime between her Ted Bundy comment and the eleven o'clock news. I'm sure my pointing out all the potential dangers knocked some sense into her, so she enlisted my grandfather to wait outside our house, with strict instructions that the bus would deposit me at 3:15 p.m. and to not be late, which would never be a problem because Grandpa Solly showed up two hours early for everything. His crispy flaked hands positioned at ten and two even though the car was in Park summoned both comfort and dread in my empty after-school belly.

"How do you do?" he asked, hoisting himself out of the car.

"Okay," I said. "You?"

"Fine and dandy," he said. "Fine and dandy."

How do you do and *fine and dandy* were pretty much the only sentences my grandfather uttered in those days. He stood silent, hands in his pockets jangling keys, dimes, and a handful of those no-name mints with the liquid chocolate centers he always had. It bothered me the way he bit into those mints. You were supposed to suck on them until the chocolate seeped out, collecting under your tongue and around your teeth.

I struggled to get the key into the front door lock without strangling myself as Grandpa Solly stood behind me, unruffled. We were sausaged in the tiny vestibule and I stepped over the mail littering the floor, making a mental note to go back and collect both the *TV Guide* and Publishers Clearing House packet. Was I supposed to play with Grandpa Solly? Recite something? Give him a snack? It was a bonanza when he made his way onto the sofa in the living room no one used, settling in with an A&P circular by his side. I knew he'd be at that post, staring at our orange walls, until 5:30, when my parents released him.

3:25 p.m.

Quick pit stop in the kitchen to corral an unopened bag of Doritos, original Nacho Cheese flavor, not the gross Taco kind that Ace preferred. He was four years older and our tastes were as dissimilar as our characters, but without him pelting balled-up napkins at my head I didn't know what to do with myself.

3:27 p.m.

Five television sets anchored our small house. We had juice with *Good Morning America* and fell asleep to the sounds of Johnny's monologue. I learned my dance moves from *Solid Gold*, how to remedy misunderstandings from *Three's Company*, and how to solve crime from *The Hardy Boys*. Later on, I'd grasp how to drum up intrigue from the ladies of *Falcon Crest* and get a sex education from the tomfoolery on *Hotel*.

Television was the Grand Poobah, our religion. We never had much to say to each other but the house was always filled with canned laughter. And so I just assumed that for the first day sort of on my own, I'd settle in with my stories.

But I couldn't find the clicker, so I went upstairs to my room.

3:31 p.m.

I opened my desk drawer a smidge, peeking inside to make sure it was still there. The Silverberg's toy catalog came out annually but I was only interested in an old copy, one featuring the bright orange Barbie Country Camper (with vinyl pop-out tent) that I very well would have sold one of my eyes for. I'd study the beautiful camper whenever I was alone in my room. Sometimes I'd place the catalog in my math book and take it to school, like a stowaway in my backpack.

I knew the camper would never be mine, nor would Barbie herself, because tenet 5 stated that Barbie was not welcome in our home. This mandate was actually put into place before Phil Donahue barged in, some time after my mother traded in her strand of pearls for the heavy turquoise beads.

This duel was unfinished, spanning four endless years. The battles all sounded the same: "Pleeeeease," I'd say. "Why not?"

"Because Barbie is a negative role model for girls," she'd say, as if reciting from some brochure picked up at Dr. Resnick's. "She's not realistic. I don't want you trying to measure up later in life."

"I won't," I said. "I won't try to measure up. I promise!"

"Oh, stop it." Throaty sounds of outrage.

"But Samantha has twenty-nine!"

"I don't care if Samantha has one hundred twenty-nine. Barbie makes girls feel bad about themselves," my mother would say, struggling with her clothes or hair. "Uch, I look terrible."

"I think you look great," my father would say.

"Oh, please," she'd answer, rolling her eyes.

When it sunk in that I was getting nowhere with Gloria Steinem, I was forced to call upon my street smarts. My Barbie desire was pretty modest. One. I just wanted one glorious plastic whore. How hard could it be to bypass my mother? I began my crusade close to home, approaching the one person I knew who could grasp my need to gussy up and accessorize better than anyone: my dad. He was a bit of a Ken doll himself. How could he say no?

Well, he said worse than no. He said he'd ask my mother. *Uch*. He was off the list.

Next up, four solid contenders: the grandparents. Why hadn't I thought of them first? Family members, yet out of the daily fray, always willing to bring gifts—they were ideal candidates. The answer to which of the four to choose came swiftly: *Nana*.

My father's mother. People pleaser, pillar of the synagogue, Nana just wanted everyone to be happy (and marry Jewish). Sweet as a Bartons Almond Kiss, possibly illiterate in a few languages, she'd ask the fewest questions. Plus, she lived across the street from the mall.

I decided that after getting the Barbie, I would leave her at Nana's, in the depths of the basement, where the cat lived and my mother refused to frequent. I drew a map in my diary, a diagram of where Barbie would be sequestered. I approached my grandmother with saucery eyes and smiled during the squeeze of the face by her slick-with-chicken-grease fingers. That's all it took. The job was done. I had sandbagged my nana.

I was finally in the Barbie game.

And it wasn't long before I was out.

My mother caught me with Barbie and there was an exchange of words and instructions for Nana to bring that *thing* back from whence it came. I was inconsolable after that, moping around the house for weeks singing Barry Manilow ballads to ease my pain.

That was two years before I became a latchkey kid. And even though I was now nine, an age at which one's Barbie interest should start to wane, mine was more ramped up than ever. I flipped through the toy catalog, and just seeing the little blond girl models polluted with sunshine and bliss as they curled the hair on the ginormous Barbie Styling Head, sweeping electric-blue shadow across her eyelids, made me want to stick forks in my eyes. Women's lib might have empowered ladies all over the country but it was ruining my free time.

It's not like I wanted much. Just Malibu Barbie, complete with fringy yellow towel and pink bulbous sunglasses, who could potentially hang out with Superstar Barbie in Cher's dressing room, where they'd meet and befriend the Cher doll herself and argue over who gets to wear the Bob Mackie dress and who would sport the fancy Indian headdress and sparkly jumpsuit when they had a soiree at the exquisite Barbie Townhouse, the one with the yellow elevator (dolls sold separately), and home of the new, dashing tenant, the Six Million Dollar Man (with bionic grip), who was angling to date all the *Charlie's Angels* dolls so he could have someone to make out with in the back of the orange Country Camper (with vinyl pop-out tent).

Nine years old and twenty-eight minutes into this Phil Donahue–imposed life of solitude, I made a decision: feminism was stupid.

3:43 p.m.

Ace's wallpaper was hot dog mustard yellow with a continuous pattern of broad orange plaid squares. The brown shag was wall-to-wall and a KISS *Destroyer* poster hung on his closet door. I pretended to browse around the room like I didn't know exactly where I was headed, but I knew full well what interested me in that room and it was in the closet behind a stack of *Richie Rich* comics. The briefcase was black, a Samsonite, with nubby skin and two slick silver locks flanking the plastic handle. I don't know how he'd gotten that briefcase, but it wasn't mine, and that was all the reason I needed to fish around in there any chance I got. Plus, I'd once overheard my mother call it an attaché case, which just made it sound even more like it should be mine.

I'd been covertly visiting it for a month, if for nothing else than to delight in the clicks as I engaged the silver locks. If my brother was at hockey practice and my parents were deep into *The White Shadow*, I could be found placing the case on the bed, clicking open the locks, and saying something businessy, like, "I have the microfiche."

When I first began snooping inside, there was not much of interest in there. Some hockey cards, birthday notes from Nana, a Cheap Trick ticket stub. In years to come, I'd discover a sandwich bag filled with crunchy greenish leaves and a small wooden pipe shaped like a corncob, the likes of which I'd never seen before. For that reason, I felt it my duty to march downstairs and show my parents. Later that night, I'd hear my father say behind Ace's closed door, "This is going to hurt me more than it hurts you," followed by the whoosh and slap of the Gucci belt. After that night, Ace barely made eye contact with me. The case would be locked forever and my time with it done, but not before I made another discovery.

There was no way Grandpa Solly would venture upstairs, so I seized the opportunity and opened the case. To my delight, there were two new items inside.

(1) A book: familiar to me, because I had its companion squirreled away under my mattress. Recently, we'd found these illustrated hardcovers marooned at the foot of our beds, with no notes from our parents, no further mention or subsequent confab whatsoever. The point of my book, *Where Do I Come From?,* was to explain how babies showed up in the world so my mother didn't have to. There was no shortage of cartoony penises and swimming sperm in top hats holding flowers. These were distressing enough, but the capper was the main character, who was naked on almost every page and looked an awful lot like Ziggy. And while I had no interest in seeing anyone's penis, Ziggy's was one I really would have preferred to keep under wraps. (Ziggy's wife, I should mention, was also a bit of a nudist and no vixen either.) They also gave us an education on how to spell *penis,* even though they said it sounded like *pee-*nus ("*peanuts* without the *t!*" it stated, which completely ruined Snoopy for me).

My brother's book, the one staring at me from the case, was entitled *What's Happening to Me?*, and I decided right then and there that I didn't care what was happening to him. I pushed it aside. Underneath lurked other bait.

(2) **A magazine:** glossy, with smiling ladies on the cover—a blonde, a brunette, and a redhead. I knew instantly where this periodical hailed from. I'd been to my father's office three times, and with each visit I was too panicked to enter the bathroom due to the neat stack of *Playboys* weighting down the top of the toilet tank. At home, *Ms.* magazines were piling up on the kitchen counter, while across town my father's magazines boasted headlines like, A PICTORIAL FIRST: OUTER SPACE SEX! INTRIGUING!

Those magazines irked me, and not for the heaving bosoms on the covers, but for the little white strip on each issue with my father's name and work address typed in black ink. The mailman would tote this magazine around the neighborhood in his mailbag, forced to handle it as he took out stacks of letters and birthday cards from nanas all over the world. And then, upon reaching my dad's office, he'd know that it was my father receiving this magazine with those ladies on the cover sporting GIRLS OF THE BIG TEN T-shirts and no pants.

There were copious pages to get through before I hit the gauzy layout of a lady in a white fishnet shirt and nothing else. Gone was Ziggy's pear of a wife. The farther along I got, the more I was faced with angles of body parts I had no business or interest in seeing. My friend's mother had given her a special gold compact with which to inspect her private parts at her leisure. I saw little reason to go rooting around in that area.

I flipped through more of the magazine through squinted eyes, until I arrived at the Tootsie Roll center of the Tootsie Pop. The centerfold. I found this to be a much more polite section, thanks to a flappy thing covering up some of the nakedness and instead of body parts I was presented with something utterly enchanting: an interview. Here, I was led into a world of deep thoughts and esoteric information. Now *this* was up my alley. I learned that Brandi enjoyed badminton and spy novels and kittens and kissing. But she hated rude people. I made a mental note to put a "Turn-ons & Turnoffs" section in my own diary.

At the bottom of the Q&A, there was an elaborate signature. I admired the way Brandi looped her *B* and drew a bubbly heart above the *i*. I hoped to one day have a great signature like Brandi's and to be able to say I was turned on by badminton. But I was done with the nudity portion of the day. I needed a palate cleanser.

4:17 p.m.

The beige push-button phone hung on the kitchen wall with a long spirally cord, allowing you free rein to walk the perimeter of the house. The living room and kitchen were far enough apart that I didn't have to worry about Grandpa Solly listening in. I dialed randomly.

"Hello?" said the voice on the other end of the line.

"Is Joanie there?"

"I'm sorry, who?"

She sounded nice enough, but old, and like she was chewing something smushy, maybe egg salad.

"Joanie," I said again.

"I'm sorry, I think you have the wrong number."

"*You* have the wrong number," I said.

Silence.

"Pardon me, dear?"

"Is Joanie there?"

"Right, then. Goodbye, dear."

Granted, it wasn't my best work but, in fairness, I was just warming up. So I called back.

"Hello?" she said, her voice more clipped this time.

"Is Joanie there?"

"Dear, I just told you there is no one here by that name and that you have the wrong number. Now please stop calling or I will alert the operator."

This was no threat for me. I continued.

"My mother is an operator." (Which *might* have been true. If you recall, I had no idea what profession she had slipped into.)

"Right, dear. Why don't you do your homework?"

"Why don't *you*?"

"That's fine. I'm going to hang up now."

And she did. So I called a third time.

"Is your refrigerator running?" I said.

Click.

I moved on.

"Hello?" This time it was a man, also old, and aggravated from the get-go.

"I am stuck in a box," I said in a teeny voice.

"What?" He was hostile, like I'd interrupted his afternoon appointment with *Bonanza*. "Miriam? Is that you?"

"Yes, it's me and I'm stuck in a box."

"Heh?" he was shouting. "What?"

This guy was useless and, if we're being honest, pretty irritating. I cut him free.

Wrapping the coiled cord around my wrist like a bracelet, I made one final call.

"Operator," announced a young, pleasant-guy voice.

"Hi," I said.

"Hello."

I then affected my best Miss Piggy voice, briefly mad at myself for not having thought of opening with this impression. "My phone is not working properly. Might you be a love and try the number just to see if it rings?"

I knew he was smiling in his operator office, I could just tell. I'd never gotten a male operator before. I wondered if he wore a blazer and what kind of chair they gave him and if he had a stack of *Playboy*s on the toilet tank where he worked. The operator call is a prank caller's last resort because an operator can see your number and probably could call the police—or your mother— but Ace once told me they had to call you back, by law, if you asked them to.

"Okay," he said. "I will try you back."

"Thank you, Kermie."

I hung up and waited. Seconds later, it rang.

"Kermit the Frog here," I said.

"Okay, kid."

"Okay, Operator."

He hung up. I remained on the line until the silence was broken by a series of annoying beeps.

4:28 p.m.

My new plan was to lie quietly and settle into despondency. Dragging my pillow onto the floor, I noticed the top of Shaun Cassidy's head. Kicking the magazine out from under the bed revealed the rest of his face, along with his pals Scott Baio, Leif Garrett, and Willie Aames. Their heads had been enlarged and placed in a quadrant, like a giant game of tic-tac-toe. *Tiger Beat* was chock-full of secret facts (*Andy Gibb's middle name was Roy*), not to mention beautiful posters of Parker Stevenson to tape onto your walls. I'd recently read the issue cover to cover, but upon another perusal I laid eyes on something I'd missed. It was at the bottom of the page.

WIN A DATE WITH GREG!

The Greg in question was starring on a new TV series, *B.J. and the Bear*, about a freelance trucker (B.J.) and his chimpanzee best friend (Bear). Together, they'd travel the country's highways getting into hijinks while trying to avoid the rascally law enforcer, Sheriff Lobo.

Now, my fantasy-date dance card was already full with Fonzie and Bobby Vinton. However, the song "Convoy" had recently taught me some trucker lingo (*yeah, breaker one-nine, this here's the rubber duck*), and CB radios seemed neat—plus I didn't really have anything else to do, so I cut out the contest form. I should note here, I was not much of a winner. There were no yellow horse ribbons tacked onto my bulletin board, no trophy cups engraved with my name. Ace always got to the Spooky Speedster prize in the Franken-Berry box first. And I'd taken no shortage of dodgeballs to the head in gym. But there was something about Greg Evigan's feathered hair and halfhearted smile that added up. I was about to be a winner.

I spent a good deal of time debating which ink from my Bic 4-Color pen to use. Settling on red, I called up those dazzling letters Brandi used for her signature, knowing it was that kind of penmanship that Greg Evigan would spark to. We were asked to write one line about ourselves: *I like badminton and spy novels, kittens and kissing.* I then crossed out *kissing* and put in *CB radios* instead. I debated a SWAK on the back of the envelope, but decided on a kiss instead, using the Tangee lipstick I'd lifted from my nana's bathroom last Yom Kippur. Just to put it over the top, I spritzed the envelope with a little Love's Baby Soft.

I would get my father to mail the contest form. He never questioned what we handed over, probably assuming it was one of those letters I was supposed to be writing to Penina Hamburger, the adopted mail-order Israeli orphan pen pal my mother'd sent away for. I knew he'd take it, along with the stack of envelopes my mother gave him, mindlessly sticking it into the brown leather purse he'd started carrying.

The potential outfit panic for my impending date set in right away. I was confident that the rust-colored crochet necktie my mother thought was cute just didn't seem cocktail-waitressy enough for my date. And what would we chat about? I didn't know a thing about badminton or spy novels. I needed some talking points, hobbies. I needed to be interesting.

Greg Evigan was an actor on television, and who knew how long that gig would last, so best to have his next project on hand. The red Trapper Keeper on my desk was stuffed with lined loose-leaf, which I smoothed out and then stared at for a while. I would author a play. It would be a two-character vehicle. The boy character would be the star of a very popular TV show whose car breaks down outside a girl's house. The girl would be lonely and sad and unattractive and bored. She was twenty-eight and a shut-in with glasses and a neck brace and had nothing to do after school.

I started writing dialogue but everything sounded dumb. Each attempt resulted in a crumpled ball of paper. I needed inspiration. Walking into my parents' room, I opened a few drawers, but nothing spoke to me. In Ace's room, I sat at his desk, smelled the rubber band that held his hockey cards together. I took the briefcase out, just to hear the clicks one more time. When I saw those girls staring up at me again, the Lite-Brite pegs in my brain lit up.

MITCH: Hi. My car broke down, as you can see. I was wondering if I could come in the house to use your telephone.

ROXANNE (*looking for car, pushes up glasses and adjusts neck brace*): Are you crazy? I can't let you in my house. I don't know you.

MITCH: Don't you know who I am?

ROXANNE: Are you Ted Bundy?

MITCH: Don't be crazy.

ROXANNE: Wait. My glasses are smudgy. I can't see that well.

MITCH: I can help you clean them.

ROXANNE: I guess you can come in and screw me with your *pee*-nus.

MITCH: Right on. Why don't you tell me about yourself?

ROXANNE (*taking off her glasses and neck brace*): I like badminton and kittens. But I hate rude people.

MITCH: I am not rude. I have a penis.

ROXANNE: All right. Let's screw.

I should note here that I had a friend whose father was a world-class pervert and, in his nightstand, on any given day, lived a bag of dried apricots and a stack of literature we could never bring ourselves to look at. But at the top of the pile was always a *Screw* magazine. Her older brother told us what it meant. And although I never actually leafed through one of them, they still managed to inspire what I imagined could very well become my new smash hit: *Win a Screw with Mitch!*

5:03 p.m.

My play was shaping up nicely but missing one thing: actors. If you had written a dirty play and needed some actors to try out some of the smuttier dialogue, who would you call? Exactly. *Barbie.* I mean, who better to talk about screwing, right? But here is just another way Phil Donahue bankrupted my childhood (see tenet 4).

I did own one big doll, Mrs. Beasley, the same one Buffy toted around on *Family Affair*. She wore a dowdy turquoise dress with yellow pin dots, and square plastic glasses, and she had a string at her waist that, when pulled, made her utter creepy sayings like, "Gracious me, you are getting to be a big girl." There is no way Mrs. Beasley could pull off the role of Roxanne. Even if you yanked that string as hard as you could, she would never agree to a screw with Mitch.

Rifling around my closet, I found an old shoebox. Inside lived the tiny loopholes my mother found in the Phil Donahue doctrine, when she couldn't take one more minute of my crusade. Enter the Sunshine Family: Steve, Stephanie, and Baby Sweets. I could guarantee that the calico dress–wearing, frizzy-haired Stephanie and turtleneck-clad Steve never screwed. Baby Sweets most probably came from the stork, even though *Where Did I Come From?* begged to differ. But they were the only actors I could get and this play needed work. Stripping the puritans, rehearsals began.

5:07 p.m.

I tried. Really I did. But those two just couldn't handle the material. I ripped their limbs off in frustration, decapitated them, then placed all the pieces back into the shoebox, along with the pages of *Win a Screw with Mitch!*, closed it up, and wrote *Ted Bundy was here* on the box top. To the back of the closet they went, laid to rest until decades later, when my parents would sell the house and hire someone to host a garage sale for them. To hell with *B.J. and the Bear*. I don't even know why I bothered. Shutting my closet door, I skulked back to the den and watched the end of *The Merv Griffin Show* until I heard my father's car in the garage.

Epilogue

I spent the rest of my latchkey days alone, just watching TV. Grandpa Solly never returned after that first day, and I insisted on my mother buying me a fire extinguisher for when the house spontaneously combusted. Shortly after turning fifteen, I adopted a bald black Cabbage Patch Kid named Cedric Imala and set up an Easy-Bake Oven on my dresser. Sure, I was too old for those things, but Nana had slipped me a little extra Hanukah money and told me to spend it any way I saw fit.

The '80s breezed in with its shoulder pads and Aussie Mega hairspray. The styles were changing yet again and it was all the rage to look as if you lived on *Knots Landing*—this intrigued my mother. She started upturning shirt collars and shellacking her hair into a helmet that could withstand damaging winds. She ditched the ties but kept the slacks. Eventually, Phil Donahue became background noise as she outlined her lips with magenta liner, filling in the rest with bubble gum–pink lipstick.

I still came home to an empty house after school but, sometimes, I'd bring a boy with me. We'd retire to my Duran Duran–postered room and he'd wait patiently as I pressed my nose up to the plastic window, watching my cake rise halfheartedly as it baked by light bulb. Later, we'd listen to Styx's "Mr. Roboto" and dry hump on the shag rug. Occasionally I'd make eye contact with Cedric Imala and think, *Fuck you, Phil Donahue. Fuck you.*

Eight Weeks

· · · · · ·

We had name tags sewn into our underwear, rations of Fun Dip and Wacky Packs ready for barter. Oversized white envelopes were dispatched months in advance, sending us to doctors for shots and signatures assuring the authorities we weren't bedwetters or asthmatics or prone to epileptic fits. While snow still piled on the roof, my mother tacked the clothing checklist onto the fridge with a sheep magnet that claimed EWES NOT FAT, EWES FLUFFY!, and still we scrambled last minute for the requisite four pairs of shorts, three bathing suits, and one rain poncho. I knew other kids, whose duffel bags and cardboard trunks aired out on lawns around the neighborhood, were bubbling like soda inside a shaken can. But as I sat on my bed, bangs hacked and crooked, I hoped that I'd contract the plague—or at the very least get hit by a truck—anything, really, so that I didn't have to get on that bus to summer camp.

I was five years old the first time I stood in the maze of sleepaway camp buses looming in the parking lot of Blue Bonnets Raceway. In its 1950s heyday, my father told me, the horse track boasted a million-dollar clubhouse for "big shots." I liked to imagine the short mustachioed man from Monopoly with his wife (a much taller broad, with her long neck wrapped in a beady-eyed fox stole) on a night out, away from the fast dealings and headaches of Marvin Gardens. But by the late '70s, the track had long since lost its luster. Now the only thoroughbreds parading around its parking lot had long curly brown hair, wore satin dolphin shorts, and answered to the names Elissa and Elana and Elyse.

Summer camps were invented in the hopes of bringing nature and outdoor pursuits to kids living in the dingy conditions of industrialized cities, the earliest Fresh Air Fund spots. By the 1920s, hundreds of summer camps had sprouted on the American landscape. I'm sure Canada adopted the idea, copying its cousin a year or two after the fact. It took us longer to get everything up north. If the camps I went to were considered Jewish camps, I had no clue. Yes, we wore white to dinner on Friday evenings and there was challah bread on the table, but it didn't occur to us that camp was religious any more than it occurred to us that the stop-motion *Davey and Goliath* show we all watched on Sunday mornings had a lick to do with Christianity. We just liked the way the dog sounded when he said "Daaaaavey."

Camp is a time to connect. In its wooded magical glory, one could make lifelong pals while sleeping in tinderboxes, surrounded by the Magic Marker graffiti of ghosts of campers past. It is a place where character takes shape. There is positive transformation and blossoming and good old-fashioned fun. In the 1970s, summer camps were still affordable and kids were sent in droves for a myriad of reasons. For those who struggled during the school year, camp could be a time for reinvention. It was fully possible to be a math nerd in the fall and a color war champion in the hotter months. For some, camp was a safe place to take on authority, others felt free enough to explore their sexuality on the baseball field or over by Canoeing. Of course, there were your garden-variety well-adjusted kids, the ones who were equally successful at home and away.

And then there was *that* kid. You know who I mean. The underdog who gets on the bus weeping and shy and scared but, against all odds, learns to rise to occasions and come out of her shell, making the best of everything, and by the end of the eight weeks picks up awards and plaques and skills and lifelong friends and lessons for the storybooks. Aww, don't you like that kid the best? Who doesn't love a kid who overcomes obstacles because she tries harder than anyone and it actually pays off? Me. I can't stand that fucking kid. Not to worry, this isn't a story about that kid.

Our cabin was a small wooden structure, painted white with dark green trim. It sat in a neat row of identical cabins on one side of a line of trees, the boys' bunkhouses mirroring the setup on the other side of the divide. Eight Shaker-style pegs outside the screen door held our rain ponchos, and the wooden porch was smooth enough for jacks. The dining hall's and rec hall's white-and-green exteriors mimicked the cabins', these larger buildings flanking the small lake at opposite ends, like parentheses.

Save for a go-cart track, it was pretty standard camp stuff. Activities ranged from softball to sailing to archery, and once a week we had a special activity called Coke Dips, which all campers lived for. While we slept, cans of Cott soda were thrown into the shallow and deep ends of the lake. As the sun rose, a voice would burst through the PA system calling "the Dip," causing mass hysteria as everyone scrambled out of their cabins, beelining toward the lake. If you were lucky enough to catch yourself a can, you gave it to your counselor, who brought it to the kitchen staff. At lunch that day, you were allowed to drink the entire can, instead of the bug juice that gurgled in those bubbling drink contraptions they also had at the mall.

There were five kids in my cabin that year. It was unprecedented to have such young kids sleeping away at camp for the entire eight weeks, so a special cabin was carved out just for us. We were made camp mascots just by virtue of being small. But even with all the special attention, a lot of us cried ourselves to sleep while clutching stuffed Snoopys, thinking of home.

For just about everyone, Camp Hiawatha was an oasis, perfection on earth. Today, way over thirty years later, many of those campers still refer to their tenure there as the best days of their lives. My memory for details of that time is tangled; I vaguely recall being in the chorus of *You're a Good Man, Charlie Brown* and a male swim instructor named Leslie pointing out a can of grape soda for my retrieval on a Coke Dip. What I remember more was traveling in a small pack of campers, being led to sporty activities I already found challenging. I wasn't homesick, because I didn't feel any more at ease back there. Being part of a pack, encouraged to participate, all that fun—I think I just felt lost.

"This is great," my father said, eating fried chicken out of a cardboard box on visiting day, his golden Capricorn necklace pendant catching the sun and memories of his own days at camp. "Man, you guys are lucky."

Maybe I was just too young to appreciate it, so my parents continued sending me off, just to make sure.

I started kindergarten the fall just after my first trip to sleep-away camp. It was a French school, housed in a large brick building that loomed over a busy residential street in Montreal. The brochure was on top of a mail stack in the kitchen and its cover featured what I believed to be a mental institution for smiling girls dressed in dark navy uniforms. Those tunics are what sold my mother. She believed in the idea of uniforms, convinced our future relationship would never be in jeopardy if we took fighting about what to wear out of the equation.

My mother brought me to school the first day, holding my hand as we crossed the threshold. The teacher stood en garde by the door, her brown wool pencil skirt static-clinging to nude panty hose. Twenty-eight kids seized the classroom dressed in kind: gray pants and white shirts for the boys, navy pleated tunics with white shirts underneath for us. I could hear kids speaking French and learned at once that no English was spoken in the classroom, which made my stomach hurt because no French was spoken in my home.

The classroom was set up with a series of tables along one side, facing a line of windows. Under the patches of light the windows let in was a domestic-style setup: a play kitchen with a fridge and oven and fake food and a small wooden washer and dryer and play ironing board with a pile of teeny rumpled clothes. I couldn't take my eyes off it. My mother's eyes were concealed behind the prescription sunglasses she'd neglected to replace with appropriate indoor eyewear. Sometimes I'd feel proud of her wearing dark glasses inside, like she was a rock star, but on the first day of French school, the kids were staring at her and I wanted her to be like everyone else. Although I couldn't see her eyes, her craned neck suggested she was checking out the small tub of hard candies sequestered on a high shelf near the door, and I'd soon figure out that on good-behavior days, Madame Larousse would give us each a sour ball to eat on the way home. If you sucked them dutifully, small shards would form and cut your tongue. I liked that part best.

We all took seats at the table. Most of the parents had left by that point, but my mother stood behind me, dark glasses in position, looking like my bodyguard. Some kids are naturally attractive, have an ease about them that others gravitate toward. I sat in my chair looking straight ahead, wooden, just like my mother. We were the dream team of people repellent. The teacher nodded at my mother, which was code for *It's time to leave your kid here with me in this French mental institution*. Understanding it was time to go, my mother scanned the room for someone to pair me up with so she could leave without my having some sort of emotional breakdown, or worse, having one of her own.

Already sitting next to me was a little redheaded girl, all freckles and good posture. My mother crouched down in between us. "Hello," she said, in her signature baby voice. "What's your name?"

The small girl looked at my mother, possibly *through* my mother, and ignored her. I immediately knew her angelic little Peppermint Patty face was a big ruse.

"Name?" My mother tried again in a tougher tone this time, staring at the kid until she finally, in a standoffish voice, answered, "Anne."

My mother gave me an isn't-this-fabulous look and stood up tall again. She hugged me from behind, my arms hanging to my knees as she gripped. To her, she'd made contact, broken the ice for me, and was now free to leave the building. I could hear her heels click and echo down the long hallway, leaving me alone with Anne, who spoke only French, and certainly not to me. I stared at the washing machine, counting down the seconds until I could line up at the door and receive my sour ball—hopefully, not the lime one.

I spent the first few weeks alone. Not (only) because I didn't speak the language, but because I had no clue how to make a friend. I'd come home after school every day and eat from the

box of Fruity Pebbles I'd hidden in my closet, trying to come up
with a plan so I didn't have to spend the rest of my days at the
wooden washing machine alone. How did people do it? How did
they make friends? The next morning, as I moped around the
classroom, it finally hit me: find the kid who looks as miserable
and uncomfortable as I do.

Gerald Wiener was round and short and a dead ringer, at six,
for Walter Matthau. He often complained of back pain and spent
half the week barfing in the classroom sink. His face was in a per-
petual squint, making him look like a human whine. Not even
his nana would call that kid happy. This was my guy.

At nap time, I'd place my sleeping mat next to his and we'd
look up Madame Larousse's skirt as she paced along the row of
foamy floor covers. Gerald started coming to my ballet recitals,
even though he reminded us at all times that the lights gave him
a headache. He was quiet, and often nauseous, but shared with
me his hatred for kindergarten at the French institution, and
confided that he, too, would rather have been at home watching
The Flintstones. When it was time to go home, we'd line up for
sour balls together, our heads hung equally low, defeated by the
day. We'd roll our eyes instead of saying goodbye, knowing there
was no way out of returning to that shit hole the following morning. But at least we had each other.

I took my crackerjack friend-making skills, along with my Yes &
Know pads, to the second summer camp I attended—this time in
Middlebury, Vermont. I was now eight years old. This camp had
dark-green cabins with white trim, and the boys' lodgings were
behind the tennis courts. Although this place was much larger, as
if the American camp had eaten the Canadian one, it might just
as well have been the same place. Canoes, flagpoles, bug juice,

beautiful senior girls named Randy and Donna with long hair and suede clogs, and days full of scheduled activities. We captured the flag in the morning, moving on to lanyard making, and then archery before lunch. Rest hours were spent playing jacks and trading stationery, or quietly devouring Archie comics instead of writing letters home.

The Canadian girls shared their Laura Secord lollipops; the Americans gave away small handfuls of the sour-apple gum we couldn't get in our towns. As summer came to a close, color war broke out, splitting the camp in two, testing mettle, seeing who could win more games or sing songs louder or, in the end, have the most spirit. When it was over, there was much sitting by the lake, usually with something burning in effigy on the water, as campers sang the last of their songs, drooping, because the best time of their lives was ending. How could they leave? Who would understand what they'd just experienced when they returned home and unzipped their duffels, which now contained everlasting memories that their mothers would just throw into the washing machine, as if it were that easy.

I knew that no matter how many sad sack letters I sent home begging for someone to spring me from this camp, unless I contracted the mumps I was there for the duration. Girls were already sharing their Bay City Rollers T-shirts and having the prescribed fun. It was time to find my rotten apple.

Amy Schecter was short and spunky with a giant supply of sour-apple gum. And while she was sporty like a lot of the Americans and I gravitated toward rest hour and doing the plays, Amy seemed pissed off all the time, and that was as good an invitation as any. My attitude was worse than hers, but Amy kept up all right. We'd sit on her top bunk while the rest of the girls played jacks, sneering at their squeals of delight when they'd won a game or danced with a boy at a social. Often we'd be warned by our counselors in meetings on the porch or the baseball field to improve our behavior or attitude or else. Amy listened more than I did, worried about jeopardizing her sporty status. Eventually I found myself in my first meeting with the camp director.

"How is your summer going?" Uncle Howie asked.

"I dunno. It's okay, I guess."

"Mmmhhh. Are you enjoying your cabin?"

"Yeah."

"And the activities are okay? The food not too bad?"

"Yeah, it's all okay."

"I see you are enjoying yourself in the play," he said.

"Yeah, I like it all right." I scratched at the mosquito bites on my leg, looking out the postage stamp–sized window in the office. Distant screams came from near the flagpole.

"I've been getting some complaints," he said.

"Oh?"

"From your counselors."

"Oh."

"Do you know what I'm talking about?"

"No."

"No?"

"I guess."

"Listen, people are complaining about you. And I don't think you want this happening. I'd separate you and Amy if I could, but we're halfway through the season and there's just no room to start moving cabins. And, frankly, it's not fair to the rest of the kids. I have half a mind to send you home, but you are an asset to the theater. And so I will keep you here. For now. But if you continue with this behavior, I will yank you from the play. You will no longer be in *Mary Poppins* if you don't shape up. Next step after that is sending you home. Understand?"

I understood. Secretly, I was thrilled because I'd never been almost kicked out of anything. I finished up that summer without getting sent home early. I did the play and drank the bug juice. I remained a pain in the ass, but mostly in my head, because I realized that being kicked out wasn't any better than being kept in. This was who I was shaping up to be, and I followed myself wherever I went.

Camp Manitou Wabing was nestled into a thousand acres of the great forests of Muskoka, Ontario. Originally founded in 1959 as an arts center, it was snapped up the following year by a father-son duo with the vision of building a specialized summer camp for older children, with a focus on arts and sports. The summer I turned ten, I would not be returning to the wilds of Vermont but back once again to my Canadian roots by attending what was now called a specialty camp. "Top of the line," my father would say. He didn't usually weigh in on these decisions but if something was fancy, he made himself heard.

Manitou had remnants of the usual summer camp landscape—rustic cabins and a lake delineated by a string of buoys and dotted with Sunfish—but the newer buildings were state of the art: tennis courts and theaters, radio stations and gymnastics tents. They imported handsome Brits to head soccer camp. There were horses in their equestrian centers, and a series of kilns in the airy, timber-framed pottery studio. Daily schedules were different at Manitou as well. At a regular camp, your bunk had a predetermined activity timetable and you meandered from softball to sailing with the rest of your group. Here, *you* made an agenda, receiving your own printout complete with a major, a minor, and a handful of other classes in between—like college, but with waterskiing.

This camp was a bonanza for parents. You could see it in their well-rested faces on visiting day, where they had the opportunity to stay at the lush inn and spa attached to the camp. They could report back to their friends at home how outrageous the place was, and how great the focus on activities and instruction was for the kids. Manitou Wabing was not your father's tetherball court. It was ahead of its time and we were lucky to be part of it. That's what my parents told me.

At ten years old, I knew full well that athletics and I were not compatible. The only interest I had was theater, so I made that my major. The director of the camp wanted each camper to fill their schedule with multiple activities to broaden their horizons and use all the facilities, but I had no interest in broadening anything. I wanted to be in plays, then lie on my bed and exude a general toxicity that would take up most of my time, leaving fewer hours for archery or basketball clinics. To this day, I am not sure how I finagled this deal, but somehow I managed to major in theater and minor in pottery and do absolutely nothing in between. So, it was settled—I would spend my summer shuttered inside the theater like veal, exiting the building every once in a while to throw a pot or ruin something for others.

There were eight of us in cabin G5, not including our big-bosomed counselor, Jordana. Five of the girls knew one another from previous summers and were instantly glued together, like one giant Camp Beverly Hills sweatshirt, already on the move and out the door to ogle the head of Canoeing, leaving me to seek out Barbara Stack from Michigan, a girl with a tangle of red hair that required much maintenance. I watched her unpack her Prell and Body on Tap and Gee, Your Hair Smells Terrific, lining her products up along the ledge of her cubby.

"This place is a dump," she said, taking out a collection of combs and the same hair picks my dad had, throwing them onto her bottom bunk. Barbara Stack had grit and troublesome hair and you could smell the bad attitude seeping out of her pale skin. I was ready to sign up to be her friend until I discovered that she was a gymnastics major, which was a focused program that would leave me without her in the cabin quite a bit to be miserable alone. Things were looking down.

There was one other misfit in bunk G5—Pam Sacks. A theater tech major, minoring in softball, Pam looked older than the rest of us, like she just needed a place to crash in between stage-managing gigs. We didn't talk much as she unpacked her duffel and I pretended to be deep into my *Jughead's Double Digest* as she folded her clothes. I noticed all the black attire she had, which was a requirement if you did theater tech, and a pile of red Adidas shorts. The last article of clothing pulled from her bag caught my eye, not only because it wasn't another black T-shirt but because it was the grooviest thing I'd ever laid eyes on.

This was no regular sweatshirt. This was a perfectly worn-in, dark-gray number, with the image of an upright alligator sporting a T-shirt with a little man motif on the chest, right above where his alligator nipple would be. The creature was smiling, not menacing in the least, pleased with himself for wearing clothes.

The Lacoste trend was a few years away from hitting Canada but all the Americans wore those coveted alligator shirts. I was not a thief by trade but I wanted that sweatshirt. I needed it. Probably couldn't go on if it wasn't mine.

To date, all I'd ever stolen was a piece of Bazooka bubble gum from this weird store located in the basement of an apartment building near my school bus stop. The gum was piled in an old-fashioned barrel, a ton of it. Thousands of neatly wrapped pieces just waiting, thousands of bad jokes, thousands of pink rectangles with a faint dusting of white powder, thousands of bubbles to blow. The way they set the stuff up, they were practically begging you to steal it. The sweatshirt was also begging.

I spent days strategizing on how to pilfer that sweatshirt. If I took it during the first week of camp, she'd know it was gone. I could wait until the last day, when she wouldn't notice until she dumped the contents of her navy duffel onto her laundry room floor. But what if she wore it the last day? Then what? I needed a better plan.

I had been cast in *The Children's Hour* as Mary Tilford, an angry girl in the 1930s who runs away from a boarding school to the safety of her grandmother's house. In order not to be sent back to the school, Mary makes up a story that her teachers were lesbians, which ends up ruining everybody's lives. I enjoyed playing the evil parts. But even more, I actually enjoyed spending the long, hot camp days in the theater rehearsing. When rehearsals were over, I'd hide in the back of the theater, skipping the other activities I hadn't signed up for. Pam Sacks was doing props on the show, so I monitored her every move. As she organized the schoolbooks and desks, I imagined ways of stealing that sweatshirt.

Three weeks into camp, our bunk was walking to lunch when I came down with a sham stomachache. The counselor wanted to send me to the infirmary but I begged for a nap instead. Saying yes to my request was easier than dealing with me, so she acquiesced. I promised that if I woke from the nap and still felt bad I would get myself over to the nurse, which was right across from the theater, where I was scheduled to be anyway. I sat on my bottom bunk, alternately staring into Pam Sacks's cubby and looking out the window at least three hundred times, just to make sure no one was lurking. When ready, I removed the sweatshirt from her cubby, stuffing it into my army green duffel bag under a few embarrassing sweaters my mother had insisted I bring. I shoved the whole thing back under my bed, then ran to lunch, although I couldn't eat due to jangled nerves. I wondered if there were many Jewish criminals.

The sweatshirt lived under my bed for four weeks, undetected. I didn't have a chance to wear it, lest I be noticed and removed from the premises, but just knowing it was hiding in my duffel pleased me. And then the system began to break down. Tensions were running high as summer was coming to a close and most of the girls were upset to leave their friends or boys they'd started kissing by that secret ditch near Arts and Crafts. There was a lot of spontaneous singing and weeping and hugs but also much bickering. My play was over, my pots thrown, and my bag would soon be repacked with the requisite four pairs of shorts, three bathing suits, one rain poncho. And one far-out terrific fantastic sweatshirt that would undoubtedly change my life forever.

When Pam Sacks finished her last show (*Anything Goes*), she finally realized her perfectly worn alligator sweatshirt had gone missing. Well. You'd have thought a child had been stolen, with all the hysterics she burst into. It started small—just some polite asking if anyone had seen it. Nobody had. The next logical step was to ask the counselors. They hadn't seen it either. The counselors also asked the kids, and still no one had seen it.

If it were me, at that point I'd have just dropped the whole affair and taken one for the team. Good lord, it was just a stupid sweatshirt. But no, Pam Sacks launched an entire investigation, taking it upon herself to climb up the chain of command. She asked section heads. She asked the boys' camp. She went to the theater and Gymnastics and the soccer field. She did everything but take an ad out in the goddamn paper. Pam Sacks couldn't just leave it alone. I mean, it was lost, all right? Stop being such a baby and let the dumb thing go.

Meanwhile, I used my acting chops to appear normal and casual. I debated asking her if she wanted help trying to find her sweatshirt but since I rarely spoke to her I thought my sudden attention would make me look like a person of interest. I considered packing my stuff earlier than planned so I could hightail it out of there when the buses pulled in, but Pam Sacks, who'd barely spent any time in the bunk for eight weeks, was now there all the time sounding the alarm about thieves and misconduct and why couldn't people just do the right thing. How much more of her hysteria could we take?

The counselors gave G5 a few more chances to come clean, since all of a sudden this was some sort of federal case.

"Pam is really upset, you guys," said counselor Jordana and her giant shelf-like accusing bosom. "Please don't make us check your bags, people."

Which is what they did on the very last morning of camp. There was a collective groan around the cabin because we'd spent an hour packing our duffels the night before. *Fine*, I thought, *let them search my bag*. We were leaving anyway. And just maybe, if I was lucky, I would get caught and not be allowed to return the following summer. Maybe there would be a small photo of me in camp directors' offices worldwide, with a typed note at the bottom indicting me as a thief, a visual warning to keep me out of summer camps in general, like those bad-check writers at the A&P.

When I first stole Pam's sweatshirt, I'd turned it inside out so it looked like a plain gray sweatshirt, which most kids had, then I'd stuffed it at the very bottom of my tube-shaped duffel. One would have to take everything out to locate it and I'd banked on the sheer laziness of the counselors.

When it came time to search my bag, I sat on my bottom bunk and hoped for the best. I used my best acting exercises. *Pretend you are innocent. Pretend you are breezy. Pretend you don't care.* Mine was the last bag to be searched and I could swear they spent way more time on it than the other girls'. This was outrageous—why were they so convinced it was me? What did I do to make them think I was the boxy sweatshirt thief? In the movies, people in my situation started yelling about how the camp had no right to treat them this way, how this was unacceptable, how they would call their lawyer. My father's friend Seymour Rosenbloom was a lawyer and I was more than prepared to throw that name out there if I had to. My father always said he was "top of the line."

The morning of the duffel search, the buses were parked near the dining hall, lined up in rows. The Americans who had to fly home left first. There was the requisite singing and hugging and promises to call and write and visit and, ultimately, reunite the following summer. I knew my parents would be waiting eagerly at Blue Bonnets Raceway, smiling and full of questions about how hot it had been or how much rain we had throughout the eight weeks. We would get in the car and drive home with the radio talking about news and traffic. Once inside, I'd wander the house, unsure of what to do with myself.

I am proud to report that because of my packing handiwork, the sweatshirt managed to hide in plain sight. It was a small victory for me, not getting caught, lasting only until I realized not getting caught also meant no photos of me in the camp director's office, that I'd be welcomed back just like everyone else. I never even wore the sweatshirt, concerned they might have sent letters home inquiring after it. I shoved it into the back of my closet, where it stayed for a month, until I balled it up and chucked it into a neighbor's trash can on garbage day. I worried long after that it would surface, like a dead body in a river.

A Lot of Living to Do

......

I was alone by the chain-link fence when the man crossed the street. He wore a tweed newsboy cap, faded jeans, and a trench coat that reminded me of the green guy on *Sesame Street* who wanted Ernie to buy an 8. The rest of the fourth graders were skipping rope or pelting balls at each other until someone cried, and I was busy singing the entire score of *Bye Bye Birdie*, alone. The man walked over to me, stopping on the other side of the metal diamond-patterned fence we sometimes got our lips stuck to in winter. He didn't say hello, just looked at me and stuffed his fat hands into the front pockets of his Wranglers.

"XYZ," I said, giving him the once-over.

"What?" he said.

"XYZ," I said again, directing my eyes to his lower half.

"What?"

Didn't this guy ever go to summer camp or have recess? Was he retarded? *XYZ, ABC gum, A-D-I-D-A-S*—these were kid codes and some of our best. Clearly he'd been a child at some point. How did he not know what I was talking about? I exaggerated my speech, going real slow so he could follow.

"X. Y. Z." His blank face was starting to annoy me.

While waiting for him to catch on, I shielded him from the other kids on the playground and also from Madame Bray, who was on recess duty and very well might have been one of the bad guys from *Scooby-Doo*. Recess had just started and I had all the time in the world to wait for this turkey to crack the code and zip up his fly. He stared at me and I sent ESP toward his zipper and, finally, after I'd pretty much spelled it out for him, his eyebrows jumped up, and he said, "Oh! You mean this?," to which I muttered, "No, doy—what took you so long?"

His eyes stayed on mine as he fiddled with his zipper. The whole affair should have taken seconds but he fished and troweled down there with real concentration, like he'd lost his keys or something. A swift nod of his head signaled that he was all set so I nodded my own head to double-check that he'd finally zipped his fly, only to see that he'd pulled *out* what was supposed to be tucked *in*. There it was, drooping out of his pants, thick and pink and a little floppy, like those Jewish salamis Zaida Max sometimes brought over from the Snowden Deli. He grinned. My ankles tingled. I shuffled back a few feet. He didn't make a move and I held my breath. Silence hung in the air like his naked wiener. And then he ran off.

He was halfway down the block when I heard a deep voice behind me.

"What are you doing?" It was Anne Irene Pasquale. A pint-sizer with rodent eyes and a mother who I was convinced was the inspiration for all those V. C. Andrews books girls read at camp. Mrs. Pasquale once made me eat fettuccine Alfredo with a glass of milk—both of which she said I asked for, both of which I despised—so I cried but finished what was in front of me anyway, worried she'd lock me in a closet.

"Well, why are you just standing here? We're skipping."

I followed her pointing finger to the group of French girls, their pink rubber rope snapping the ground.

"It's okay," I said. "I'm gonna stay here."

"Too good for us?" said another girl, who'd marched over to collect Anne Irene Pasquale.

"No," I said, trying to sound like a hellion.

Nathalie Tremblay put her arm around Anne Irene Pasquale, as if she were her property. "Come on, Anne. Let's go."

There were only a handful of English-speaking girls at Collège International Marie de France, the French private school I'd attended since kindergarten, an institution known for its challenging academic programs and educators who hailed from France, thereby teaching us Parisian and not French-Canadian French. The leaflet boasted children of all ethnic diversities and claimed to be nondenominational and open to speakers of all languages. Loosely translated, that meant 99 percent white Catholic French kids and one lonely suburban Jew who was forced to sit outside of catechism class on a bench, and who would get flashed by a perv during recess.

Suffice it to say, the French speakers hung around with their kind on one side of the playground, leaving the bilinguals, who spoke English only when they felt like it, on the other. I rarely understood what was going on and waited for pity or translation and the occasional invitation to play. Bilinguals who spoke to me were hard to come by and I was not prepared to let Anne Irene Pasquale go, even if her mother made me eat cream-based sauces.

"She doesn't have to go, you know," I said. "It's a free country."

I had no idea if Canada really was a free country, since I barely understood French and couldn't follow a thing in geography class. But I'd once heard it on TV so I thought I'd bench-test it. Nathalie Tremblay didn't care what I said. She crossed her arms and stared me down. Taller than all the fourth graders, she was rumored to wear Tickle deodorant. Her bangs were curled under and the braids that fell over each shoulder were neat and tidy, like two Marathon bars fresh out of the wrapper.

My insides were still buzzy from the wiener incident, flipping a ruffian switch I didn't even know I'd come assembled with. Gathering strength in my weak ankles, I kicked Nathalie Tremblay with my Frye boot. This was not Nathalie Tremblay's first time in the ring, because she had maneuvers. As I hurled my leg toward her, she grabbed the stacked heel of my boot, biting her bottom lip with the enormous teeth that made her look like a beautiful rabbit. She held on. I tried digging the heel of my other boot into the ground but I was no match for my opponent. It took a good three seconds for me to lose my balance, falling hard onto the cement, bringing Nathalie Tremblay down with me. Anne Irene Pasquale took off in a panic either to tell or to hide, leaving us in a heap by the hopscotch court. We sized up the passing clouds for a few minutes, still tangled in our fall.

"I like your boots," Nathalie Tremblay said.

"I really like your teeth."

Stepping into Nathalie Tremblay's house was like crossing the border into a foreign land, a dark little country decorated with mismatched furniture and chintz drapery. A small black upright piano took over most of the living room. There were a few houseplants and I noticed a green plastic watering can left on the rug. I thought of the young blond guy with the bowl haircut who showed up every Thursday with his own special watering cans to take care of our indoor potted plants. Peter Plant, I called him, but to everyone else, he was the Plant Guy. Our house had a lot of "guys." We even had a live-in Filipina housekeeper who slept in the basement. Riza was in charge of operations around our cramped three-bedroom house, calling my parents ma'am and sir and ironing underwear.

Nathalie's mother liked me to call her Mrs. Tremblay, which soothed me because there was never any question who the adult was. She had just come in from their square of a backyard, bringing sprigs she had cut from the lilac tree and placing them in a glass vase on the kitchen table, which made the whole inside of the house smell like we were outside. Mrs. Tremblay did the laundry, carrying a small plastic basket around from room to room with folded clothes for all three kids to put away. Mostly they threw the items at the back of the closet and she never said a word. She went to the grocery store, with coupons and a neat list.

After school, Mrs. Tremblay held on to her strand of pearls, her only decoration, as she leaned against the kitchen sink listening to our news of the day. I took in her plain skirt and cardigan. She looked like a television mother and I wanted to hug her.

"Thanks for the cookies, Mom," said Nathalie Tremblay, finishing her milk and Fudge Stripes. Mrs. Tremblay had poured a glass for her daughter from a large aqua Tupperware pitcher, and inside the vessel was a plastic bag of milk. Nathalie told me her brother drank a lot of milk and, when her mother opened the fridge door, I saw at least four backup pouches on the top shelf, like IV bags fat with dairy instead of medicine or blood. Never in my ten years had I seen such a lineup of the stuff. Jews rarely drank milk as a beverage, not because it was against our religion but more because we collectively just thought it was gross. In our house we had Diet Pepsi, and Ace only drank 7 Up. I wanted nothing to do with milk but I was obsessed by those sacks of it.

"Let's go upstairs," Nathalie said.

The second floor of the Tremblay house was even better than the first. All the beds looked like they'd had other lives, maybe at their grandparents' house or a distant cousin's in war-torn Europe, and my favorite part: nothing matched. The hallway floor was hardwood scattered with area rugs, and two of the four bedrooms had wall to wall. The windows were open and a breeze swirled in.

We had never opened a window in my house because they were painted shut. I spent many nights in bed thinking up complicated egress plans should a radiator suddenly explode and attempt to burn the place down. My parents didn't seem to mind the lack of fresh air, as it didn't interfere with the year-round use of the central air conditioning system. Meat-locker-temperature air pumped through the house, blasting from white holes in the floors and ceilings.

But the real showstopper at the Tremblay house arrived every night at 5:30 p.m. Mr. Tremblay was a giant, bearded and menacing like some beastly version of the guy on *The Life and Times of Grizzly Adams*. Nathalie's father taught clarinet in the public schools by day and sold lumber for firewood after hours. He had a red pickup truck with his name painted on the side. Every night, he'd stomp into the house with his oversized half-unlaced work boots tracking bits of mud all over the floor, the likes of which would have given my own father a heart attack.

I thought of my father returning home from a day of making ladies' blouses. Hanging up his suit on color-coded hangers, slipping on his pressed denims, the Yorkshire terrier snuggled at his feet as they fell into a deep snooze to the background sounds of *Barney Miller*. Sometimes I'd watch him sleep. The rise and fall of his Cartier necklace, the naturally curly hair that was also permed poufing like a cloud around his head, the snug-fitting jeans he'd assured me were the ones real cowboys wore and were also "very in."

When Mr. Tremblay returned from his day, he'd stagger around for a few moments, crash into furniture, then yell at it. Nathalie told me that one night a few weeks earlier she'd had to call the operator because her father was all liquored up and swung a small machete at his wife's neck. It was the wild, wild west at the Tremblays'. I wanted to stay forever.

I don't think Mrs. Grizzly Adams found the comings and goings of her house as glamorous as I did, because with each visit her nerves seemed more frazzled. She grasped her pearls tighter, and I noticed her hands shaking as she poured the milk. Mrs. Tremblay may not have appreciated what she had, but I was stinking jealous that Nathalie got to call the actual police when her father nearly sliced open her mother before her eyes. Who knew this stuff even happened outside the hum of the television droning from my parents' room—that there were men out there who whipped out their privates, that husbands brandished real live swords in attempts to slit their wives' throats. Currents of danger and sizzle never breezed through our sealed windows. And how did Nathalie even know what to do? I didn't know how to turn the oven on.

I decided then and there that I never wanted Nathalie to come over to my place because all we'd do there was listen to records on my hi-fi and watch the Yorkie hump his Charlie Brown towel that everyone called his girlfriend. Or my father would tell her that dumb story about how during Ace's Hockey Night in Canada–themed bar mitzvah, he forced me to pop out of a cake. Worse, she'd find out about the deal he was trying to broker with me, the one about how he'd absolutely get a nose job but only if I got one, too.

How could I bring Nathalie over for any of that? Yes, my father was well-meaning, everyone liked him; you couldn't help it. He was kind and golden retrieverish and he often carried Freshen Up gum in his purse. He drove my brother to early morning hockey practice and walked the dog down the driveway to pee because my mother wasn't outdoorsy. You never even saw his skin crawl when his father came over to see the new car and Zaida Max called him a big shot, which he said through a smile, and Nana Esther sighed, assuring him the car was beautiful. Yes, my dad was all right. But, if we're being honest, it was a goddamn bummer that there would be no situation in which my father would pull a knife on any of us. There was nothing going on at my house, ever. The only action we saw took place on *Quincy*.

It was all fun all the time at the Tremblays', and on the rare occasion that we'd find ourselves with nothing to do, I'd bring up her father, hoping to hear the latest installment of doom. She was always pissed about him and we spent a good deal of our after-school hours holed up in her room, eating Fudge Stripes and hatching plots of murder and revenge. Here, finally, I had something to add, since I'd clocked many hours in front of *Guiding Light* and knew all about how to get back at people.

"We should slash my dad's tires," Nathalie said, biting the chocolate backing of the cookie with her sparkly beaver teeth. "Or put thumbtacks on the driveway."

"One time at summer camp, they put Saran Wrap over the toilet," I said, hoping to keep our nefarious activities indoors; I was scared to be outside at night.

"We could poison him. Like put Drano in his beer."

"We could leave something at the top of the stairs that he could trip on," I said. "He could fall down the stairs and get amnesia."

"That would be loud," she said, and we paused to imagine her ginormous father plummeting down the stairs. "No! I got it."

She explained to me that the cordwood business was an all-cash one. That even though Grizzly Adams was tricky and no one knew how he'd act at any given time, eventually, no matter whom he insulted or tried to stab, he'd always step out of his jeans just before passing out in his bed and not wake until morning. It was like clockwork, she said. Nathalie got out a composition book she had laying around to illustrate the plan. She drew a bed and her father's giant outline in it. Then, on the floor next to it, she sketched out his crumpled jeans and a wad of cash as a lump in the back pocket, a bubble arrow pointing toward the potential loot.

"What if he wakes up?" I asked.

"He doesn't. I swear. Once I poked him with a broom."

She continued with the diagram and explained that my job was to secure a sleepover for the coming Friday. It was then the heist would go down.

I spent the next few nights tucked in my bed, imagining Mr. Tremblay out in the world. How, after teaching clarinet to small children, he'd probably get into the red pickup with his name across the door and start with the drink. I liked to think he had a small cooler on his front passenger seat filled with Labatts, which he'd dig into as he drove down the streets of Montreal, throwing out the empty bottles when he was done with them. He'd also toss bundles of wood out the window and onto the front steps of his clients without even getting out of his truck, just like our paperboy, whom my mother was constantly annoyed with because then you had to walk down the front steps to collect the news.

When he was finished with the wood, he'd probably stop into an old-timey saloon, one that had a dartboard but also played Kool & the Gang. There, he'd drink more, regaling the other patrons with stories of stupid kids with no talent, punch a few people in the parking lot, and drive home. Sometimes I'd picture my father and Mr. Tremblay out for dinner together. My father would admire the authenticity of Mr. Tremblay's costume, the suede vest with denim work shirt and the perfectly worn boots he'd kill to have. In turn, Mr. Tremblay would watch with curiosity as my father sipped a nice Cabernet, wondering why he was so tan in February and what the hell he carried in that purse.

With Friday approaching, I did whatever I could to not let my grit fizzle. A few weeks earlier, I'd never kicked anyone on the playground or been flashed. With a little more time maybe I could even transform into one of those kids people gave nicknames to, good ones like Lefty or The Possum. Who's to say I couldn't slip into the role of badass elegantly? So what if I'd never tangled with a drunk? I was out in the real world now. I was in charge of my own pluck.

The Tremblay dinner table was set with a casserole of shepherd's pie next to some waxy beans and that Gentile pitcher of milk. I was put at the head of the table, in Mr. Tremblay's seat, since he was probably out beating people up. It was delightful knowing he could be home any moment and physically remove me from my chair, lifting me by the scruff and holding me at arm's length like we were on *Tom and Jerry*. However, I managed to get through the main course and the little cups of pudding Nathalie sometimes had in her lunch with no surprises or random acts of violence, which, if we're being honest, was kind of a disappointment.

We were clearing the table when the front door finally blew open. And there, in the doorway, stood a sweating, staggering man—as hammered as I'd hoped. Ignoring all of us busy in the kitchen, he stomped up the stairs, work boots tracking bits of dirt and gravel through the house. We continued to clear, careful to not make too much noise. There was stomping above our heads, then a current of pee hitting water but no flush. It didn't take long for a loud thump to follow, signaling Mr. Tremblay's fall into bed. His snoring began, exaggerated and cartoonish, so ridiculous it sounded like he was faking. The family dried dishes and put leftovers in the fridge, keeping hushed so as not to wake the bear. I imagined it would take a lot more than clinking forks or the suction of the fridge door to disturb the beast, but they were better schooled in the drunk-man arts, so I followed suit.

Nathalie's sister, Beatrice, was tasked with table wiping, and we were excused since I was the guest. If we timed it right, Nathalie told me, her mother would make herself a cup of chamomile tea and spend the next thirty minutes listening to Beatrice's piano practice as Dave, the brother, went outside, claiming to join a street hockey game but really hiding behind the car smoking KOOLs. The sounds of "Für Elise" plinked up the stairs, competing with the drunken snoring. Panic and dread sizzled through me at the thought of potentially getting killed. *Man*, I thought, *now, this is livin'*.

"Okay," Nathalie said. "I'll go in and take the money. You be the lookout."

"No fair," I said. "I want to steal."

"Uh, it's my father who's the drunk."

"So?"

"So I get to steal the money."

"No fair."

"It is *too* fair," she said. "At least I asked you to do it with me."

"You always get to do this stuff," I said, teetering on the cliff of a fit.

"If he wakes up and sees you, he might kill you."

"You said he wouldn't wake up."

"He's not going to wake up."

Nathalie's argument was weak but, after thinking about it, I remembered I was, too. For sure I would have barfed or fainted but I felt I should at least try to get a horse in the race. If being friends with Nathalie Tremblay had taught me anything, it was that you had to fight a lot.

I took my post in her doorway, which provided a clear view of both the top of the stairs and her parents' room. We wished each other good luck and off she went, creeping into the drunk's bunker. My insides became ferrets and I could barely stand still. I wondered if I might pee. When Nathalie got to the jeans, she turned to face me and we stuffed fists in our mouths to stifle the war cries inching up our throats. Nathalie composed herself by taking exaggerated breaths and shaking out her hands, stuff to make me laugh and prolong my anxiety that he could open his eyes and grab her neck, or mine. This stake-raising business was terrifying. I'd never felt giddier. Nathalie nodded and winked, then reached into the back pocket and pulled out a roll of fifties. She sprinted to her room and I shut the door behind her, and together we laughed like maniacs while counting our haul.

"I swear he'll never notice," said Nathalie. "He brings this much home every day."

Later that night, as I fussed on the floor, trying to not feel trapped by the sleeping bag I was sausaged into, I thought of how my father would call me into his room every Thursday before *Mork & Mindy* and hand me three dollars, which I'd stick in my own pockets and then spend on grape Bubble Yum. This money was different, dirty and hard earned.

The first thing we bought with our dollars was a small metal box apiece, complete with teeny keyholes and locks. Mine was red and Nathalie's was black. She gave me some string and we both wore our keys around our necks, under our sweatshirts. Then we went downtown to Phantasmagoria Records and bought *Zenyatta Mondatta* by the Police. I knew I'd have to hide it between my Bobby Vinton records in case my parents saw.

Nathalie started pilfering money, almost nightly, without me. I was sulky not to be part of things anymore even though she still often shared, keeping my lockbox full with the sneezing powder and sparklers and Silly Putty we paid for, and the Kissing Sticks Nathalie stole for us from the drugstore. It was great to have all that stuff, but things were getting crazy at home and she often wanted to come to my place instead. Once there, she'd say I was lucky that my parents wore Calvin Kleins and she didn't mind that the windows couldn't open.

I longed to be part of the action back at her house but, if we're being honest, I knew that all I ever was, all I'd ever be, was a passenger in Nathalie Tremblay's getaway car. I liked all the souvenirs I got along the way, but what I really wanted was her spunk and mettle. Why was it that everyone else came assembled properly? Even that playground flasher seemed to be doing all right. Confidence certainly didn't seem to be a problem for *that* guy. He felt okay enough with himself to spill it out to strangers on the street. Where do you even get that kind of moxie? Why wasn't I cut out for an existence like that? Life was bullshit sometimes.

By the end of fifth grade, I was doing so poorly academically they wanted to hold me back a year. I was sent to a bilingual public school for the sixth grade, where for the first time in my life I understood how to spell words and do long division. Eventually, Nathalie moved on to a public high school where she'd wear raccoon eyeliner and French older boys. I heard she even bought some hash from a tenth grader and carved the word *fuck* on the front door of her house.

We didn't see each other as much anymore. I made a *few* new friends blessed with familial turmoil, but nothing ever as good as what happened at the Tremblays'. Sure, there was divorce and stuff, maybe an abusive uncle, but none of it compared to the charms of a machete-wielding drunk or the enchantment of banditry or those gorgeous sacks of Christian milk.

Letters to a Low-level Depressive

· · · · · ·

To Whom It May Concern:

Robbie Levine wants a hand job. Also, he'd like to be called Robert now, since he is going to be a playwright, possibly also a screenwriter, and wants to be taken seriously. He'd like for me to start taking myself seriously, too. He also wants the hand job request to be taken seriously. Robbie/Robert Levine wants a lot.

I'm writing to you because Lisa Dorfman's basement party is coming up and I'm not sure what to do about Robbie's request, or who to ask about it. My mother whispers the word *bathroom* when she has to use it, so I imagine that upon hearing my dilemma her head would explode in the restroom and we'd never get the smell of Aussie Mega out of there. I can't turn to my best friend, Wendy, because last night she ate another whole pack of Ex-Lax *and* six peanut butter–flavored Ayds—she's convinced she's fat—and her mom is so mad she made her stay home from school today. I bet she's watching *General Hospital* with a tub of Baskin-Robbins, then making herself barf. If I had to guess, though, I think she'd tell me to definitely do the hand job because

I'm lucky to have a boyfriend in the first place, and also that I am not fat. Plus she thinks he looks like Magnum, P.I.

My brother, Ace, is supposed to be writing college essays, but he's playing air guitar to AC/DC in his room. If my friends call the house these days, he tells them I can't come to the phone because I'm dead, so he's no use. And my father—well, who can ask their father about these matters? Not to mention that when he found out I smoked that More menthol in the park last week, we had to have a sit-down in the den, where he looked uncomfortable and said something about how he'd "tried a couple of marijuanas in my day and good thing I didn't like them."

This leaves Riza, our Filipina live-in housekeeper. But it's awkward enough she lives in the basement and irons my father's jeans. So I am turning to you. I wasn't sure what to call you, so I used the whole to-whom-it-may-concern thing, because we learned it in English class. Please reply as soon as you can. Lisa Dorfman's party is next week.

Yours truly,
High School Kim

Dear High School Kim,

So nice to hear from you! You can just call me Kim, or Middle-Aged Kim; whichever is fine. Let me start this letter by saying there is usually a rule in movies about all things relating to time travel, instructions on how you are free to divulge what happens in the future but no one is allowed to do anything that will change the course of history. I'm not sure if our correspondence constitutes time travel, but if it does, don't worry about it. You know we don't pay much mind to rules. And not because we think we're Fonzie or anything, but more because we are apathetic.

Just to make sure there was no revisionist history about our inertia, I did some research. After scouring all our high school yearbooks, my memory serves. There wasn't a poem or art project with our name under it, there was no team involvement of any sort, and for just about every class photo, we were absent. I'm sure I don't have to remind you that our high school was pretty small—with only two hundred and fifty kids in total, sixty in our graduating class—so to not make any showing in the yearbook is next to impossible. It took work to not be represented in any capacity. So, good for us, I guess.

A side note: You know how high school in Montreal lasts for five years, from grade seven through eleven? Be prepared to have to explain that one for the rest of your life when you move to the States, because it doesn't work that way here. Also, they say "eighth grade," not "grade eight." (Yes! You are going to college, in the States, where you will remain for good after you graduate. I know, right? Feel free to pay even less attention in science. You won't be using it in your daily life and it doesn't matter.)

All this aside, yes, I am happy to give you guidance on hand jobs. Or anything else that might come up for you. I don't get out much and I love giving advice. Remember how we dreamed of writing an advice column for *Seventeen*? (That never happens.) Anyway, here we go. . . .

Robbie Levine, first love, thirteen years old. That guy's intense, huh? Not even five feet and already calls you "darling" as if he drinks Cognac and teaches the classics. And the way he had his whole life planned out? So focused, such an overachiever. I wonder if we believed some of that might rub off on us, perhaps during all that dry humping to Jackson Browne at his house.

Don't you love that house? Nestled in the cul-de-sac, all that laughing inside, so vibrant, the endless amount of siblings? Are you still wearing that silver ID bracelet? The one he got for his bar mitzvah but gave to you when you started going out? It was so heavy. Such a reminder that you had a pulse, that you were connected to something. First love is intoxicating. At once private but fully out there for everyone to see, even your teachers. It was everything.

Have you sneaked to the second-floor bathroom, the single one with the lock, to make out yet? What about all the letters, have you guys started writing those? I still have a box downstairs filled with all the high-school letters—mostly from friends, but there are still some of those letters from Robbie. Your first love letters written in his neat, loopy cursive on his monogrammed notecards saying things like how you were the most special girl he'd ever known and how it would be a long time before he met anyone as unique as you and that his love for you has grown an "awesome extent."

And guess what? I found one that says, and I quote, "I deeply respect you for sticking by your standards." I'm guessing that's the hand job part.

Wow, look at me, waxing poetic instead of answering your question. The kids will be home from school momentarily, so I should probably end this. I'm assuming by the time you get my reply, you'll have already given the hand job right there in Lisa Dorfman's backyard while the rest of the kids slow-dance to REO Speedwagon. After, he'll give you a box of yellow stationery that he had engraved with both your names on it: ROBERT & KIM. But, on the off chance this gets to you before it all goes down, I say go for it. It's so not a big deal. Plus it will be one of the first times in high school that you actually accomplish something.

Yours truly,

Me

P.S.: Act surprised about the stationery.

Dear Middle-Aged Kim,

I got your letter just after Lisa Dorfman's. Thanks for the reply, I guess. Do you think, next time, if I ask you a question, you could just give me the advice and not tell me all the stuff that happens in the future? Maybe some people want to know, but I don't. I think it's kind of depressing.

Thanks,

Kim

Dear H.S. Kim,

Depressing? You don't know the half of it. Wait until the end of the school year, after the hand job and the stationery and all those letters claiming he'll never love anyone like he loves you. Cut to—your mother signs you up for theater camp and Robbie/Robert decides he'd like to go, too. You sit on the bus together and just before you get there he says, "Hey, I've been thinking. Let's stay going out this summer but let's not tell anyone." And you say, "Um, okay."

Um, okay! How's that for depressing? So you guys settle into camp—well, he settles into camp. He's all well adjusted and confident, so he instantly gets whisked away by some famous kid who is about to leave to star in a movie, but not before he introduces Robbie to all the players. They pal away arm in arm, and you, shy and sad and wet-dog pathetic, stand alone with your duffel. He gets cast as Danny Zuko in *Grease* and proceeds to make out with twenty-two girls (yes, you keep count). You play an old lady, an aging performer in some geriatric home for geezery actors in this Noel Coward snoozer that no one wants to come see because it's not a musical. We're not even good in it.

You know what else we're not good at, right? Exactly. Camp.

We suck at camp. We're all lonely and awkward and we have no confidence, so making friends is a real bitch.

As luck would have it, though, some of the more attractive campers take pity on us because Robbie/Robert is a man-about-camp and we're—well, we're us. They try to boost us up, nudge us to meet other guys, which, ironically, we do. And then, you know who resurfaces? You guessed it. Robbie/Robert now loves you again, so you break up with the other guy, who actually gets kind of mad and throws a chair at you during rehearsal.

Obviously, R/R goes back to conquering the rest of the girls, leaving you to roam the halls of the derelict, creepy hotel the camp is housed in, alone. No guy will come near you now for fear of upsetting Danny Zuko because he's the greatest. God, you love him.

I can't remember much else from that summer, except I think you end up stealing someone's jean jacket, possibly someone on kitchen staff. And then, to top it all off, when you get home, we get a perm.

All the best,
Me

Dear Kim,

Oh my god! And then what happens? Do we break up for good? Please tell me! I can't do my homework until I know. Please write me back as soon as you get this.

Oh my god,
Me

Dear You,

You might as well sit on that leather chair you like so much in the den. Not only because what I am about to tell you will be hard to hear but also because your mother is about to hire a decorator and all that squishy worn-in leather furniture is about to undergo some serious lacquering. In a matter of months the whole house is going to be all glass bricks and black shiny everything. Even that toilet downstairs, the one in the guest bathroom by the front door, is going to be replaced with a black toilet, which, I will warn you now, is very daunting to use. Things are about to get uncomfortable for you, literally and figuratively. You might want to get a pack of those powdered donuts from the bread drawer. And some Doritos from the chip cabinet. I hate to be the one to tell you this, but . . .

Yes, you break up. By the beginning of grade 9, you're officially kaput. When the decorator redoes your room, you pick a black water bed, in which you will spend many hours floating on the lukewarm mattress, weeping to the sounds of Sérgio Mendes swearing he's "Never Gonna Let You Go." Wendy will stay on the phone with you all the way up until *Knots Landing* comes on, and even then she'll remain on the line as Abby Ewing threatens Valene. Wendy will try her best to make you feel better, mostly by reminding you how lucky you are not to be fat.

In years to come, you and Wendy will take a Jewish teen tour to Israel, where Wendy will subsist on Diet Coke and, literally, one carrot a day. She will lose an entire person in weight and become so thin she looks like a profile. When you get off the plane, her mother will burst into tears at the terminal and blame you for what has happened. But until that time, Wendy will be of sound enough mind to be a good friend.

Meanwhile, life moves on, but you will not yet be over Robert Levine. What you are over, though, along with mostly everyone else in your grade, is the whole preppy thing. Everyone will get Flock of Seagulls haircuts, pierce their clothes with safety pins, and discuss Nietzsche at their lockers. You will embrace this trend by embracing Robert Levine's stepbrother, whose nature is darker and jeans pegged, with whom you will remain obsessed for a total of five months. This gets you back onto the cul-de-sac. The making out now happens in the basement where you spend good after-school hours watching *Koyaanisqatsi* and being very avant-garde. You'll pretend you understand Philip Glass's music and the themes of life being out of balance, but in reality the whole thing makes you feel kinda dumb. And really nauseous.

When the stepbrother dumps you, you will take to the water bed again and shortly thereafter resume your Robbie/Robert obsession. You will keep your perm over your eye and get through the days as best you can, but you will not find meaning in anything except television, mostly *The Love Boat* and *Mama's Family*. You will start watching *St. Elsewhere*, convincing yourself you have the featured disease. In the afternoons, you will stare at Chuck Woolery on *Love Connection* and wonder where it all went wrong. You will crank call Robbie/Robert, hanging up as soon as you hear his perfect voice. You will watch *Dirty Dancing* on VHS at Wendy's, rewinding and rewatching as much as she wants, just so she'll listen to you cry. You'll hatch schemes to make him fall in love with you again. Since Wendy has more classes with him that year, you beg her to report all the things she's seen him do or eat during the day, what shorts he's wearing, and which girls he's potentially making out with in your special second-floor bathroom. You call this part "the news" and you'll tack on a special section at the end wherein you tell each other all the bad things you've heard other people saying about each of you. You will spend most of ninth and tenth grade like this (especially the first nine weeks of tenth grade when you are home in bed with mono). You will try to grow out your perm. You will debate getting bangs or wisps, gathering the ends of your hair and placing them over your forehead to see which would look better.

Finally, you will arrive at eleventh grade, your terminal year in high school. Last chance to apply yourself, maybe even try. You get cast in the senior show. Robbie Levine also gets cast. He will play the lead in *The Crucible* and you will be the wife he cheats on. You want the role of the sexy miscreant who sleeps with Robbie's character, but instead you play his sad, cold wife. You have similar acting styles—you cry loudly and he screams loudly. You are both acceptable but are both convinced he should win a Tony.

The highlight of the theater season happens while you both are in the wings, waiting for your cues. Sometimes, you make out. He may or may not have a girlfriend but you don't care. You make yourself available any time he is ready. He makes up some stuff about how kissing each other will help you get into character. Or how this is how real actors are, loose and free. You don't care about the reasons, only that you are back on the other side of his make-out. You love the theater. Now you are jazzed about life. You even sign up to be on the yearbook committee (although you ultimately get fired . . . something about not doing any work). Eventually, you meet another guy who doesn't go to your school and you will love him, but deep down you furiously, rabidly, dementedly love Robbie Levine for almost longer than I should tell you. He goes off to college and has a swell time. And you go off to college and—well, maybe I'll just leave that alone for right now.

So, there you have it! The *Reader's Digest* account of your high school career. Hilarious, right?

Write soon,

Me

Dear You,

Does anything good ever happen to me?
   Sigh,
   Me/You

My Darling (ha-ha) Kim,

That's the thing! All kinds of good things happen to you—you just can't see the bright side of anything. You don't know how. Your insides feel like a hollowed-out canoe but nothing is actually really wrong. You have friends who write things in your yearbook like, *You're a great kid!* And *I never would have survived Mr. V's math class without you!* You waste all kinds of years pining for Robert Levine, but you actually end up having a decent array of boyfriends. You are relatively healthy, no one you know dies for years to come, and you don't even have to get a job until you're out of college!
   Don't let the turkeys get you down,
   Me

Dear You,

I just want to ask one last thing. I read once in my mother's *Cosmo* magazine that a lot of people have a rough time in high school but you shouldn't worry if that's the case because it all gets better. Is that true? Does it get better?
   Me

Dear Kim,

Nah, they don't know what they're talking about. It doesn't get better. It gets worse. You're not going to see the light of day until your forties. You live in your head too much and you're going to take just about everything personally and feel sad most of the time. Don't worry, though, you're not going to become an alcoholic or anything. You have a Jewish constitution and booze doesn't really agree with you. Instead you'll sort of become addicted to sadness and negativity. Sometimes, while still living under our parents' roof, you'll feed the malaise with Doritos and water it with Diet Pepsi. You'll not be able to identify what's wrong, or talk about it with anyone in your family, so you'll keep it to yourself, hide it in the back of your brain somewhere, but it will ooze out all the time like that toy slime you wanted when you were nine, the one that came in the little lime garbage pail but our mother said we couldn't have because it would stain the rug. Eventually you'll go to a few colleges, then move to New York and get jobs you think you aren't very good at and make lots of friends you are convinced don't really like you and spend much time not wanting to go to parties you are invited to and get morose because no one asks you to be in a book club even though the last thing you want to do is be in a book club but would it kill them to ask?

I know I said that thing in my first letter about not changing the course of history, but I think they should make an exception for you, because if we're being honest, you're kind of a sad sack. People say to enjoy yourself because life is short. Sorry, kid. Full disclosure here, but life is long. Really, really long.

Love,

Me

Dear Kim,

Maybe you shouldn't write me anymore. You're depressing. And kind of a downer.

Kim

Dear Kim,

You don't know the half of it.
    Be well,
    Me

There's No Business

. . . .

My favorite records, when I was nine, featured ORIGINAL BROADWAY CAST RECORDING across the front of their cardboard covers. I could identify the eleven o'clock number of any musical, owned a satin show jacket, and knew the entire *Liza with a "Z"* concert album by heart. If I was a middle-aged gay man in my youth, no one said a thing. It's possible you heard my rendition of "The Ladies Who Lunch" from Stephen Sondheim's *Company* during my nana's Passover seder, at which I'd performed regularly. Zaida Max had requested the Four Questions, but I knew he'd rather hear my interpretation of a drunken toast to the rich ladies who wasted their days at luncheons instead of finding meaning in their lives. My family would prod their gefilte fish as I, third grader, finished strong with

Does anyone. Still wear. A hat?
I'll drink to that.

I could barely ride a bike but was expert at mimicking Elaine Stritch's tone. I already came assembled with most of the cynicism required for the number, everything else I'd picked up from the droll musings of my favorite TV show, *Maude*. Squirreled away in my room memorizing lyrics, belting them into my mic-shaped soap-on-a-rope, was how I spent many a childhood afternoon.

Riding the city bus to school each morning, I'd pretend to practice piano on my green vinyl book bag. We didn't have a piano at home, nor did I play a single musical instrument (minus the kazoo and one song on the push-button telephone), but still I slouched over the phantom ivories, doing my best Schroeder, hoping someone would notice. At recess I'd walk around with my feet positioned in duck formation so that I might be mistaken for a dancer. I was saving up my allowance to buy one of those silk piano-key scarves and a pair of Capezio dance shoes to go with the burgundy Danskin wrap skirt I'd forced my mother to buy. These were the accessories I was sure every last one of those orphans in *Annie* owned and were probably the reasons they were chosen to be on Broadway.

When I was ten, I wanted to go blind. What, didn't you see *Ice Castles*? Somewhere between Tom Skerritt's turtlenecks and the scrappy rasp of Colleen Dewhurst's voice, I wanted in. I dreamed of being Lexie, with her curled blond bangs and poly-ester skating costumes. Mind you, I didn't have a lick of athletic ability, but somehow I knew, deep down in my weak ankles, that if I'd ever bothered to apply myself, I, too, could do a triple axel. So what I wasn't thrilled with the whole catastrophic-fall-amid-the-metal-tables-and-chairs-causing-the-life-altering-blood-clot part, I'd still take it. Because, oh, how I wanted flowers thrown at my blind self while Robby Benson stared deep into my unsee-ing eyes, Melissa Manchester's voice in the background begging the world not to let this feeling end.

I wanted all those things. Who didn't? But what I wanted most was for that big-city coach—the one with the cowl neck

the entire way to my apartment. It was on this route that I was stopped by a homeless fellow in a Davy Crockett hat.

"You got any change in that box?" he said, fiddling with the tail on his head.

"No," I said, using the rude tone I'd mastered in my brief tenure in show business. I held on to my office box, the one filled with the pens and Post-its and rage of my fellow shit-canned employees around the world. The man just stood still, giving me the once-over. Then he leaned in and said, "You should smile more."

"*Pffft.*" Off I marched.

"Bitch," he said, rather loudly.

I channeled all the scrap I could muster, spun around, and marched right back to his judgy face and dumb hat. "Hey!" I waggled a finger near his eyes. "*You'd* be a bitch, too, if *you* just got laid off!"

I could still hear him laughing as I fought the wind over the Mass Ave Bridge.

I spent a month holed up in my apartment, watching television, eating toast, when Casting & Co. called to offer me my job back. (I know, settle down, I, too, was surprised.) This time, I vowed to do things differently. Oh, sure, I'd still have a terrible attitude, but this time I'd dust off my old acting skills to make it *appear* as if I were participating. Which I did until I couldn't fake it anymore. It was time to take this show on the road.

Entry Level Redux, Manhattan

New York City: birthplace of the discovered. Here, it would all be different. Here, I would be different.

The first thing I did was enlist a telephone-answering service called Bells Are Ringing. This is what all the soon-to-be's did back in the early '90s. Being part of a phone service triggered something in me. It made me finally want to apply myself. All the energy my high school teachers and various educators spent begging me not to be lame finally paid off. A fresh city meant a new life's ambition: becoming the top client Bells Are Ringing ever had. I wanted to be more than Caller 580—I wanted to be highly esteemed, the most fun, the gold star. I didn't even want a job anymore, just my position as number-one caller-inner.

Jeffy was instantly my favorite, and I his. We hit it off right away. He, the upbeat wannabe Broadway dancer answering phones until Tommy Tune came a-callin', and I, the sassy work for hire who clocked in at least three calls a day even though my resume hadn't garnered one bite. By the end of my second week, we had inside jokes and he was calling me "hon." I adored nothing more than being called "hon," especially by a gay phone operator. My mother subscribed to *Ms.* magazine so that I could avoid being called "hon," but nothing made me feel mightier.

I loved Jeffy. We'd stay on the phone for five- to seven-minute clips. I didn't even need a job or friends or a place to go because I had Jeffy, and he had me. A job would only get in the way of our relationship. However, with only seventy-eight dollars left in my bank account, Jeffy suggested perhaps it was time to get working.

I spent many unemployed days walking the streets. When moving to NYC, one wants to look like a real New Yorker. You don't want your clothes to give away your place of origin. You adopt a New York face, which is a combination of purpose and unflappability and superiority and *Don't bother me, I'm going somewhere important, but if you get hit by a bus, I will definitely help you*. Nothing fazes you. If someone yells in your face or is masturbating in Central Park, what do you care? You're a native.

You know to complain about the incompetence of the cashier at your local Duane Reade. When out-of-towners tell you your city is great but they wouldn't want to live here, you wave off their nonsense by telling them you can eat pad Thai at three a.m. if you so choose (but you rarely do). You say the crowds give you energy, even if they give you panic attacks. And you walk wherever you need to go. Well, that part I just told myself. Real New Yorkers take the subway, but I was terrified of it. I grew up watching *The Warriors* and *Fame* and *Welcome Back, Kotter*—I knew what roguery took place underground. I spent my dwindling dollars on cab rides.

When Jeffy called to announce that I'd finally gotten a real appointment at a talent agency, I put on my interview pants and took a cab to 250 West Fifty-seventh Street. The lobby had a small newspaper stand with an impressive candy display, and a company directory on the marbled walls that I consulted three times upon arrival even though I'd memorized the floor, checked, and rechecked at home and twice in the cab. I'd never heard of the Agency, but after some due diligence I learned that the founder, who lived in Los Angeles, had a Hollywood actor pedigree and had started a West Coast agency that represented the likes of James Earl Jones and Bette Midler and Jean Stapleton. I was to meet the agent in charge of the New York office.

"Have a seat, honey," said an ascotted fellow with thick plastic glasses low on his nose. Head down and eyes peeking over the top of the tortoiseshell rims, he said, "You might want to sit for a moment. She'll be back soon."

Back at the electric typewriter, he hummed as he clacked and clicked, and I wondered who *she* was—Jeffy had told me I was to be meeting someone named Paul. There were no framed headshots on the wall the way I'd imagined, just stacks of half-opened envelopes on a messy desk, and a few sad chairs, on even sadder carpet, lined up near the door. Half the office was windowed, yet still it managed to feel dark inside. The only difference between the Agency's office and my prior agency job in Boston was the address.

Twenty minutes later, a man entered the office with a stack of *Variety* magazines in hand. He had black hair and wore black jeans, black Reeboks, black glasses, and a light-blue button-down shirt that was mostly tucked in. One of the bottom buttons was undone, revealing some hirsute-stomach business I tried to ignore as he lumbered to the back of the office. A few seconds later, the telephone rang and I was told Paul would see me now.

Paul slid a client list across the desk, one typed into three columns on letterhead, on which I recognized one or two of the 150 names. He talked for many minutes about Broadway and *Law & Order* and something to do with LORT contracts, to which I nodded like I knew what he was talking about. There was a washed-up, tired feeling to every corner of the office, every rug and chair and envelope. I expected New York show business to be shinier than the *Broadway Danny Rose* feel I was channeling. Regardless, it was a foot in the door of real New York living, so I did all my best nodding and promising to be a very good employee.

Jeffy called two mornings later to tell me Ascot called, and so I called Ascot, who put me on the phone with Paul, who let me know I could start next week, which actually thrilled Ascot, as he was dying to get out of there to pursue his lifelong dream of experimental theater writing. The Agency would be my place of work for the next three years.

JOB DESCRIPTION (AS PAUL EXPLAINED IT)

Answer phones: Self-explanatory. Please be polite.

Upkeep of headshots & resumes, plus handle incoming: Make sure there are at least thirty headshots on file at all times. Open all headshots that come in mail. If anyone looks interesting, pass to me.

Prepare daily submissions: Each morning, an envelope will arrive via messenger, which will contain what we call a breakdown. This is a write-up of each project looking to hire and a description of roles they are setting up auditions for. I will write on the breakdown who I feel is appropriate. You type out list, collect the headshots, and mail or messenger in.

General office and client paperwork maintenance: If the copy machine breaks—well, you get the idea. Oh! This is the most important. You see that black filing cabinet over there? That has all our clients' union papers, their SAG and AFTRA contracts. These are very important and need to be checked monthly to see whose are up for renewal. Once they need to be renewed, you type up the new forms and send them in. Okay? You got it? It's *very* important. (Reader alert: Chekov's gun.) (Stay tuned.)

JOB DESCRIPTION (AS I EXECUTED IT. FOR THREE MONTHS. AND THEN . . .)

Answer phones: Oh, God, stop ringing, already.

Upkeep of headshots & resumes, plus handle incoming: I'm sure there are enough in the files.

Prepare daily submissions: Really? Submit these thirty actors for *Stomp* (a percussion show), when only one of these actors has percussion experience listed on his resume? Is anyone from here really going to star opposite Tom Hanks? I'll send it tomorrow.

General office and client paperwork maintenance: Oh, is
the copier jammed? Does anyone really need staples? I'm
sure those pesky contracts are fine where they are.

When I first moved to the city and started at the Agency, I
imagined life would be like *The Mary Tyler Moore Show*. I'd move
into a darling apartment with a sunken living room and a new
best friend right upstairs. During the day, I'd pal around with
my coworkers and be the apple of my boss's gruff eye, although
really he had a heart of gold. At night, my Rhoda would come
downstairs and together we'd lament our hilarious work shenan-
igans and share head scarves.

In reality, my neighbor was a shut-in and the studio I was
subletting was littered with take-out containers. There was no
camaraderie at the office like at the WJM newsroom. The day-
to-day work was tedious. Sure, there were perks. Paul loved
going to the theater, which he did almost every night. If there
were extra tickets, he'd give them to me. Many a time that meant
sitting in a church basement suffering through an all-woman
production of *The Cabinet of Dr. Caligari*, but sometimes it meant
Lincoln Center, where I went to the opening night of *Arcadia* and
found myself sitting in front of its author, Tom Stoppard, and
right across the aisle from Regis. I saw Carol Channing return in
Hello, Dolly! when she was 107 years old and they had to put a
net over the pit lest she fell off the stage. I even attended opening
night of *Damn Yankees,* starring Jerry Lewis, then off to a party
at Tavern on the Green. On those evenings, I really felt like I was
a part of things.

But the next morning I was back to sweeping the cinders. And
although I had little experience or talent for the job, I wanted to
be in the thick of it all the time. I wanted to turn down offers for
our too-busy clients and wear sunglasses indoors. Instead of tak-

ing a long look at myself, I decided instead to find things wrong with my boss. His eyebrows were too thick, he whined when he spoke, what did he do all day besides read the trades? How could I be expected to work under such unprofessional conditions? Our clients weren't landing big roles. Some made money as long-standing soap-opera characters and we had a few up-and-coming Broadway performers, but this was C-level stuff.

I decided it was time to move on. I alerted Jeffy that I had sent out one resume and asked him, even though I wasn't that kind of lucky, to please keep an ear out for the potential call, which, lo and behold, came in. I interviewed on my lunch hour and actually landed the job. It was the most Hollywood thing to ever happen to me, and I took that as a sign.

Unfortunately, I was too scared to quit, so to remedy that, I started phoning it in. The submissions got lazier. Sometimes if we were low on resumes I'd just omit them from the packet. If the copy machine jammed, I pretended I didn't see. I talked to my friends on the phone instead of ordering the office supplies or keeping tabs on those very important contracts sitting innocently in file folders, expiring. It did occur to me that Paul might do occasional spot inspections of the contract files, so instead of dealing with them as instructed, I hid them in the top drawer of my desk. At least I had the decency to give my notice two days before Paul found said contracts in the desk drawer. But Paul still got mad. Really mad. I took my lumps, though, let him scream at me as he stomped around my desk a few times and then, like a maniac, yanked the phone cord out of the wall.

"You may not use this any longer. You may not talk on the phone. Or answer the phone. Or touch the phone. Just. Do. The. Contracts. And then, you are fired!"

"I'm not fired because I quit!" I said. Okay, I didn't say that. I did, however, want to remind him that I'd already quit, but even

I knew enough to stop talking. Paul didn't speak to me for the remainder of my time there, which, if you ask me, was rather unprofessional. On my last day at the Agency, I walked into his office to say goodbye.

"Good luck to you," he said under his breath, but I think he actually said "Good luck to *them*."

Last Stop: Show Business

It is said that the entertainment industry is the only place where one can fail up. When I walked into the SuperAgency—a boutique agency, which was a smaller operation than the big guns like William Morris or CAA, but which represented actors you definitely knew by name or face—I knew I had finally stepped in real show business. Here was the big-fish/small-pond situation I'd hoped to find for myself. Finally, after all that nonwork, I'd arrived. Should you find yourself working in the talent agency world as an assistant, here are some signs to confirm that you, too, have officially entered real show business.

1. The letterhead is very nice. Also, each agent has a stack of special note cards, which usually are in a bookmark shape, with their names emblazoned on them. They are of thick card stock and get placed in scripts or submission packets with small notes inscribed. Assistants dream of having these cards.

2. You will use a headset to talk on the phone. Not only does this look official, it leaves your hands free to organize note cards.

3. You will be forced to learn a new language—a *slanguage*—which you'll absorb by studying the copy of *Variety*

you will be told to read only after your boss has finished consulting it and throws it in the trash. To get you started, a few of the more important words:

> *ankled* = fired
> a *shingle* = a small business
> a *ten percenter* = an agent
> *Gotham-based* = New York City–based

Not to worry, you will catch on quickly but, if you're lost, ask a fellow assistant because . . .

4. No agent will talk to you.

5. It's no longer Robert De Niro, it's Bobby. And *Marty* Scorsese and *Sandy* Bullock and everyone's best pal, *Jimmy* Caan.

When I first started at the SuperAgency, an awful agent/creature was running the show, a Hydra of sorts. And, just as the Greek myth suggested, when one head got cut off, two more grew in its place. Word came from HQ in Los Angeles that our boss had been set free and, until further notice, two senior agents would temporarily take over—one Hydra gets ankled, sprouting two new heads of talent. This new thing was a creature so powerful that it caused assistants to hide in their cubicles or scurry to the bathroom to weep.

Had I been in a movie, audiences would have seen a greenish sky looming over Forty-second Street, cockroaches and rodents running to get the hell out of the area. Something wicked—well, two things wicked—this way came. The audience would shout warnings at the screen: "Get out of there!" "Run!" But who listens to moviegoers who yell at the screen? Instead, I stayed at my desk, reminded on a daily basis of my stupidity, incompetence, and general dislikability.

My direct boss was a comedy agent. Mind you, she represented young stand-ups way before stand-ups made any real money on television, so she wasn't taken seriously and also suffered at the hands of the new boss ladies, whom I'd come to regard as Roald Dahl's infamous duo from *James and the Giant Peach*, Aunt Sponge and Aunt Spiker. If you are not familiar with these aunts, one was rail thin and the other a roundish ball, and they were the relatives forced to take young James in after his parents get eaten by a rhinoceros. They watched over him, sure, but they were mean, abusive, and never let the young boy out of their sight to play with other children. Agent Sponge and Agent Spiker were, to put it plain, hideous to us. They were the agents you see in movies but don't believe really exist. Calling us names, pitting us against one another, throwing the contents of our desks across the office. Sponge and Spiker seemed to take great pleasure in the insults they hurled our way, the mind games they played on us. It was degrading.

In fairness, I was still a lackluster employee, complete with bad attitude and lazy work habits and a real talent for stirring the pot, but they treated every assistant this way, even the ones who made an effort. We knew better than to tattle on Sponge and Spiker, especially to their clients, who loved their agents loyally and somehow found their unctuous personalities delightful. The upside was that it bonded we lower-level employees. We were tight, a band of not-so-merry assistants, and I, the most miserable and aggravated of the bunch, led this group daily to our two-dollar beans-and-rice plates at the dive across the street, where we'd spend our entire lunch hour dissecting each mean thing said to us that day, picking apart Sponge and Spiker limb by limb like a group of four-year-old boys with a handful of daddy longlegs. It just made us feel better.

In the spring of 1986, we'd learned that two high-powered agents had been poached from William Morris to breathe new life into the SuperAgency. The assistants whispered about it in the bathroom, wondering whether these new agents chose these positions or left William Morris to *spend more time with their families* (slanguage synonym for *ankled*). No matter, in our eyes their arrival ruffled Sponge and Spiker, and that was good enough for us.

The office was not nearly big enough—literally or figuratively—to hold our new SuperAgents. Reshuffling ensued. Sponge and Spiker let everyone know they were staying put. SuperAgent One looked around the place, to see which room was grand enough to hold him and his deal making. As he paced the office we were already mushrooming out of, his assistant walked behind him, surveying the scene. You could tell she meant business in a way none of us did, due to her smart slacks and serious glasses. You knew by just looking at her focused eyebrows that she'd never slum by the Xerox machine to waste time or complain. SuperAssistant walked with purpose, her headset (with dangly cord) always on her head, ready to plug into any phone at a moment's notice should one of their top-shelf clients call in or, more importantly, if her SuperAgent felt thirsty or needed the air conditioner turned up a degree.

She was at once hateful and enviable. We felt silly in her presence, as if we didn't take the nature of the buying and selling of actors seriously enough. SuperAssistant had a super show-biz attitude—her work was the most important, most serious work of all. She was taller, cut from a better cloth, and at the end of the day she found the lot of us ridiculous. SuperAssistant was Pac-Man buzzing along the maze, we the Pac dots she ate to get to the next level.

SuperAgent One eventually decided he'd move into the oversized conference room, the only area large enough to contain the lot of us comfortably. There was a rarely used mini–conference space, stuffy and crowded, one that barely fit six chairs, and you couldn't get in or out without knocking something over. This was now our only place to meet, with clients or with each other for the officewide weekly council. It was the least impressive room we had. It was also where my agent was moved, told she'd have to vacate the premises any time any meeting needed to be held by anyone in the entire office. The real estate of it all spoke volumes, letting my boss know they thought her work was comedic—but not in the good way. They took away her view and her desk and her pride and, surprisingly, her assistant: I was to start working for SuperAgent Two, effective immediately.

"We're gonna make a lot of people a lot of money and have a lot of fun doing it," said my new boss, SuperAgent Two. I sat across the desk from him, per his request, as he unpacked the boxes he'd had messengered over from the William Morris Agency. Removing three oversized drums of vanilla protein powder, a case of protein bars, and one red binder, he placed them on a shelf overhead. The final check of the box produced a Rolodex, with one thousand teeny white index cards neatly fanned into place. He didn't bark at me for help. Instead he flashed his expensive teeth, then asked for my opinion on some wall-art placement, movie posters he'd had framed, autographed by clients. This behavior was SuperAgent code for *I will not demand you pick up my dry cleaning or the pieces of my personal life, just maybe the odd lunch—not that I really eat food—when we're too busy making deals together. We are pals here. Equals, even. I plan to learn from you as much as you learn from me. I am the cool parent.* I was dubious of his nature, believing it was a gimmick, something to reel in clients and disorient producers. SuperAgent Two was Good Cop to the rest of the agency's Bad.

I was the only assistant whose desk was positioned in her superior's office. This station left me little wiggle room to slack off or talk to the other assistants freely. I spent a lot of time by the copier or the other cubicles and most of my day involved the phone, just like in my two previous jobs, but in real show business this was called *rolling calls*. Your boss gives you a list of numbers in a certain order and you do the actual dialing for him, and when the designated person answers, your line is "I have SuperAgent Two for (insert important show business name here)." If I wasn't on the phone, I was typing up submissions or organizing files or calling actors to check their availability and desire to audition for certain jobs. It was basic assistant stuff but the agents made it seem like open-heart brain surgery performed on the president of the universe.

The two things that kept me going in this line of business were (1) my fellow not-so-merry band of assistants and (2) the information. I loved knowing what movies were coming down the pike, what television pilots got picked up, which producers were nightmares. I even liked chatting with the actors on the phone, especially SuperAgent Two's clients, because they, for the most part, were lovely and fun and flirtatious and took the monotony out of the day.

Now officially three years into real show business (and five years into sort-of show biz), I wondered every day when I would move up the ladder and become a junior agent, even though I'd done nothing except the time to deserve it. But it was the goal, after all. I was finally making a few bucks (although it was very few), so when was I going to make a difference? In the back of my mind, I still longed to be discovered, even at the SuperAgency. Sometimes I'd have to put an actor's audition on a videotape if they couldn't be in Los Angeles in person, and I'd do my very best reading, still hanging on to the possibility that a producer or director would hear my excellent work and ask who the reader was and hire me to be in the movie. If I went to a Broadway show, I waited for an actor to get the stomach flu, believing a stage manager would run over to the house seats I sat in and ask me to take over. I was ready, Mr. DeMille. But, until that happened, I felt the least show business could do for me was bump me to Junior SuperAgent so I could make some deals and get my damn note cards already.

One morning at the end of April, I was called into Spiker's office. Occasionally, one of the agents would pick up the phone and let you know they needed you and you'd have to walk into their office so they could tell you the same thing they very well could have just told you on the phone, but it was a great show of power to have us jumping in and out of our chairs, standing at attention in front of their desks. SuperAgent Two was at a meeting out of the office and I was minding the store, as he'd asked. When I arrived at Spiker's door, I saw Sponge sitting on the guest couch inside. My scalp began sweating. *They are firing me*, I thought.

"Get in here," said Spiker. "Look, you've been here awhile now."

"Three years," added Sponge.

This is going to take forever, I thought, desperate to flee. I stood, working my thumb cuticles, ready to be *ankled*, probably not before they read me a long list of all my shortcomings.

"We're going to give you your first deal," said Spiker through her thin lips and toxic face.

"It's for my client," said Sponge. "So mess it up and die."

They laughed like it was the best joke on the planet. Spiker put her head in her hands and I saw a red sore on her scalp. Sponge lifted her porcine legs off the floor as she laughed. They told me that SuperAgent Two was aware of the deal I'd be making for them, that *he* supported the decision, and that it was a theater gig.

In the SuperAgency world, film deals were the best, then TV, then Broadway. About ten rungs below that were the regional theater jobs, and they only submitted actors to the top ones. About twenty-seven rungs below that were the odd touring companies that they made fun of, drawing straws to see who would take the lead on them. This is the deal they gave me. But no matter, it was a deal. If I made this one properly, I'd get franchised—meaning I'd be able to negotiate SAG deals and be an official junior agent. It was my moment. All that Sondheim singing and pretending to be Liberace on the bus, all those hours filing and walking the city hoping something would happen to me, led to this. My very first deal.

The job was for a B-list client, one who used to be a series regular on a decent sitcom. The gig was for a tour of *Death of a Salesman* at the Coconut Grove Playhouse in Florida. It was my understanding that after its run at the Playhouse it would tour the rest of the state, followed by a national tour and eventually hit Broadway. And although Hal Holbrook was starring as Willy Loman, no one had high hopes. It was a theater project—in Florida and this is why it was given to me. You don't cut your teeth on a Bob Redford picture, I was told. For a brief moment, while they were describing the deal, I thought it might be some twisted joke, like Carrie being asked to the prom. I hoped I, too, had telepathic ways to collapse the SuperAgency before they spilled the pig blood on me.

"They are offering him eight hundred dollars a week," said Sponge. "Which is fucking ridiculous."

"Totally," said Spiker.

They both looked at me and I could see that they needed me to do something, I just didn't know what. I nodded. Sponge and Spiker looked at each other and cracked up at my expense.

"Okay, genius," Sponge said. "You are going to tell the pro-

ducer that you find that number insulting. That this actor was
a very successful part of a very successful television show, that
they are fucking lucky to have him. You say that you'd take two
thousand a week. Plus a nonshared dressing room. And a case of
Perrier."

This was the New York minute in which I realized I wanted
nothing to do with any of this. I didn't want to make this deal. Or
any deal. I had no interest in being an agent. I had trouble asking
a storekeeper to break a dollar for quarters, so how was I going
to ask some real live theater producer for a sum I found ridiculous? In my eyes, that actor should have been delighted to get a
job offer in the first place. It's not like he worked all the time, or
ever. Half the time the agents turned down jobs before consulting with the client because they'd found the money insulting or
the role beneath them or the project too piddling. I never really
paid attention to what they were saying because all I had to do
was Xerox and mail stuff. Now I was in the game. And for the
first time in eight years, I found the game completely ridiculous.
I was all about the show and wanted nothing to do with the business. Business gave me hives.

The call was to take place the next morning. I spent the
remainder of the day at my desk with my head down, trying to
figure out how to get through it. Whose big idea was this, anyway? I wondered if I could quit just to avoid the call. Sponge
and Spiker, against their will, told me I'd be franchised after I
made my first deal. It's what all the assistants wanted, what I
thought I wanted, but now no longer wanted. What I wanted,
I realized, was to leave my *Gotham-based shingle*, to *spend more
time with my family*. Please *ankle* me. I will be a terrible *ten
percenter*.

In bed that night, I conjured up all the sports movies I'd seen in my life for inspiration: speeches from coaches, slow-clap moments. *You want fame?* Debbie Allen shouted at me in my head. *Well, fame costs, and right here is where you start paying. In sweat.* I didn't have this in me. I didn't want to pay. I didn't want to sweat.

The next morning, I sat at my sliver of a desk, facing the wall. I put my headset on, then took it off, deciding I needed to use the receiver instead of talking into a small mouthpiece. I wanted to hold something heavy and real, maybe even twist the cord like I used to do with the beige wall phone in my childhood kitchen. The world got a lot better when I found out that SuperAgent Two would be out of the office and I'd be able to handle my business with no one eating PowerBars behind me. Or listening.

2:30. It was time. I dialed the number.

"Irv Shatz." He answered his own phone. This threw me. His voice was craggy, like he'd swallowed a bag of sand. Even from the way he said his name I knew he was old-school, probably called women *dames* or *broads*. For sure he said *gams*.

"I'm Kim, from the SuperAgency," I said. "I'm calling about Ron Ralston?"

"Who?"

All I'd done was introduce myself and already he hated me. But I was already in the dentist's chair and the drilling had started and I just couldn't get out.

"What can I do for you?" said Irv Shatz.

Did he not know why I was calling? Was he not aware we were about to start negotiations for Ron Ralston, an actor with a pleasant face who looked like he was very nice to his mother?

"Um," I said.

"I made the offer when I spoke to the other girl. Last week," he said.

"Well, I'm the girl making the deal?" I said, trying to find my inner Swifty Lazar. I leaned back on my swivel chair but slid out and had to shimmy back so as not to slam into the window.

"I'll say it again: eight hundred a week, eight weeks. I told the girl I wasn't gonna budge. This is my best and final. He's got better things to do? I'll get someone else."

I was losing Irv Shatz and I was losing the job. It was so precarious holding someone's career in my hand; I was now a surgeon massaging a heart. One wrong move and he remains unemployed. I needed to put on my *we're gonna make a lot of people a lot of money* voice. If I did this, I'd have seniority over SuperAssistant. I'd be able to give her dirty looks and maybe even brush past her smart slacks on my way to an agents' meeting. Opportunity. It only knocks once.

I thought of my high school boyfriend, who'd had his life mapped out in his mind from the age of six. He'd planned what college he'd attend and the entire career path he'd follow. He was the only person I'd ever met who actually set out what he wanted to do and succeeded at every checkpoint along the way. I recalled a phone call we'd had when I'd started on this road to SuperAgenting.

"You know you're going to hate that, right?" he said. "That's not the career for you." I remember hanging up and calling him a tool in my head. What did he know? I could eat PowerBars and lunch with Marty if I wanted. Good luck living out your planned life, overachiever, you know what they say about life and plans. (I don't care for footnotes, so let me note right here that high school boyfriend is now a multimillion-dollar-making film director. *Pfffft*. Whatever.)

"Eight hundred a week," Irv Shatz said, again. "Best and goddamn final."

This was it. Curtain up. Light the lights. Just follow your cue, like Sponge and Spiker said. He says eight hundred and you breeze in with two grand and the Perrier. They're just words. Go. I took a breath and fixed my posture. And then, in the meekest voice I had in my repertoire, a voice so quiet I wasn't even sure *I* heard me, I kicked off my real live show-business career and said, "Okay."

"Good," said Irv Shatz. "I'll have the girl send over the paperwork."

I put the receiver on the cradle, then swiveled my chair to look out the window. I didn't make anyone a lot of money or have any fun doing it. I actually screwed up someone's chance to make more money and drink fizzy water out of small green bottles whenever they were thirsty in the privacy of their nonshared dressing room, maybe even to go to Broadway. Unsure of how to admit to the mess-up, I lied to Sponge and Spiker and told them Irv Shatz just wouldn't budge. I don't think they believed me, because Sponge ended up calling him back, probably saying I was mentally challenged, and she was able to go back in and negotiate properly, with skill and confidence, with guts.

Ron Ralston went to Florida with a better bankroll and no shortage of beverages. I, in a move still beyond my comprehension, got franchised and would now be considered a junior agent, while still playing the role of SuperAssistant. Why anyone agreed to this, I'll never know. I was terrible at my job and a nuisance in the office. This promotion would allow/force me to start finding my own clients to represent, sending me out to church basements and dank theaters all over town in the hopes of lassoing some talent. I felt guilty for not telling the truth about my negotiation but realized maybe they found this trait appealing and agenty. If, my first time out, I was able to lie (albeit to the wrong person), maybe I wasn't such a loser after all. Maybe that's why they patched me through to the next level.

A week after the negotiation, I sat in front of SuperAgent Two and gave my notice. He nibbled on a PowerBar, storing little pieces in his cheeks so he could say goodbye.

After eight years in this racket, I finally decided to break up with show business. One of the number-one rules in show business is Don't work with kids or animals, and so, just to spite the entire industry, I decided to become a dog walker. Maybe what I needed was an alternative lifestyle. I had visions of myself communing with nature, considering perhaps that what I had to offer couldn't be contained indoors. Not everyone was cut out for office life, right? It was time to take my talents elsewhere.

I kicked off my new career by walking my friend's mutt, Dixie. I didn't have to sit down and hear about the phone answering and filing I'd have to do. There were no contracts to keep up or deals to make when walking an animal, just a leash and a plastic bag. And, who knew? Maybe I'd find the Murray and Ted Baxter of dog walking out in the park. My business multiplied rapidly, and in a matter of weeks I had a few clients, all from the same building. A Havanese named Baxter. A white fluffy thing called Norm. And when word got out about me, a short businessman put me on retainer. His foxlike dog, Duke, needed to be walked once in the morning and again later in the afternoon. He didn't even care what time I showed up.

Every morning, I'd strap on my overalls and headphones blasting AM talk radio and head out to pick up one of my clients, then take him to the park. Together we'd go for long walks. He'd sniff around and I'd imagine all the books I could be writing if I didn't have to spend so much goddamn time walking these dumb dogs, who, if we're being honest, were beginning to get on my nerves.

Instead of going to the park, I started watching TV in the dogs' apartments. Eventually I'd drag them outside to pee, where'd I'd sit on a bench and give the animals dirty looks. Seemed as though dog walking, like show business, was just not all it was cracked up to be. At least it didn't take me eight years to figure it out. Norm's mother was the first to fire me. She didn't think I was serious enough because I didn't leave notes on her kitchen counter with recaps of what Norm did on our walks and how many times he did his business. My friend kept me on, as did the short business fellow. I took their faith in me as a sign to just keep moving. I stayed with the dogs for seven months even though we hated each other.

I never did get discovered. Not on the city bus, not in the cookie aisle at D'Agostino's, not in the business of show. I did, however, make a discovery: I was bad at jobs. I realized that Tom Brokaw was wrong—not everyone could make a buck. I don't even want to talk about making a difference.

This Is Our Story?

·······

The first time I saw Buzz, he was walking down Beacon Street. He wore a tie-dyed T-shirt with an unbuttoned baby-blue oxford over it and carried a navy backpack, a sheet of loose-leaf crunched in the zipper. A swirl of his black hair escaped its ponytail, and the faded jeans he chose that morning seemed to be falling off, defying his canvas belt. Stopping at a huddle of boys, Buzz listened, then laughed by throwing his head back while keeping his mouth wide open, like Guy Smiley.

"There!" said my friend Mitzi, pointing her Camel Light across the street. "There he is!"

"That guy?" I said.

"Yes!"

"*That* guy?"

She grabbed my arm. "Yes. That's him. Isn't he cute?"

"Cute?" I said, looking for my smokes. I was wearing a black off-the-shoulder snug-fitting shirt, a man's suit vest, jean shorts over multicolored floral tights, black John Cougar Mellencamp–inspired western shoe-boots, and a top hat. "That guy looks ridiculous."

"He went to camp with my sister," Mitzi said, as if that changed the fact that he resembled Tiny Tim without the warble and ukulele. "I think we know a lot of the same people."

"He's still ridiculous."

"You're wrong."

We smoked, sitting on the fourth stair of the building's front stoop that served as Emerson College's student lounge. Most of our classes took place in the converted living rooms of old brownstone buildings that dotted the Back Bay of Boston, but the steps of 130 Beacon Street were social and cigarette-smoking headquarters. Buzz traipsed along, eventually disappearing around the corner as Mitzi news-briefed me that he, like us, had transferred to our school sophomore year. He was a Jew from a fancy Wasp town in Connecticut and went to summer camp in Ontario, Canada, which is where he met Mitzi's sister. He majored in advertising, had a girlfriend who went to another college in the area, and when he drove his off-white 1973 Super Beetle he wore a signature wool hat with earflaps, no matter the season, which he called his Driving Hat.

"Come on," Mitzi said when he was no longer in sight. "You don't think he's even a teeny bit cute?"

"No."

I replay the original Buzz sighting of 1990 in my head often, wondering how I got here. *Here* is a rental car we've secured at the Cancun airport, a red compact we will sit in for two hours along a highway that is crumbling, not unlike my life, and even in my state of despair I am able to see the irony—or is it a metaphor—and I add *messed-up road* to the running mental list I began before we left, entitled "Signs."

That morning, to the untrained eye, I might have looked like

I was minding my own business in the vestibule, waiting for the town car to arrive and speed us to the airport. Buzz didn't notice me inspecting his Plane Pants, which were really just cargo pants from the Gap. Buzz didn't like wearing jeans on a plane, as he found them too constricting and without enough pockets. After spending four months locating the perfect pair of travel bottoms, he then gave them a moniker, which was not unusual for Buzz, as evidenced by his Club Shirt in college and the recently scored Dog-Run Jacket from Filene's Basement. The Plane Pants were equipped with deep pockets, and I spent a good amount of time lacing my Pumas, pretending I wasn't searching for a lump that could pass as a small velvet box. When that proved fruitless, I asked if I could get some gum from his backpack, which he obliged, making it clear there was nothing concealed in his bag either. I tried to stay optimistic by switching the nature of my investigation, focusing less on hard evidence, more on behavior.

But I should have known better than to flirt with optimism. Buzz was not a morning person, or a big conversationalist, so it was usual for him to be quiet and dazed as we waited. To clarify, Buzz is a talker—so chock-full of information they should farm him out for weddings to keep topics flowing—but he is not a conversationalist.

Me, I can easily go ten rounds on *Do you think the laundry ladies hate me?* Or *Do you like the bus?* Or *Do you think our deli guy hates me?* But on these subjects, he has nothing to add. On the morning of our Mexican vacation, Buzz was acting just like Buzz. Not squirrelly, not like he was concealing anything. Signs were quickly turning into omens. I sat on the dirty lobby floor, eyes on the Spackle-colored sky, comforted that I was not the only rain cloud on Columbus Avenue that morning.

• • •

I wasn't always like this. As a kid, nuptials were not my thing. I didn't have sunny yellow wallpaper or the disposition to match. I didn't wear headbands or the Esprit sweaters my mother pushed me toward in the store, and I certainly never ripped out pictures of wedding dresses, cataloging them in a binder for my eventual big day. It's not that I was against the event. I wanted to marry Duran Duran as much as the next person, but I could never imagine myself in a poufy white dress.

Having been raised by a nineteen-inch color Zenith, I thought this is what weddings were. Dresses of any kind were not welcome in our closets because my mother was a feminist. Minus the burgundy velvet floor-length skirt with bustle she wore to my brother's bar mitzvah, I never saw my mother in a dress. She wore suit pants, with panty hose underneath, because Marlo Thomas said mommies were people and people wore pants. As I came of age in the '80s, things got more confusing. From the neck down my mother looked like she worked for IBM, but above the shoulder pads she glazed her face with pinks and blues and molded her hair into a domed helmet that would make Joan Collins look like she'd given up.

It's possible my mother was trying to convey messages of strength and equality, but to me they were filtered through a colossal game of visual Telephone. We didn't have intimate talks, because my mother was private. So I learned to focus on what was physically in front of me, which was usually a bag of mixed messages. As a result, in the sixth grade I never took off my steel-toed boots, because we were feminists. But I was also encouraged at thirteen to buy blue eyeliner and small jars of Indian Earth because it made us look less tired. My father must have wanted to be a feminist, too, because he also started wearing bronzer.

When I moved out of my childhood home, I was confused. Finally living on my own, I would get to the bottom of what it meant to be a grown woman. I achieved this by doing the opposite of everything I'd seen my mother do to date. Skirt buying became an addiction. I renounced hairspray. And I took not being vain to such champion levels, Buzz often said I looked homeless. As a strong woman, I would have solid reasons for my actions and belief systems that I'd share with others. No accessories for me. I was going to have substance. I was also going to have lists. Because what better way to show you meant business than bullet points? When friends started talking emerald-cut rings and three-tiered lemon-chiffon cake with raspberry cream, I hung the following list above my toilet.

WHY I DON'T WANT TO GET MARRIED:

1. Jordan almonds are stupid.

2. You can't wear a veil if you wear glasses.

3. Dancing is dumb.

4. Chicken, beef, or fish?

5. Don't have enough friends to invite so would appear like loser at own nuptials.

6. Can't call in sick to own wedding like you do for other parties.

7. I don't like parties.

I lived my life with limp hair and strong convictions for many years. Now, in my late twenties, I suddenly found myself in one of those movies where someone gets hit in the head and sees things differently and learns lessons and switches bodies with

Fred Savage. Now, seven years into this relationship, I ached to get married.

Tulum is a sleepy pueblo, on the eastern side of the Caribbean coast in Quintana Roo, Mexico. It is home to a well-known archeological Mayan ruin but not known enough to warrant a call from my mother reminding me of a *Dateline* she saw recently and to please watch out for kidnapping and decapitation. Today Tulum has a "hotel zone" and nightlife and an ATM and a gym and there is talk of an international airport, but back in 2000 tourism was limited to a few Mayan-style thatched huts for lodging and a mellow quality that made Buzz repeat (frequently) that it was a place for "travelers, not tourists."

This was a return trip for us. Two years earlier, we'd driven this same fissured road to spend six days on a divine beach we had just about to ourselves, minus the odd stray dog, the stunning woman with mermaid hair covering her boobs while practicing naked yoga in the distance, and the small group of fellow travelers we dined with occasionally even though one of them, a gay blind man named Blair, was so detestable that Buzz and I spent the better part of the week debating the karma, rules, and social implications of having a problem with the sightless. Mostly we just wanted to know if we were allowed to hate the blind guy.

One had to be vigilant driving this route from Cancun so that a Mexican crater didn't swallow up your rental. There were no dividing lines to hint at where you should be driving and seemingly no road rules at all. This kind of driving was Buzz's Super Bowl. Back home in New York, if I slammed on the pretend passenger brake or gripped the handle above the window where people sometimes hung their dry cleaning, Buzz would just shrug and say, "What?" On the Mexican highway, however, I had sunk deep into the bowels of a slump and couldn't even be bothered to police Buzz's driving. Instead, I pressed my forehead to the window and seethed. I thought, *Drive like an asshole, see if I care. Get into a head-on collision and get us both killed. I'll just look at your stupid run-overed face and say, "What?"*

Up ahead, I noticed the green highway sign with white lettering that read, EXCUSE TO DISTURB YOU IMPROVEMENT THIS ROAD FOR YOUR COMFORT. Last visit, Buzz and I enjoyed this sign a great deal, quoting it often, followed by general laughing and pats on the back for our hilarious senses of humor. This time, Buzz hit my arm to signal its presence but I ignored him, leaving him to laugh alone. He didn't even notice. (*Signs.*) We turned right, heading toward the very end of the Boca Pailla road.

"I'm starving," Buzz said, turning off the car. "You?"

I didn't say anything.

"Guacamole?" he said. "Maybe fajitas."

He got out with our bags, disappearing into the hotel, not noticing I was still locked inside.

Mitzi ended up in Voice and Articulation class with Buzz, Thursdays at 8:30 a.m. They became fast friends sitting in the back, learning of sibilant *s*'s and dentalized *d*'s. Since fast-friend making was not my strong suit, I just glommed on to Mitzi's choices. I learned right away that Buzz was charming, if not a nincompoop, but pretty focused academically for someone who drank so hard he spent more than a few nights asleep on a stoop on Exeter Street. No matter the damage he'd done to himself the night before, he'd show up to every class with books in hand and a ring of Pepto-Bismol around his lips.

We were creatures from different parts of the zoo. He, a quasi-Deadhead sporto part-time vegetarian/alcoholic with a rotating stable of girls passing through his bedroom. Me, an occasional agoraphobic listening to DJ Jazzy Jeff CDs and the original soundtrack to *Les Misérables* while still making crank calls. He made dean's list three years running and I missed the first month of Novel into Film because I couldn't locate the classroom it was held in.

In 1990, Emerson College was about 35 percent male, and half that population was gay. These were the statistics I attributed to Buzz being so lady lucky. To this day, he contends that I, like the rest of the female population, was in love with him, which is completely false, as I was perfectly busy being obsessed with a flamboyant Richard Grieco lookalike we dubbed Booker.

Pretty soon after our newfound friendship, Mitzi lost romantic interest in Buzz and moved on to a senior with a Hollywood pedigree. Buzz ended up with a model-singer Mariel Hemingway doppelganger as his main course, with a lazy Susan of dark-haired coeds and one art major who did her photo thesis on Buzz as Jesus in a toga. I didn't like Buzz as more than a friend, but you couldn't help but appreciate the guy who, for Valentine's Day, mailed me a flappy, almost wet, slice of deli turkey in a small white envelope and, for my birthday, gifted me a three-pack of those plastic rain bonnets my nana used to wear.

I moved to New York in the fall of 1992—three bucks, two bags, and all that—in order to become a talent agent and marry Adam Sandler. My previous Boston boss knew a working actor in the city whom she'd convinced to let me sublet an apartment from. The rules were simple:

1. Keep it clean.

2. Pay rent on time.

3. Never receive mail, never check the mailbox. Do not play music, talk to anyone, be seen coming in or out of the building, get deliveries, or keep the lights on too long. And please, take the trash out under cover of night.

And, as with the rules in *Gremlins*, I followed none of the above.

The studio apartment was dinky at best, the only piece of useable furniture being a double bed. It served as sleeping place, dining area, hangout spot, guest seating, and a surface for my clothes since there was no closet and I was forbidden to use the dresser. Hostile about that rule, I rifled through his top drawer the first day I moved in, only to find a men's navy-blue G-string with a golden zipper on the crotch. I made a mental note to go against my snooping instincts for the duration of my sublet. The walls were layered with chipped white paint, and the pipes clanked so loud and often it sounded as though a trapped chain gang was trying to get out.

The kitchen was galley-style, delineated by a thin chrome rail covering the linoleum, over which I tripped hourly. I was thankful for the television, though it housed a poltergeist that turned the thing on and off for sport whenever the mood struck. The one window did not let in any light but was generous with the sounds of the hookers outside who, after midnight, laughed or fought or splattered vomit onto the sidewalks below. I often thought of my mother turning her nose up at a bellboy showing us to a perfectly fine room on a family trip—"Uch, this is not what I asked for," she'd say, annoyed by the wrong view or unacceptable bathroom—as I sat on my borrowed multipurpose bed/couch/chair, eating cold sesame noodles with my fingers while trying to ignore the International Male undies hiding in the drawer, and watching the television as it turned itself on and off.

Buzz was living with his sister in a fifth-floor walk-up on the Upper West Side. She was in the advertising game and got paid quite well while wearing suit pants and heading to an office every day. Naturally, we thought she was a sucker. To us, it was like looking at our parents, who'd chosen boring lives, not cool ones like ours would be once they got off the ground.

Mitzi resided in Chelsea, with her gray cat and boyfriend, where she hosted parties for the new friends I didn't care for. My sublet was in Murray Hill, which, at the time, had a few Indian spice shops, an Irish bar or two, one Chinese restaurant, and an overall depressing quality that made every hour of every day feel like 4:30 on a November Sunday.

Since I wasn't allowed out in the hallway, I stayed in a lot, as did my neighbor across the hall. I had moved to Manhattan to look for a job, but I spent the first two weeks as a New Yorker doing nothing but keeping my eye on the peephole of my door lest my mystery neighbor emerge. When it comes to things that do not matter in the slightest, I am nothing if not tenacious. For five days I kept watch but there was no movement. On the sixth day, I saw a skeletal appendage sticking out of the door and a sliver of bordello-style wallpaper, deep red and possibly textured. The light inside was yellow and dim and I felt the presence of a kindred spirit, someone who understood the value of staying home and also loathed overhead lighting.

I watched as the arm collected a paper bag from Meals-On-Wheels. I'd come to figure out, from going through the mail too large to fit into his mailbox, that he was a vintage-instrument enthusiast and also in the midst of dying at home. This put a damper on my plan for him to emerge and be the Rhoda to my Mary. With that hope dashed, I had nothing left to do with my days except send out a few resumes and watch *Rudy* on an endless loop, weeping each time at the end as if I never saw it

coming. When Buzz called with a job opportunity, I knew I
had to say yes.

Mitzi had somehow already gotten herself a job at MTV where
she was in a position to hire, and she recruited Buzz to work on
various lip-syncing and sometimes spring break–style gigs, where
he'd spend the week in Lake Havasu, Arizona, wearing a headset
and sleeping with random coworkers. But the jobs were finite and
sometimes Buzz found himself out of work, like me.

The stint Buzz called me about had something to do with
the *New York Times* and data compiling. Some corporate babble
I had no understanding of, but it would be a few days' work for
$200 and I needed more Chinese food money.

I consulted my bus map for the stealthiest way to get to Buzz's
place on the other side of town. Sure, I was still too scared to take
the subway, but I found the bus the city's most pleasant surprise.
It had a way of making you feel six and eighty-six at the same
time.

Slow and steady up the five flights, I stopped at each landing
to catch my breath and also see if any pigeons were hanging out
on the windowsills, waiting to flutter. Buzz's sister was moving
on up and getting her own apartment in three months, and I was
slated to move in as the new roommate. I spent nights in my sad
sublet wondering how I'd handle the birds taunting me in the
stairwell. At least my typical uniform—denim overalls with one
strap unfastened—was like a bear bell for those damn birds.

"Nice suit, Mr. Green Jeans," Buzz said when he opened the
door. He couldn't resist mockery of any variety and his specialty
was clothing one-liners.

"Shut up," I said, squeezing by him, since two people could
not fit into the skinny front hall of the place.

The compiling station, as we'd come to call it, was set up on a
small foldout table in the middle of the room. On it was a stack

of Xeroxed sheets, two barely sharpened golf pencils, and a *New York Times* tucked into the blue plastic bag you saw all over the city on Sunday mornings. The actual work was mind numbing, involving one of us reading data aloud and the other one jotting it down. About eight minutes in, Buzz suggested we take a nap. I should note here that Buzz and I had napped together a few times at school because we were often very tired. And college was sometimes boring.

We got into Buzz's bed-in-a-bag sheets, the factory seconds set his mother had gotten him at an outlet center. He might have made fun of my clothing choices, but I found his attempt at an adult's room high-rolling comedy. The dry-mounted Picasso's *Flowers* and Van Gogh's *Starry Night* to let the ladies know he dug fine art and was sensitive but not gay. The oversized Michael Jordan *Wings* poster above his bed, just because he was "the greatest athlete who ever lived." Every piece had been selected to get a reaction from an overnight guest. The black milk crate housed a digital clock radio he'd pilfered from his childhood home (*Awwww*, they'd think, *he's nostalgic*), a CD player with a Tuck & Patti disc all queued up (*Wow, he really is romantic*), and a candle for mood lighting (*This guy cares about details*).

We got into his bed, organizing ourselves in a platonic tangle. "Do people really fall for this?" I asked, staring at the posters.

He closed his eyes, settling in for our two-hour nap. "Every time."

When Buzz kissed me, with his Tiny Tim face all crunched into mine, I didn't pull one of those movie moves where after a few seconds I realize what is happening and push him away and tell him he had the wrong idea, mister. I mean, he did have the wrong idea—a weird, mortifying, awkward-beyond-belief idea—but the work was tedious and it was February and he did have the better apartment, which was also all the way across town from mine, and so it just seemed more convenient to stay where I was.

The compiling work lasted a few more days, but our mutual unemployment and general ennui kept us together for random afternoons and a handful of nights over the next few months. Out of sheer languor, we'd become the dog-eared pages of a squirreled-away copy of Judy Blume's *Forever*. There was no way I could share the news with friends that I was now part of the group who lay under Michael Jordan's arms and fell asleep to the musical stylings of Tuck & Patti. I told myself that it was fine—hilarious, even, which was usually how I chose sweaters, not men. I made a mental note to quit this new hobby in another month when I was slated to move in.

I moved in and the extracurricular activities didn't stop and so we were forced to have words. We covered the casual nature of our dalliance, how our friendship came first, and, of course, how we should and would be seeing other people. I assured him I was fine and totally seeing other people. Plenty of other people. He started staying out later and later, sometimes not returning home at all. I knew his new schedule because I stayed in my room for a month listening to Paula Cole and crying to Mitzi, who tried to help me even though our friendship was also in the midst of fizzling out because she, too, was seeing other people.

One Tuesday evening, Buzz and I headed to our local supermarket. The Associated was two blocks away and smelled like rat pee, but it was closer than Fairway, which required one of those red wheelie granny carts to bring home the seltzer and bulk rice, and our wheel had recently fallen off. We were standing by the freezer case when Buzz yanked me down to the ground.

"What are we doing?" I asked.

"Nothing."

I watched Buzz crane his neck but still try to hide in plain sight. I stood up and noticed a cute Semitic faux bohemian with long, dark, wavy hair and a patchwork suede coat straight out of *Rent,* who was picking change out of her shiny, hot pink Kate Spade wallet. This was every girl Buzz dated at summer camp. Buzz begged me to crouch down again, which I did, wondering when I'd turned into Lucy Ricardo. I'd like to say I marched out of there, head high and all that, leaving Buzz to deal with the Jewess at the checkout, but I leaned against the freezer until she left, paid for Buzz's three bottles of seltzer, and carried them home in silence.

It was grim in the apartment over the next few weeks. But it was rent controlled and people in New York City lived under all kinds of weird circumstances to keep their housing. I knew of at least two couples in the midst of divorces, still living together in a classic six.

Two years after the compiling job, Buzz and I were still up to the hijinks. Sometimes I'd call it off, sometimes he would, but eventually we'd end up back together. We rented '70s movies and ordered in Chinese and hung our heads in shame together when our racist dog barked at anyone who wasn't Caucasian. We ate silver-dollar pancakes and bacon at corner diners, where we'd end up on the street in a fight, yelling at each other, often pausing to note Matt Dillon walking across the street, or C. J. Cregg from *The West Wing* approaching, then carrying on with our shouts. We were a contradiction, and sometimes our differences were a balance, other times a tug-of-war. We were forever calling it off, then returning to our shared apartment, each taking to our bedrooms on opposite sides of the ring, agreeing that this time we should just end it for good. At one point, we decided that I should move out, so I took the dog and relocated to a friend's apartment down the street, since she spent weekends in the Hamptons.

Morose, I called my mother, who, when I told her, sighed in my ear and said, "Well, I'm not going to tell your father. It will kill him."

Even with our enforced separation, Buzz called me every day to see how the dog was or what I was eating for lunch, and by the end of the weekend I was back under Michael Jordan's wingspan. A month later we resumed with the pancakes and the outdoor fighting.

"This is ridiculous," Buzz said. "Either we break up or go on vacation together."

His logic was a pretzel but, somehow, in your twenties, this stuff makes perfect sense. We marched down the block to our local Liberty Travel, where a zaftig woman in a floral sundress assured us she could put us in a lovely property in Naples. Florida. In July. After some gentle prodding, we agreed to a week on Captiva Island, Florida, in a resort called South Seas Plantation, where we saw manatees and rode bikes and ate at restaurants with names like Cap'n Al's.

And then, because it was July, Buzz went and got first-, second-, and third-degree burned and could barely take to the bed since even the crisp white sheet was too much on the damage he'd done to himself. I watched TV and applied the aloe. The whole trip was comical. And restorative. And repellent. And lovely. And ridiculous.

We returned home vacation drunk, sobering into business as usual in the weeks to follow. The night before Buzz was to take another trip to Florida, this time with friends, we ate cheap sushi we'd brought in from Teriyaki Boy.

"I think I love you," he said, holding a sliver of faded pink ginger.

I rolled up the paper chopstick sleeve. "Um. I might love you, too."

"Should we give this a real try?" he said.

"Like, now?" I said. "Or when you get back from Florida?"

"Now."

"Okay."

And then, like seventh graders, we were officially going out.

"Why are you moping?" Buzz asked, watching me poke the small lump of wasabi resting on its fake grass.

"I don't know."

"You don't know?"

"No. I mean, you know."

"I know what?"

I could hear our neighbor's Jack Russell terrier running in the hallway. Probably chasing a pigeon. "*This* is our story?"

Buzz chewed, mouth open, and stared at me for clarification.

"From here on in, this will forever be our story."

"What are you even talking about?"

"I mean, we made out because we were bored and then I moved in and you dated people and I cried and then we brought in bad sushi and now we're a couple."

Buzz took a sip of beer. "So?"

"So, this goes on our permanent record. If we ever get married or have kids, this is what we will have to tell them. This is all we got. It's not that good a story."

"Ah, don't worry about it," Buzz said, his sleeve dipping into the small tray of teriyaki sauce. "I don't think I'm the marrying kind."

I stared out the window, at our view of the brick wall.

• • •

Many people ask how they will know when the right person walks into their life. My question was always, How will I know when it's time to walk out? The question and level of optimism are different, but the answer is the same for both: *You'll just know.*

We sit in the open-air restaurant facing the dazzling Mexican beach, and I find myself hostile at the beauty. The beach is just showing off. And then come the stupid birds. They coast and swoop and I think, *If I wanted to see goddamn birds I could have stayed in the stairwell of my apartment building.* At least the sky is on my side. The weather is turning (*signs*), and I am grateful for the support.

It's possible that Buzz is on a different vacation. He looks relaxed and already suntanned even though we just got out of the car. His personality now cranked up to high, he is euphoric because it is feeding time. He eyes the specials chalkboard. Buzz is a consummate overorderer. There is not an abundance of choice at the restaurant, but the options all feature avocado and fresh salsa, our favorites. It is Christmas morning in those too-close-together hazel eyes. Soon he will ask if I want to share that gross chicken *pibil* dish we got two years ago that I didn't care for or insist I try the shredded-pork tacos even though we both know I dislike that kind of pork. The small table will soon be over-crowded and the waiter will have to do some fancy maneuvering to fit the various plates on our table. It will appear that we are dining for twelve. He will ask the waiter so many questions and rearrange the menu offerings to get exactly what he wants. And then he will eat with his mouth open and go on about the chicken and the guacamole and "God, don't you just love fajitas?" and I will want to stick salty tortilla chips in my eye.

You'll just know.

The food comes, so all the water glasses and sugar packets must be removed to make space. The waiter smiles and pretends to wipe his brow when he has unloaded his tray. After a round of *gracias*, Buzz places his forearm on the table, leaning in to start the eating. He is focused, an Olympian going for the gold. He makes pleased little noises as he chews. He doesn't even realize I am sitting across from him with that shoulder blade pain I thought was a tumor but Dr. Shapiro insisted was stress. I have had enough.

"I just want you to know," I say, my voice calm and measured, "that I will be here on this vacation. I'll sit on the beach with you and eat and swim in those sinkhole things. But, when we get home, I will be getting my own apartment."

Buzz does not look up. Instead, he dips chips into the homemade salsa. When finished, he reclines in his chair and inspects my face. He leans onto the table and says, "A one-bedroom or a studio?"

"What?"

"When you move out," he says, "will you be getting a one-bedroom or a studio?"

The tears that were about to spill onto my mango quesadilla dry up. I suddenly feel like spitting. "I don't know!"

"Well, would you mind staying close by?" he says, resuming the chip dipping. "So I can still see the dog?"

In a move I learned from *Knots Landing*, I push my chair away from the table, with great emphasis on the floor scraping. I want to throw a drink in his face, push all the plates and glasses and silverware to the tiled floor. Alas, it is not Sweeps Week, so I walk out of the restaurant. But I walk really, really fast. Once at the room, I jam the key in the lock and, no matter which direction I jiggle it, the lock won't give. I long for the credit card swipe key but know deep down I can't use those properly either, and

I wonder why I can't just open a door like a regular person. I hear Buzz behind me because, much to my daily chagrin, he is a mouth breather. Without turning around, I throw my arm behind me with the key pinched in my fingers, which is code for *You open the door, idiot*. Buzz unlocks it with ease and I blaze by him and take to the bed. Curled into the fetal position, I start to cry. Grape-sized tears travel in all directions off my face, many ending up in my hair, which has already conspired with the humidity to make me look like Gabe Kaplan.

Even through my snarfling, I can hear Buzz unpacking his clothes and locking his passport in the safe. I start conjuring all the ways he could possibly die on this trip. Shark attack. Ripped apart by jungle critters. Ceramic iguana from the coffee table to the back of the head. There would be a pool of blood on the pale tile and I could run to the front desk, speaking in the bits of my childhood French, which, I'd later tell in court, was used because I didn't know Spanish and was in a panic and Canadian. One could get away with a lot more if you were from the Great White North. They would ask what happened to the loud, handsome fellow who made all the jokes and tried to get a discount on the room. I'd whisper how he fell out of bed, which, besides making him dead, would also make him look like a moron.

"Kim," Buzz says to my back. "Let's talk. This is ridiculous."
Unpacking is ridiculous. "Leave me alone."
"Come on. Don't be like this."
"Go away. I'm serious."
He sighs. "Kim, look where we are! Please stop crying."
I continue crying.
"Let's just talk. Turn around. Look at me."
"I don't want to look at you."
"Turn around."
"No."

Buzz gets on the bed and tries to physically move me. "Kim. Turn. Around."

"*Uchhhh.* You're an asshole," I say as I flip myself over, only to be faced with a small black velvet box, its sparkly contents blinding my puffy eyes.

"Will you marry me?" Buzz says.

"Fuck you," I say.

"I had a whole thing planned for tomorrow morning but I thought you might have a heart attack. Plus, you broke up with me at lunch."

He places the ring on my finger. "You still haven't answered me, technically."

"Are there any tissues in this stupid hotel?" I say.

I am covered in snot, and my fake sporty shirt that says SHARKS is drenched in self-pity. He kisses me anyway.

We are engaged.

"Are you still going to get your own apartment when we get home?"

Buzz is pleased with himself that I had a nervous breakdown in his honor. I start crying again.

"Seriously?" he says. "Again with the waterworks?"

I weep the very last tears I have left in my sockets. "*This* is our story?"

The next morning, before he even opened his eyes, Buzz said, "You moving out of the hotel room?"

I had been awake for an hour, clutching my face.

"What's with this?" he said, pointing to my cheek.

A pain in my mouth had started in the night. A paring knife to the gums.

"Open," he said.

I shook my head.

"Just open."

"Don't touch it."

"I'm not going to touch it."

Buzz always swore he wouldn't touch the sliver of wood in my foot or the weird wrist cyst that sometimes sticks up, but he always did. However, before I could even open my mouth, I suddenly needed to excuse myself and run to the bathroom. Which is where I stayed for the next three days. I didn't know what was taking revenge on me. I'd brushed my teeth with bottled water, I'd squeezed my face tight in the shower so as not to let a drop in by mistake, I didn't eat lettuce. Instead of being fetal on the bed, I was prone on the cold tile. And the pain that started that morning was teetering on the edge of unbearable. (*Signs.*)

"Should I find a doctor?" Buzz said to me.

"Here?"

"Yes, here."

"No."

Not only was I scared of what kind of doctor we'd find in the middle of the jungle, but I couldn't admit defeat. Buzz often told me that basketball players play with broken feet and concussions and the flu, whereas I skipped work if I felt sweaty. Plus I'd convinced myself that all the symptoms I'd ever experienced up till now had led me to this moment and I was definitely dying in the bathroom of the various tumors I knew were rotting my insides, along with the lupus and typhoid fever. Why didn't I take care of these things years ago?

"You're a vision," Buzz said, the next day. My hair was a giant tangle, a Mexican bed Afro. Spanish saltine crumbs were stuck to my legs and arms, and crumpled tissues trailed toward the trash can like ellipses. I was now beyond what a cold compress and glass of iceless ginger ale could fix.

"Should we just cut our losses and go to Cancun?" Buzz said.

Even plagued with dysentery and a mysterious life form growing out of my jaw and exiting through my cheek, the word *Cancun*, especially during spring break, was grim. How could I take Traveler Buzz out of this postcard and plop him at Señor Frog's with a group of lacrosse bros?

"No," I said.

"Why not?"

"I don't want to ruin the trip."

The sun was bright, the sand sugary, the turquoise water Elysian. Buzz stared out the window, then back at me. "I'm going to make some calls."

Worlds shifted when Buzz made calls. Deals were made, discounts had; companies never even saw it coming. When people saw Buzz in action, they all said the same thing: "Next time I buy a car, I'm bringing you." There was nothing he wouldn't ask for. He was the guy who'd asked the CVS clerk if she could do better on a four-pack of Duracells. I apologize for walking into a store. It was spring break in Cancun. Girls were wild, boys were pillaging—no way was there a room to be had.

"We're leaving in the morning," Buzz said, returning an hour later. "Three fun-filled nights at the Hilton Cancun."

We would say goodbye to our eleven-room boutique eco-hotel for travelers not tourists, where the only sounds one heard at night were the waves and the faint whir of some weird lemur I was convinced would kill me in my sleep.

The Hilton Cancun had 426 rooms and 7 pools. The lobby thumped. Clumps of families stood by the gift shop wearing bathing suits and snorkel gear, Cheez-Its and Oreos spilling from their oversized beach bags. Groups of office types gathered in the lobby in their casual attire, checking out one another's pale legs or arms, which were usually concealed in their air-conditioned offices. Staff was everywhere, smiling, with trays of drinks or maps or ready to mop up some guest vomit. Everything was shiny.

"Go sit on the couch," Buzz said, as he had business at the front desk. I ambled over, looking like a kidnapping victim moments after being rescued from a chained radiator. I sat on the white leather as small children walked by with curious faces, covertly grabbing a parental hand. The hum and chatter and unnatural lobby light mingled with frosty temperatures gave me the panicky feeling usually reserved for large malls.

Buzz held my elbow and guided me toward the elevator bank, then led me down the long, carpeted hall. He swiped the room key (effortlessly) as I heard kids thumping on the floor above. Housekeeping pushed the large cart past me, and even through my dying haze I peeked to see what there was to steal. Buzz shoved me along even though he swore he wasn't pushing.

"Get into bed." His tone was bossy.

The room was small but immaculate. Six pillows on the king-sized bed stood at attention. A dark wood unit (maybe walnut, I don't know my woods) housed a television. A windowed door covered an entire wall, looking out on one of those slivers of balcony that were just there for show, and a small dining table with two chairs.

The blanket and sheets were facelift-skin tight and I barely had the energy to fight with them to get in. Not wanting to ask Buzz for help, as he was busy reading the room service menu, I managed to get in by myself, then felt accomplished and athletic. I rubbed my legs around the cool sheets, settling into position.

Buzz handed me the remote, told me that he was going to stretch his legs and walk around. He closed the door and I could hear his flip-flops smack down the carpeted hall. I pressed all the buttons on the remote until the television turned on. *The Cosby Show* was on. In English.

"I fucking love Cancun," I said to myself.

At sundown, Buzz ordered room service. I was still only gumming saltines, so he ordered dinner for one. He looked small slouching at the table near the sliding door of the nonbalcony, eating room service shrimp fajitas to the sounds of Rudy Huxtable.

The doctor's office was in the basement of the hotel.

"It never occurred to me that hotels had basements," I said, still dying but rested and ready for conversation.

"Mmmmhmm."

"What, you don't want to talk?" I said to Buzz.

"I don't have anything to say."

The doctor introduced himself as Dr. Alvarez and excused himself for a moment, letting us know he'd be right back. He patted my head before exiting.

"Is that Alfred Molina?" I said.

"I don't even know who that is, but no."

"You know, Alfred Molina, the actor," I said. "He's in everything."

"I don't know who he is, but this guy's Dr. Alvarez and he is in the basement of the Cancun Hilton. Why would he be Alfred Molina?"

I shook my head. "You're no fun."

Dr. Alvarez returned and had me sit on a folding chair.

"What do we have here?" he said, smiling like Santa Claus waiting to hear about the Cabbage Patch dolls I wanted.

I reported my symptoms and when they'd started. As I mentioned the stomach issues, he nodded.

"*Sí, sí, sí,*" said Dr. Alvarez, explaining the affliction. "Happens to many, many tourists."

Travelers. I didn't have the energy to correct Dr. Alvarez. Buzz sighed, because not twenty-four hours earlier he was a traveler and now—well, he was part of the group who felt proud of themselves for shouting *hola* whenever they could.

As for my face pain, he looked into my mouth and said that indeed something was there but he didn't know what it was. This was out of his area of expertise. He suggested a dentist and I nodded with interest but there was no way I was hitting a dentist's office in another basement. Dr. Alvarez spoke in a clipped Christopher Walken–style cadence.

"As for the stomach. I give you. This medicine. So you can. Sit. In the seat up there," he said, pointing to an airplane in the sky. "And not. In the seat. In there." Dr. Alvarez laughed as he motioned toward the bathroom, and then went to get me some medicine. After I took the pill, Buzz made me sit by the pool and get real air, convinced that was all I needed to fix this phantom pain hammering my face.

Three days later, my home dentist explained that although I'd been told I was part of the 1 percent of the population who had no wisdom teeth in her head—which, he joked, didn't mean I wasn't wise—he'd found out I did indeed have one and it was growing sideways out of my gums and straight into my cheek. The dentist had never seen anything like it and called in a colleague and three hygienists to see.

"Congratulations, sweetie," said Paulina the hygienist, touching the ring on my finger. "Did it just happen?"

Had I been in regular form, I would have regaled this stranger with tales of sun and sand and stories of love past and future and way more information than she'd bargained for. But as the dentist poked at the disfiguring and insistent tooth, I just nodded politely, sucking in the nitrous, enjoying the flight above the room without retelling the backward tale of casual sex and shrimp fajitas. *That's your story?* she'd say, as I wiped my sweating palms on my jeans, staring at her central-casting white spongy shoes. *It is*, I'd say.

Maybe I'd say more, because I'd be high on laughing gas. Maybe I'd tell her that I like our story because it embodies us perfectly, that it is at once lovely and ridiculous. That of course there is love and like, but there is also Alfred Molina. Buzz brings so much to our story. He brings humor, he brings intrigue, he brings the plot. He is always willing to go to Ikea, and his charm is mayoral. He explains *The Hunt for Red October*–style movies to me and knows I have a weakness for celebrity impressions. He is versed in which donuts I like and will always do the talking at a party so I can be uncomfortable in peace. And while he actually believes his dishy good looks might signal to others that he's been in a bar fight or two, to me his handsome face skews more nice Jewish Colombian drug lord who went to summer camp. He's man-about-town to my woman-stay-at-home. He's a gamer and fiercely loyal, and although he is admittedly dead inside, I know that sequestered somewhere in there is a neon— albeit murmurish—heart that flashes and hums when you need it to.

We were married seven months later, in an old movie house in upstate New York. The guests ate Twizzlers and popcorn as Buzz and I walked down the aisle together. Yes, my mother wore pants. Our vows spoke of love and honor and all that, adding in a much worked-on line that promised there would be *no situation in which we can't find laughter*.

Buzz still uses this line most days, usually when making fun of me.

"You don't even understand the vows," I say.

"*You* don't," he says. "We're finding laughter."

"No. *You* are finding laughter at my expense."

"Have you met you?"

And so goes the marriage. This is our story.

A Very Special Episode

· · · · · · ·

The floors of the funeral home were shiny, like Granny Smiths in the supermarket. It smelled like lemons, not dead people, and everyone was mingling and kissing like they were at a bar mitzvah. My mother, all of a sudden, was starring on *Falcon Crest*, leaving fuchsia, egg-shaped marks on the cheeks of guests, drooping her head at the mumbling of the words *sorry* and *my sympathies*.

We were instructed to move operations to a special room earmarked for family members of the deceased, and I watched my parents and Ace excuse themselves from the ballooning crowd. When I felt Buzz's hand on my back pushing me in the same direction, I rooted my shoes, not wanting to budge, but instantly lost the battle, as my soles were unscuffed and those lustrous floors tricky.

"Stop pushing me," I said.

He pressed harder. "I'm not pushing you."

"You're pushing."

"I'm *guiding* you," he said. Buzz was no abuser but I still contend he'd already shoved me through the revolving door at the airport that morning, no matter what he said. "Just go."

He slid me closer to the portal of a room I imagined vice presidents were squirreled away to in the event of an assassination attempt. Down the hall of Paperman & Sons, past the bathrooms and a sign announcing the services of Bella Steinmetz and Hershey Finkel and our own Pearlie Segal, I stood outside the Family Room. The lighting was pleasant enough, though that piped-in organ music swirled through my brain, summoning flashes of endless hockey games, and days in Samantha Narvey's basement, listening to her play "When the Saints Go Marching In" on the electric organ as her father cracked their greyhound for peeing on the sheepskin rug.

I'd read somewhere that when adults return home to spend time with their parents, it's not uncommon to revert back to the same behaviors they exhibited at, say, thirteen years old. As I sent poisonous darts at my mother's hairsprayed helmet on the day she was to bury her own mother, I chalked it up to statistics.

The sign on the door said FAMILY ROOM, but clearly the definition of family had a different meaning for all, because the place was packed, mostly with my parents' friends. Dark-suited men huddled; a knot of women in black outfits showcasing chunky jeweled necklaces whispered about the golf club. My parents were the only one of their group not to join the Club, and I'd spent my entire youth hearing golf gossip at dinner. My mother didn't play golf or tennis or even really go outside, but it was a gathering place for well-to-do Montreal Jews and she felt left out. She'd lament the summer weekends because all their friends were at the Club, and although I'd never set foot in the place, I hated it.

• • •

The call about Grandma Pearlie came on Wednesday, six a.m., Eastern Jewish Standard Bad News Time. Apparently she'd died the day before in the early afternoon but my parents waited to place the call. I've never studied Judaism but am sure somewhere in one of the books it states that all tragic news must be delivered before sunrise. To this day, if the phone rings in the early morning hours, I start calculating who is dead. I remember reaching over Buzz to get the phone and barely hearing my mother's words but also somehow knowing exactly what she was saying. Her voice was small and far away, and I said "What?" at least twice before I heard the sentence, "Grandma Pearlie died." I don't remember hanging up, only Buzz gathering me in as tears dripped onto his white Approved Sleeping T-shirt.

The only death I'd encountered to date was when my brother's hamster ate his pregnant hamster wife, leaving their unborn children in various stages of chewed up, but I was sheltered from the carnage because no one let me go down to the basement to see. I was six years old; there was no funeral. Somehow, because my parents married young and came from small families, I'd managed to avoid death altogether. Even when our Yorkshire terrier died I was away at college and dodged my father's misery during the disposal of Milk-Bones and leashes and that full-body navy snowsuit with hood that the dog hated.

I'd seen plenty of dying and funerals in movies, which is how I knew to dig out that pair of black pants from the back of my closet, the ones I'd bought to make me look serious at work. They were called Editor Pants, from Express, and they were kind of a big deal because they cost more than twenty bucks and also came with a name. I was supposed to get them altered but never did, so they scraped the floor as Buzz pushed me along the halls of Paperman & Sons.

When someone died on *Guiding Light*, all they focused on were oversized black hats and decanters of brandy and revenge. But clearly there were other major parts of death and funerals. Like the toffee-colored guest book I couldn't stop obsessing over. *Who the hell would come to my funeral?* I wondered. This caused instant hostility toward my charming and likeable best friend in Manhattan, who would, for sure, have way more people show up to her death.

"You're still standing out here?" said Buzz, returning from the men's room. I pretended not to hear him. He *guided* me again and I kept my head down, thinking it might keep well-wishers at bay. I had a hard enough time making small talk under regular circumstances. I knew I'd earned a get-out-of-jail-free card, being a mourner and all, but I didn't have it in me to say anything to anyone, and although I didn't want to discuss my grandmother with these people, I couldn't bear to hear about their golf game or kids either. And I certainly didn't want to talk about the weather, which is my least favorite topic, unless I bring it up.

And so I used some of the techniques I'd perfected for pretending I was crazy on the streets of New York if I felt some weirdo following me down Avenue B. It was basically a lot of face acting—alternating looks of concern and surprise, all the while arranging my eyebrows in different stages of ascent. I'd learned some of the moves from a relative who often wore fur coats in June and believed the FBI was tapping her refrigerator. I launched into these maneuvers while facing away from Buzz so he wouldn't think I was having a stroke. It was just as I was organizing myself at the optimum angle that I saw it. Right there in the middle of the room, minding its own business.

As with most of my death experiences, the only coffins I'd ever seen were in the movies and on TV. Those were usually deep cherry or rich mahogany with satiny interiors fit for the likes of Liberace. Fancy stuff. But the one in front of me, the one that housed Grandma Pearlie, was pale and cheap looking and instantly made me feel the way I do when I catch a glimpse of an old person eating meatloaf alone in a diner. It was so rinky-dink that it looked like my father put it together in the backyard. Well, maybe not *my* father, since he carried a purse, plus it's no secret that most Jewish men don't usually wield hammers. We know better to leave the fix-it stuff to the Gentiles. But *a* father, in *a* Christian living room somewhere, might have put this casket together on Christmas morning.

Grandma Pearlie was in a box. Why did my mother choose this Ronco Fantastic Casket kit for her own mother? I imagined the choices at her disposal, all the colors and sheens and snazzy interiors. My mother has never left the house, never even left her room, without makeup. So why box up her mother in this? I overheard someone mentioning that the box was pine, but to me pine was the bedroom set Bonnie Caplan had in seventh grade. This thing wasn't the smooth four-poster bed and matching dresser with full-length mirror; this pine seemed like it might give you splinters if you touched it the wrong way.

"What's with the box?" I said to Buzz, who muttered something vague about Jewish law. My family was Jewish a couple of times a year, and mostly that entailed eating roast chicken or a light meal of dairy after my nana made us fast. What I knew about Jews came from that Mordecai Richler book they made us read in high school and from my religious tenth-grade boyfriend. I did recall him once telling me that the reason Jews bury their dead so quickly is to avoid humiliation for the deceased. Clearly whoever wrote that rule never saw the grapefruit crate my grandmother was stuffed into.

And it's not like Grandma Pearlie was religious. As a matter of fact, when Grandpa Solly occasionally went to shul, she stayed home to watch *The Price Is Right* or take a bubble bath with the oversized bottle of Fa bubbles that lived on the side of her tub. Did all the Jews at Paperman & Sons get this box? There were some pretty fancy Jews in Montreal and I couldn't imagine them choosing this option to send their families off to wherever it was Jews believed in, even if it was the law. My father drove a chocolate brown Jaguar and wore custom-made cowboy boots with his suits, my mother wore sunglasses indoors; they loved being fancy. It certainly was not glitzy to send off one's loved one for all eternity in something that looked like I'd made it at summer camp.

I wondered what Grandma Pearlie looked like jammed in there. No matter how tight I scrunched my eyes, I couldn't make out her face. All I could picture was E.T. in the scene where he was dying, all gray and shriveled. I thought of how I was quasi-claustrophobic and had to sit on the aisle at the movies so I could evacuate if need be. I made a mental note not to be put into a box when I died. I decided then and there to be cremated, even though a college friend once told me her uncle was cremated and her aunt got a Ziploc in the mail that said REUBEN SCHLOSS— CREMAINS on it in Magic Marker. His whole body fit into a sandwich bag. If you looked closely enough, she said, you could even see chips of bone.

"I have to get out of here," I said to Buzz.

"Are you all right?"

"No. It smells like lemons and people are dead."

I left Buzz alone in the Family Room, seeing as my parents and their friends preferred him anyway, and escaped to the bathroom. It was unnerving how still and squeaky clean the place was. I knew there were two other services taking place that day and yet there wasn't a person in sight. Except for one man

I noticed in the distance, dressed in a brown suit that had seen better days. Grandpa Solly. I had been avoiding being alone with him since I got to town. We were not the kind of family who said *I love you* out loud, ever, so how could I possibly have the words, or the courage, to speak to my grieving grandfather. Plus, he'd been a little off as of late, as evidenced by his entrance to my parents' apartment that morning.

"Moe is a bastard," he said, whizzing by me when I opened the door for him.

"Not today, Daddy." My mother was by the window, outlining her lips with fuchsia pencil, filling in the rest with Pepto-pink lipstick, the same shade she wore fifteen years ago when I was in high school. It was rare to see her apply makeup in public. Mostly it was done behind the closed bathroom door, her version of Superman's phone booth. In all my years, I had never seen her undecorated or undressed. I have never really seen her.

"I'll tell you one thing, if you think I am going to talk to him in this lifetime, you got another thing coming." Grandpa Solly followed my mother, hands in his pockets. He jangled quarters and those generic stripey mints, the same ones he'd toted around when I was a kid. He didn't say much but you could always hear him coming, like a janitor. He was also carrying a small duffel bag that appeared to hold a change of clothes.

"Jesus, Daddy," my mother said. "Your teeth are going to crack in half."

"Well, if they do," he said, "I'm not going to that dentist of yours. Son of a bitch will soak you for all you're worth."

My mother *tsk*ed. "Fine. Just get dressed."

"I am dressed. Nothing wrong with these trousers."

"Mom would have wanted you to wear your navy suit."

"That's *your* story," he said, walking away toward the wall of glass windows. He stared out onto the city, carrying on with the pocket rumpus. I wasn't used to Grandpa Solly talking back to my mother—or, really, talking much at all—but I'd heard my father say something about how he'd recently wandered in off the street to an assertiveness training course at the Jewish Y, which may have had something to do with his new behavior. Plus his wife was dead.

There were laugh-track sounds from the den, where Ace and my father were on the couch together, dressed in dark suits, very busy staying out of things. Grandpa Solly walked into the guest bathroom and locked the door. I could swear I smelled cigarette smoke. My mother made phlegmy sounds, then snapped her hairsprayed helmet in my direction. "Why isn't anyone ready?"

"You have lipstick on your teeth," I said.

"I go down to that McDonald's on St. Catherine. About six in the morning," said Grandpa Solly, returning from the bathroom. He smiled and I saw that one of his teeth was missing. One near the front. "I walk or take the bus. Sometimes I ask the paperboy to drive me. I have coffee and talk to the guys."

I wondered when my grandfather got "guys." Grandpa Solly wasn't a guy's guy, but more of a sit-with-the-ladies type. He could spend hours at the little shopping center near their apartment, sitting on a bench, reading circulars or staring out the window while my grandmother picked up her watch from the jeweler or the latest hardcover from the public library located upstairs. She'd bring him Styrofoam cups of coffee with eight sugars from the PIK-NIK and ask him how he was doing. "Fine and dandy," he'd say. "Fine and dandy."

Imagining him talking to the guys seemed inconceivable, as I could count the words he'd uttered in my lifetime. When calling our house, he'd say, "How do you do? Let me get Pearlie," as if we'd called him. He was her built-in studio audience, even near the end, when her brain frazzled and I'd sit on their salmon-colored velour couch for an hour as Grandma Pearlie asked me when I was heading back to New York on a continuous loop. In groups his silence was even more pronounced. At holiday gatherings, he was unapparent, remaining mum and seated as the coffee and cookies were served, not leaving the table with the other men to watch the game, even when Zaida Max asked him where his dress and pocketbook were.

It's possible there were guys at one time, eons ago. Grandma Pearlie'd often told of being taken to the Yangtze on Saturday nights for egg rolls and chicken chow mein, then back home to a running gin game for the men, while the wives played bridge and drank coffee. There were eight gin players, including my grandfather, but I knew they'd all died, and Grandpa Solly brought the same box of chocolate to all seven shivas, referring to himself as the Last of the Mohicans.

Perhaps there were work guys. Back when he stood at the far reaches of the old-timey pharmacy, beyond the soda fountain and under the sign that said PRESCRIPTIONS. With a cigarette stuck to his lips, he filled customer orders, calling out their addresses or phone numbers when they walked in instead of their names, every one of which he knew by heart—his parlor trick. He'd bring home boxes of Turtles and an assortment of bars, because Grandma Pearlie preferred chocolate—candy and ice cream and brownies—to food. There was always candy on hand at the apartment, but it was usually squirreled away in cupboards and cabinets, and I'd spend all my time there on a scavenger hunt with no clues.

Mostly what I knew about my grandfather were the things that concerned me; the other Solly facts were murky and would surface only as time moved on. Although his last name was

showcased in giant neon letters over the front window—SEGAL'S
REXALL DRUGS—it never surfaced that the store belonged to one
of his brothers, one who put him through pharmacist school in
exchange for over thirty years of service but refused to give him a
piece of the business. If there was hostility, I never saw it or heard
it mentioned. Sometimes what went on in my family was cloudy
and the list of what wasn't talked about lapped what was. This
aggravated my prying nature, or perhaps ignited it. Here I was
thirty years old and couldn't bring myself to ask my mother why
she chose the coffin any more than I could ask my grandfather
what was going on with the new personality.

"How do you do?" Grandpa Solly said.

"Oh, you know" was all I could manage.

Grandpa Solly leaned in toward me, smiling like one of those
mustachioed cartoon villains. "Did you see Moe the bastard?"

Grandpa Solly laughed and, jangling his pockets, meandered
to the glass entrance doors to stare out the window, full of pleasant beans.

People picked their seats like they were going to a movie. Some
knew exactly where they wanted to sit, while others whispered
in the aisles, deciding. My parents and brother sat in the first row,
next to Grandpa Solly. In a move that will endear Buzz to me
for life, he pushed me again, but this time into the row behind
my family. I didn't want to be tucked into the first row, with
direct access to my grandfather's face, even if he wasn't crying
but, rather, humming, as if he were at the circus.

The rabbi walked onto the small stage toward the Box. Lacing his small pale fingers together, he welcomed us in a girlish
voice. When he started comparing my grandmother to Rebecca
from the Bible (neither of whom he'd ever met), I tuned out,

counting backward from ninety-six slowly, like I do when I can't sleep. I kept my eyes forward, not looking behind me to see if the rows were filled. I knew I couldn't handle it if the place wasn't sold out. What if only a handful of people show up to your funeral? That leather guest book peacocking in the vestibule, a wink reminding me that my own funeral would definitely be one of those *Mary Tyler Moore* parties—a real clunker, where there is not enough food to feed the small group who bothered to show up. *Seriously, people*, I thought, stewing in my own juice. *Would it kill you to come pay your respects? I died, for Christ's sake.* And it's not like Buzz would do anything about it, except to say I didn't even like parties, so what did I care? *Screw all of you*, I thought. *Screw everyone. Except you, Grandma Pearlie. Please forgive me. Amen.*

The rabbi continued on about sunsets and lives lived.

"Can't hear!" shouted a voice. "In the back! Louder! We can't hear a thing back here!"

I could feel all heads turning to see where the voice was coming from but I knew exactly who was responsible for stopping the service. Zaida Max, my father's father. He sounded pissed, too, like he'd paid for the good seats to see *Fiddler on the Roof* and got this.

"Shit," my father said.

Zaida Max could be a prick, but he was also an orphan, so we let it slide. He was matinee-idol dashing and very alpha. At home, he had a personal lounger and no one could touch his television. Nana Esther would run to and from the kitchen for him, bringing plates of honey cake or dishes of ice cream. A Jewish Edith and Archie Bunker.

The rabbi cleared his throat and raised the volume, back to our program already in progress. I continued counting but then felt bad for not focusing on my grandmother, so I moved on to my own reflections about Pearlie. How she had a certain smell—a mix of fresh lipstick and Kleenex. How tiny she was. Sitting together at Murray's in a small booth as she ordered her egg salad on toasted rye with a cup of black coffee, followed by a single scoop of chocolate ice cream, preferably one that came in that little silver dish. That buzzy sound that happened in the back of her jaw, one that would drive me mental if anyone else made it. These were the things I'd have said if my mother had asked me to speak at the microphone instead of Ace, who became the official family eulogizer that day. I was fine with keeping my thoughts in my head, convinced that if I'd mentioned any one of those sentiments out loud someone would cluck a tongue because I was doing it wrong.

Grandpa Solly leaned over to my mother. "You see Moe, over there? The bastard."

Even with her back to me, I could hear her say, "Enough, Daddy," in a wait-until-your-father-gets-home tone. He laughed when she got mad. He sounded like Barney Rubble. He didn't care what she said to him but I did. Why wasn't she cutting him a break? He was staring at a shipping crate and she was scolding him. *Let him act the way he wants! His wife is in a box!*

I might as well have been sitting on my water bed wearing an oversized Benetton sweater, the one with the giant *B* on the front, as I stared at my Richard Gere poster, plotting all the ways I could ruin my mother (this might have been the revenge portion of funerals I'd seen on the soaps). So what if I was thirty-one and sitting in a pew? I couldn't help myself—it was bubbling out of me like apple pie guts stuck in an oven too long. I seethed at the back of her head, hating the architecture of her hairdo. I was mad that a monsoon could rush into the funeral home and her sculpted helmet wouldn't know the difference. The outdated pink lipstick she still wore enraged me, the way it stuck to her teeth. I was pissed at her teeth.

"Very nice service," said Grandpa Solly, as we sat in the limousine on our way to the grave site. "Too bad it wasn't for Moe the bastard."

"Uch, Daddy, can we not talk about bastards right now? Can we just ride to the cemetery in peace?"

Grandpa Solly laughed, watching the lampposts and cars go by as if he'd never been on a street before. "Would you look at all these cars. . . ." His foot was twitchy, he couldn't sit still. "Why are we in this limousine? We could have taken my car."

"You haven't driven in ten years," my mother said.

"So what?"

"So, you don't even have that stupid car anymore. You got rid of it ages ago."

"Then we should have taken the bus. Nothing wrong with the bus. What do we need to be fancy for?"

Ace and my father were sitting in the little leather jump seats, facing the wrong way. We all knew my mother had to face forward in a car or she'd get nauseous. It did seem curious that a car from a Jewish funeral home had backward-facing seats when it was pretty standard that fragile constitutions ran rampant throughout the religion. The driver was a maniac, unable to handle the length of the vehicle. He was no stranger to the brake, and every turn he took caused my mother to squish into my leg.

"You don't take a bus to a funeral. Taking a limo is what you are supposed to do."

"Well, I sure as hell hope they aren't soaking you," Grandpa Solly said. "Never heard of having to ride in a car made for rock and rollers and bastards."

My mother closed her eyes, made tight little fists. I could see the belt on her men's slacks moving up and down in quick spurts.

"I mean, what are we trying to prove in this crazy car?" he said. "We shoulda gotten a lift from 68 Glenmore."

Ever the pharmacist, he called family friends by their address instead of their name. My mother made a whole host of phlegmy noises and Grandpa Solly hummed and smiled, asking Ace when he'd be heading home to Connecticut, and wasn't it nice that he was able to make it back to Canada. My father rubbed his index finger back and forth over the knee of his crossed leg, Cartier bracelet clinking against the gold bezel of his Breitling watch. The driver was Mario Andretti all of a sudden, trying to make all the lights, shaking us up like cans of soda. Buzz zoned out.

"Why *did* we take this dumb car?" I said.

Buzz sighed. Ace and my father looked out the window.

As they lowered the box into the grave, I didn't know where to look, so I called up some more obscure *Happy Days* episodes from the deep recesses of my brain. The one where Fonzie's dog Spunky gets depressed. Richie Cunningham getting arrested for being the Kissing Bandit. Chachi setting fire to Arnold's. Joanie leaving Milwaukee to tour with Leather Tuscadero. Inspiration Point. Mr. and Mrs. C. Ralph Malph. Potsie. Al. Rosa Coletti. *Shortcake. Aaaaaay.*

And then, Grandma Pearlie was gone. The episode was over. *The one where the grandmother dies.*

We were stuffed into the elevator: my parents, Ace, Buzz, and I. Solly had strict instructions that he wanted no part of a shiva—

"no deli meat or bastards"—and we were, instead, to "come up to the house." At the twelfth floor, we filed out, and just like on every Jewish holiday I'd ever spent there, Grandpa Solly stood waiting for us at the end of the hall, outside his door, feet planted on the moss-colored nubby carpet, arms waving like we were a rescue plane overhead.

"How do you do?" he said from his end of the hall, like we hadn't just seen him. As if everything were normal. I almost expected Grandma Pearlie to be inside holding a just-set bowl of Jell-O with suspended grapes and pineapple cubes or exhaling smoke rings out the balcony window, even though she claimed not to inhale.

"Okay, what's he doing now?" my mother said.

As I got closer, I noticed the telephone in the hallway. The green rotary phone sat by itself outside the door, as if it were being punished. Next to it was a bag from the A&P.

"Daddy, why is the phone out here?"

"I don't wanna talk to that bastard."

I had no idea who this bastard was, if he was even real. I'd tried to get it out of my mother earlier but she was already at her limit with discussing Solly.

"You have no idea what I've been dealing with," she said to me before we left for the funeral home. "He's on the streets all day. He's been locking himself in my bathroom and smoking. He keeps denying it but I can smell it! And he looks like a rummy."

The rest of the group walked into the apartment, but I was locked on that phone. I loved its avocado color and the sandy noise it made when my grandmother placed her finger in the rotary dial, winding it clockwise, gracefully letting go. "Regent 9," she'd say, then announce all the other numbers as she dialed. I couldn't bring myself to step into the apartment. Instead I imagined what it might feel like to kick that phone. Really smash it down the hallway. Watch the spiral cord flail off in slow motion as it soared through the halls of the Belvedere. I would scream "Regent 9" as it crash-landed, making a muffled dying ring against the carpet. Any sound would have been better than the series of ticks and clicks I could hear coming from my mother, even while standing out in the hall. *Uch. Tsk. Pfft.* These were her noises. Her punctuation.

I truly could not get myself inside. The spit-polished lemon floors and the freshly dug grave had nothing on walking into the small two-bedroom with the hidden candy and library books and the dull sounds of a baseball game on the transistor. I knew if I stood in the hall much longer my mother would come out and we'd be alone and I'd have to be nice and have that *One to Grow On* moment she deserved but I could not give.

So in I walked. For the second time that day, I was floored by what was in front of me. We all stared around the living room, not saying a word. You could have heard a brownie crumb fall to the carpet.

"Take whatever you want," said Grandpa Solly, delighted by his handiwork. "I have no use for any of it."

It remains unclear when he did this, but at some point in the past few days Grandpa Solly had managed to get down to basement storage and lug the plastic lawn furniture up to his living room. He'd found card tables and folding chairs and placed them around the room. Their couch was missing. Set on all surfaces were wedding china, glass bowls that used to house spaghetti and meatballs or that stuffed cabbage my mother liked, cookie sheets, brownie tins, Bundt pans. There were collections of straw, leather, and beaded handbags. Slippers, winter boots, and lines of shoes all in a row. Hangers perched on doorknobs displayed pants and raincoats. Decks of cards stacked the windowsills, pictures and ashtrays and necklaces piled on the one upholstered chair he chose to leave in place. Books remained on the shelves and art on the walls but there were pieces of scrap paper taped up all over the place, filled with scribbly handwriting and random phone numbers. We were in the middle of a freak garage sale.

"What are you all waiting for?" said Grandpa Solly, like we were shy about digging in. "Start taking."

No one budged.

"Daddy, this is ridiculous."

My mother had officially hit the limit with her father's misbehavior, which was the only cue I needed to start shopping. Yes, it was disturbing—both this new shell he'd cracked out of and the death sale before me. But I still wanted something to take home. A piece of her. A souvenir.

"Who needs grips?" he said, holding up a tattered suitcase. "Here, Kim, take the grips."

"Daddy, this is nonsense. She doesn't need a suitcase. What is she going to do with any of this stuff?"

"Well," he said, "what am I going to do with it?"

"Just keep it!"

"For what?"

No one had an answer for him, so we milled around the room looking for bargains. My mother stormed off into the tiny galley kitchen, helmet about to blast off. My father followed. Buzz excused himself, something about needing air. Ace went to the bookshelf to look busy. He flipped through hardcovers with library stickers affixed to the spines, fingers squeaking along their thick plastic jackets. Who would return them? He picked up a Stephen King, and dollar bills fell to the floor. He looked at me and I looked for my mother, who was, thank God, in the kitchen, huffing about crumbs. There were shopping bags in corners that we were supposed to fill, removing all traces of Grandma Pearlie as we left. Some of

the bags contained wads of cash. I went to the den to see if
there was any candy, noticing that their double bed with rose-
colored chenille spread no longer lived in the room any more
than Grandma Pearlie did. Had he stopped sleeping? I went
back to the living room.

"Daddy," my mother said, walking back into the sale, "you
need to have someone clean in here."

"Why?"

"It's a pigsty."

"No, it's not."

"Daddy, it's terrible in there."

"It's fine."

"It's disgusting."

"It's fine," he said, shooing her away. "You can eat off the
floor."

"There are crumbs all over the floor!"

"I can take care of myself!" he said, slamming a fist on the
dining table. A muffin tin went flying.

My mother sucked in her breath, her stomach disappearing
into the folds of her black slacks.

"I don't need a goddamn girl in here to clean," he said under
his breath.

"Why don't you just sit down?" my mother said, annoyed.

Grandpa Solly started pacing. Around the dining room
table. Behind the chair, up and down the hallway to his bedroom, going on about the bastards. Grandpa Solly. The silent
man who held the crook of my grandma's elbow when she
walked down a flight of stairs. Who placed pink carnations in
a vase by her bed the day she came home from cataract surgery. Who sat quietly by her side as she watched TV, jangling
that change instead of making conversation. Grandpa Solly was
losing his marbles in front of us. They spilled out of his head,

along the carpet, under the lawn chairs, behind the remaining upholstered chair.

I sat on the fuzzy pink toilet seat lid, knees together, feet apart. The Oil of Olay was there, just waiting for her. It was the only room left intact. Her tortoiseshell paddle brush was still on the hand mirror, next to his comb. There were silver strands tangled in the bristles.

I thought about my own death often, wondering what could be festering inside my body, giant tumors plotting to bully the rest of my organs into a slow and painful demise. It had been a hobby of mine since early childhood. I'd spent so many hours planning the ways one could die that I never even considered what actually happens when you do. Does it hurt? Do you know it's happening? Are you presented with answers right before you go, like a parting gift? I wondered if Grandma Pearlie had secret information right now, tucked away in that box. Pretty clever to lock up all those answers and bury you deep in the ground so they don't get out. Seal them up in a sandwich bag.

When I was at the funeral home, a young mortician asked me if I would be speaking at the ceremony, a few words about the dearly departed. I told him I was not much for audience partici-pation. He smiled, probably used to all kinds in his line of work and skilled at dealing with all forms of deflection.

"You know," he said, "there are many ways to voice your thoughts, other ways to say goodbye. Sometimes people write notes to the departed. We can put those notes in the casket for you."

"Ew," I said.

"Ew?"

"I mean . . ." I laughed, biting the inside of my cheek until I tasted salty blood.

"Would you like a pen?"

I told him I always carried a special pen but would be thrilled for some casket-worthy stationery. I sat in the bathroom stall for half an hour, trying to come up with something Grandma Pearlie would be fine with for all of eternity. I wondered if I should open with a joke, but figured she already had to live in that crate, so the least I could do was be respectful.

Dear Grandma Pearlie,

I will always think of you when I have egg salad or Turtles, and if I have a daughter, I promise to name her after you. I love you.

I added my signature at the bottom, like I was giving her an autograph. It was the first time I'd said I loved any one of my family members. I folded the paper as many times as the letterhead would allow, placing it in the firm hand of the Jewish mortician.

Once back safe in Manhattan, I thought about that letter constantly. Should I have taken more time with it or asked Grandma Pearlie questions about herself or pulled the old *wish you were here* bit, pretending like everything was fine? I hoped she read it. I hope she saw it all. The people who came to pay their respects, the speech Ace gave. But not Grandpa Solly going off the deep end.

Word came from home that Grandpa Solly had started spending his days outside the apartment, walking the streets from morning until night, still looking like a bum. "What am I supposed to do," he'd say to my mother, "stare at these four blank walls all day?" My mother would call him on the hour, waiting for him to answer, to let her know he was fine and not hit by a bus, but when he finally answered she only knew how to express her concern by snapping at him and using that tone she usually reserved for waiters.

He was giving her a run for her money. Gifting A&P shopping bags of cash to various tenants in the building, sitting in the waiting room of a family friend's law office all day, shoplifting from the mall. All this behavior seemed so out of character for the grandfather I knew. And then one day, my mother called to tell me who was pregnant and who else had died and maybe I wanted to send a card.

"How's Grandpa Solly?" I said, changing the subject.

"Uch, I don't want to talk about it," she said. "It's getting worse. He's off his meds again."

"His what?"

"His pills. He decided he didn't want to take them and flushed them all down the toilet at our house. He was smoking in that bathroom again, if you can believe that."

"What pills?"

"Oh, please, Kim, you know about those," she said, now aggravated. "The antipsychotics."

The what? Turns out Grandpa Solly wasn't quiet my entire life because he was, well, quiet. He was mute because he was depressed. Manically, maniacally, psychotically so, and taking some heavy medication to boot, or at least when he felt like it. Wasn't this a nugget I should have been privy to? What else didn't I know? Had my father once been a woman?

On soap operas, when people found out this kind of hidden information, they were told that it had been kept secret for their own protection. Is that why no one had ever said a word to me about sex or puberty or money or mental illness or reality or the fact that my great-aunt Rita and -uncle Moishe lived together for their entire adult lives in the same apartment and were not indeed married but instead brother and sister? Seems I was shielded from quite a list, sequestered in a suburban Jewish witness-protection program.

My family was riddled with mental illness—schizophrenia, suicidal tendencies, garden-variety depression—and now I had a new one to add: some version of mania, although my mother resisted giving it a title, or much validity, as if he'd made it all up as an excuse to stay home from school. Was it really for my protection, like *Guiding Light* had led me to believe? Or was it that if my mother looked at her father closely, officially diagnosed with the big daddy of depression, she would have to stay out of Superman's phone booth and look at herself, at me? I finally understood that it was just easier to hide in the bathroom, making herself up and talking about the weather.

"I have to go," I said, avoiding the deeper questions about my grandfather's illness, resigned to just researching the symptoms on my own, like I usually did.

As I waited for my mother to have the last word on the phone call, I decoded that I'd been terrified of returning home to bury my favorite relative, to see my family, because I might actually be faced with an unfiltered, raw moment. Something real. The funeral, the Box, Grandpa Solly—they were ice water to the face but we were expert at taking cover. Out of habit and reflex, I wanted to blame my mother for not showing me something personal and authentic that day, but it finally registered: She just didn't have the chops. The coated face and phlegmy noises were gadgetry to help her survive it. It was hair-raising to venture out, so she stayed tucked in. It was what I was used to, how we were trained to handle our family business. And although I insisted that I wished it were different, I think I preferred it that way. We stayed quiet on the phone for a moment.

And then, "I miss my mommy," she said, behind that signature baby voice.

I'd like to say I stepped up and gave her what she needed. That I thawed, even just one degree, but I remained my thirteen-year-old self, deciding that if she couldn't give me that one real moment, I couldn't either. She was the mirror. And I said goodbye.

Lemons & Limes

....

I was supposed to be resting. If I didn't lift anything over ten pounds, avoided exercise, strenuous activity, sex, and air travel for the next twenty-four hours, they assured me nothing would happen.

"But let's just *say* I did something," I said. "Like by accident. What *could* happen?"

As I began listing potential calamities, Buzz gently shoved me out the door while giving instructions to my doctor. "Don't feed the bears," he said. "Please!"

They all shared a big laugh, including the technician. It's true, they were right—amniocentesis was hilarious.

Buzz was itching to get home. Not to make sure I was in the proper state of repose, but to open the small kraft paper envelope he held in his hand.

"You get them to write down the sex of the baby and put the results in an envelope. Then you can open it at home and not in the hospital, so it's not all clinical and stuff. It's genius!" was how he sold it to me. "Where are the envelopes?"

He was hopped up about this latest harebrained scheme, which meant he'd suggest it to every pregnant lady waddling through town, and he'd be so persuasive that I guarantee they'd all follow suit. Buzz is a snow-to-the-Eskimos type; sometimes his enthusiasm is infectious, like pox.

I spent the days leading up to the amnio researching *potentially disastrous outcomes for lengthy needles jabbed into amniotic sac* while he busied himself looking for office supplies. But, as spooked as I was about the procedure, I was even more anxious about showing up with the wrong kind of envelope for the occasion. I have absolutely no time for plain white security envelopes or a chewed-up pen from the bank. Plus, I wanted my ob-gyn to think I had good taste in stationery.

With the procedure now behind me, and the husband off to work, it was time to get on with the prescribed twenty-four hours of idleness. I was now free to indulge in my favorite pastime: watching reruns of *The Cosby Show*. The fetus (aka the Junior Mint) was resting comfortably, blanketed in beans and rice and cheese and those cheap, fat corn-syrup jelly beans from CVS (two packs for a buck), but I was in distress. I'm sure Rudy's fish, Lamont, was an excellent pet, but his funeral was not the sole reason for my aggravation. Finding an agreeable position was challenging and, according to that damn oversized book you were supposed to read, any way I chose to arrange myself would do irreparable damage to the five-month-old fetus, which now had genitals and was the size of a banana. After much flailing, I settled on my back, which the oversized book frowned upon, so I smoothed the throw blanket and kicked the book onto the floor. That's when I heard it.

It wasn't exactly a crash. Nor would I classify it as a boom or a slam or a smash or a thump. I think it was somewhere between a clatter and a clink, but a very menacing clatter and clink. Gripping the remote, I made a quick mental list of probable causes:

1. Serial killer

2. Rapist

3. Murderer

4. Cat burglar

I knew, gauging by the prickles of sweat piercing my scalp, that it wasn't just a potted plant losing a battle with the May breeze. Something was downstairs. I'd seen enough ADT commercials to know that intruders don't enjoy company, so I turned up the volume on the television and threw a few more books onto the floor, hoping that, like most of the symptoms I was usually plagued with, it would just go away.

We had been renting a duplex apartment in Carroll Gardens, Brooklyn, for two years. It was in a handsome four-story brownstone—complete with thriving front garden labored over by a previous tenant—on an extra-wide tree-lined street, with parking right out front. The whole thing seemed very delightful, but apparently it was just on the border of no-goodnik territory. When we signed the lease, our curmudgeonly landlord grumbled, "Well, don't get too excited about the area. It's not perfect or anything. It's still pretty rough around the edges."

The bottom two floors were ours. We had our own entrance on what the Realtors referred to as the "garden level" but the locals called "the basement," and we occupied that as well as the entire parlor level above. The stoop was shared with our upstairs neighbors and, in an emergency situation, we could escape through two giant doors that served as a wall in the Junior Mint's room, which opened into the parlor hall. The floors were oaky, the ceilings covered in original tin. I loved the place. But on my day of supposed rest I began to take umbrage with it. My sole job was to stay still and make sure the Junior Mint's house didn't spring a leak. And now I was forced to be some sort of hero and deal with an interloper downstairs.

I am not a graceful person by nature, but I did my best impersonation of someone stealthy, imagining I was stepping over those red laser things, the ones you always see in spy capers. But even with my catlike swiftness there is nothing quiet about a hundred-year-old brownstone staircase. I stopped halfway down and peeked. Everything seemed in its place. Dining room was clear of prowlers. All rapists were home, safely tucked into their beds.

Puh-link.

I froze. The kitchen. It was coming from inside the kitchen. Practically hanging off the banister, I craned my neck as far as it would go, and then I saw it. I saw it I saw it I saw it. Darting back upstairs, I shut the door behind me. There I did a little jig of panic. New plan. I grabbed the phone and used the Junior Mint's giant doors as a means of egress. Once outside, I dialed Buzz.

"Everything okay?" was how he answered.

"No!" I said, cupping my hand over the mouthpiece.

"What's wrong?" He sounded worried. *One in 1,600 women may suffer a miscarriage as a result of amniocentesis.* "What happened?"

"There. Is. A. Squirrel. In. The. House."

Silence. Sigh. "A what?"

"Squirrel! There is a squirrel in the house! In the kitchen! He somehow managed to break in, gnawed his way through the screen. He is on the counter right now eating limes!"

"There's a squirrel in the house!" he shouted to someone in the office. There was raucous laughter like it was the goddamn Christmas party.

"It's not funny!" I said, my bare feet sticking to the warm concrete steps. "And don't *tell* people!"

"Sweetie, I'm in a meeting. I gotta go."

"*Go?*"

At the time, Buzz was working for a late-night comedy-show host. I could now hear him in the background doing squirrel material.

"Well, why did you even answer the phone, then?" I said, like I was nine.

"Because I thought there was actually something wrong."

"There *is* something wrong!"

"I'm sorry there is a squirrel." I could hear his dumb smile. "But I really have to go."

And, just like that, he hung up.

Uch. Now I needed another new plan.

When you read about hurricanes, earthquakes, and tsunamis, there are often accompanying stories about the wonderful spirit and efforts put forth by the victims' neighbors. When we lived on the Upper West Side in a fifth-floor walk-up, my neighbor in 2B once pulled a gun on me and my dog because we were in his way. I decided then and there that I should probably leave my neighbors alone. But this street felt different. Although most of the neighborhood was beginning to fill up with ironic mustaches, our street clung to its old world–ness. Our block was a beef stew of old mingling with new, traditional rump roast with just a drip of truffle oil. There were always so many brownstone dwellers out and about, chatty and nosy fixtures standing in front of their short iron gates, wanting to complain about parking or tell how things used to be before I moved in.

"*Marone*, it was somethin'," said a visiting grandson. He was returning from a little stint in jail and was visiting his grandma (Gloria, at number 28 just up the block). He even offered to show me his gun, which he said he kept buried in her backyard. "Street hockey. Gangs. We had it all."

"Man, it was the best," said the cousin who'd picked him up from the clink. "That was before the blacks and the Jews brought in the AIDS . . ."

Yes, it was time to enlist the neighbors. I couldn't miss. The street was lousy with them. The natural first choice was . . .

Punchy: Squat and dense, with a white band of Friar Tuck hair semicircling the back of his head, he was a ruffian from another era. Pretty high up the ladder, we were told. The entrance to his house was covered in a bulletproof cage and he was forever pacing the street, talking on the phone while walking his beagle, whose likeness was tattooed on his left hamstring. "Let's just say," said Donna, the crusty retired gym teacher from up the block (my strong second choice), "you don't gotta worry about your car being stolen on his block, if you get my drift."

Neither Punchy nor Donna were in their usual spots. Neither was Gloria, the red shopping cart pusher and teeny grandmother of the returning convict (a distant third option on the list). Oh! The Mayor! (Change him to third choice and move Gloria down one on the list.) Where was he? You couldn't miss him—about five foot five, a rounder, more avuncular Frank Sinatra. There was a brief period when we first moved in where I was convinced he hated me, so I went on a three-month campaign, complimenting his dog and inquiring about the neighborhood's history to win his affection and, once in his good graces, would hide in my vestibule to avoid the rehash of his trips to the new Costco. I would have sold my pancreas to have him stop by now.

There were, of course, the last resorts: my direct next-door neighbor, Frank the Racist, who looked like Santa with a tucked-in golf shirt. He used to like us before we left our trash can out and it accidentally blew into his yard, knocking over the woven lawn chair he sat in to make sure no one dinged his Pontiac Bonneville. He was not home either.

And then there was that guy directly across the street, Dominic Jr., who barked unnerving threats and profanities from his window. Once a week the SWAT team would come, all puffed up in full regalia, and cart him off to the slammer for a few days, just to cool down. "Troubled in the head," Donna would say, clucking her tongue. "His poor mother."

Where the hell were all those players? On any given day, it took forty-five minutes to get down the street. Now it was the Upper East Side at three a.m. I had some good action for these people, stoop fodder for months to come. I was actually doing them a favor. Where was the Mayor? What about that little mobster beagle, didn't he need to go out by now? Donna? Gloria? That hot-dogging SWAT team? I would have even settled for Dominic Jr. But the neighbors failed me.

I paced the sidewalk but worried that was considered exercise. I sat down, waiting for the affable UPS man. I'd forgotten about him. He was so delightful that you just wanted to bake him a pie. And his arrival was guaranteed, because the nut job at the top of the block, the one with the corner lot, had a bit of a QVC problem. Her lawn was overrun with American flag pinwheels and light-up angels and tin butterflies and glass balls, all punctuated by a large ceramic gnome in a bathing suit and sunglasses, holding a surfboard, with a sign that read, IT'S FIVE O'CLOCK SOMEWHERE. As a super last resort, I'd wait for the ornery mailman.

And then I saw him turn onto the block. His name I couldn't tell you because he was the only guy on the street who didn't speak. He was tall and undernourished, with a gazelle-like grace that suggested he might have once been a mime. I could guarantee there wasn't a speck of dust under his fainting couch. For sure there was a cat. He had kempt brown hair and an amiable face and it wouldn't have surprised me in the least if I turned on the news to learn the authorities had uncovered eighty-three severed body parts stuffed behind the veal stock and rainbow sherbet in his freezer. I could already see Donna on the local news, shaking her head and noting how quiet he was and what a shock this was to their neighborhood that was once so pleasant before the blacks and the Jews brought the AIDS, and now *this*.

No matter—these were desperate times and I needed a hand, so I put all thoughts of his freezer out of my mind. Plus, if he did cut me up for parts, think how bad Buzz would feel for hanging up on me.

"Excuse me," I said, hustling down the stairs, holding my back. "Hi! Hey! Excuse me?"

He stopped halfway down the block, squinting in my direction. I hurried to meet him, affecting a waddle in an attempt to appear drenched in pregnancy.

"Oh my god," I said, out of breath. "This is kind of mortifying, but I'm pregnant and there is a squirrel in my house. It just scratched its way through the screen with its gross little claws and is now in my kitchen eating limes."

He scrunched his eyebrows together and just stood there.

"My husband is at work and I kind of feel like a fifties housewife, needing a man's help and all that. Between you and me, I have a little rodent problem, like jump-on-the-table kind of problem. Do you have a ton of mice in your place, too? It's all the construction. Our landlord told us to get a cat. Anyway, I'm kind of freaking out and I never do stuff like this, but I was wondering if there was any way you could help me get the thing out of my house?"

I am not a street accoster, nor do I touch strangers, but I found myself placing a hand on his back and scooting him toward my house. He was skeletal, probably bruised easy, and I could feel his body tense up and leaden. I pushed harder, he dug his pristine gray New Balance into the sidewalk.

"The thing is," he said, as I tried to maneuver him past his stoop as if everything behind us was in flames, "I'm scared of squirrels, too."

Here, I did what anybody else would have done. I pretended not to hear him.

We stood together inside the parlor-level foyer, the entrance atop the stoop. I gave him an intricate lay of the land, revealing how best to serpentine his way through the house to capture our infiltrator. He looked around for a weapon, considering either a broom or the oversized golf umbrella my upstairs neighbor probably swiped from a hotel. He settled on the broom, giving him more of an air of old-ladyness than he already brought with him.

"Now, where is it, again?" he asked, and I could tell he was stalling. He was starting to get on my nerves.

I mapped it out one last time as we huddled together in the vestibule. He held the broom, I my sagging belly. *Good grief*, I thought, *let's go, already. . . .*

"Um, I'm Mitchell," he said.

"I'm Kim."

With the broom positioned like a fire hose in his delicate hands, Mitchell pranced down the stairs. I certainly hoped he was more menacing when chopping up bodies.

"There it is!" he whispered, looking up at me from the bottom step.

I shot mental poisonous darts at him. And then, propelled by what I'd pegged as fear mixed with a growing mutual hostility, Mitchell charged the squirrel. He sashayed along the softwood floor and I could have sworn I heard him making a buzzy sound. Shortly after takeoff, Mitchell lost his footing, causing the unwieldy broom to knock a glass of seltzer off the coffee table. The room was on mute, save for the hiss of dribbling soda water.

It remains unclear if it was the shattering noise or Mitchell's timid *shoo* or just a fluke, but the varmint looked our way, sighed, and then waltzed out from whence he came. New York critters are so laissez-faire. They don't even scurry. They just break in, take whatever they please, and leave when they are goddamn ready. Just like that, it was over. If we're being honest, I was kind of disappointed. I was hoping for just a little bit more of a duel. Mind you, this meant Mitchell could finally go home.

"Thank you," I said, but he was already gone. Mitchell glided home eyes-to-shoes, avoiding the neighbors, who were now, all of a sudden, securely back in their usual places. I'd see Mitchell sporadically in the years to come but our exchanges were relegated to the block walker's head nod. We never spoke of the Great Squirrel Incident of 2004. Returning to the scene of the crime, I picked up the lime with a paper towel and threw it in the trash, then secured the window, vowing to never open it again. Crisis averted, I returned to my regularly scheduled programming already in progress: *The Cosby Show* (the one where Theo and Cockroach scheme to pass a test on *Macbeth* without reading the play).

There is something delightful about forced bed rest. It was early May, but my hair was already starting to frizz and the locals were beginning their discussions of when to install the window units. If I weren't on lockdown, I'd have felt pressure to have one of those early-warm-day celebrations, complete with Frisbees and grilled meats and people. Being urged to take to the bed was a box with ribbon and a bow, especially after the break-in.

The results of the amnio were scheduled to come in somewhere between five and seven business days. Sure, it would feel

like eons, but, on the bright side, it would afford me some socially
acceptable crazy time. It is not uncommon to be anxious when
waiting for test results, and I loved scanty pockets of time when it
was appropriate to be mental. I told myself to relish this moment.
And I did. For seven minutes.

At the eight-minute mark, I replayed our first trip as expec-
tant parents to the ob-gyn. I was deep into an article about soft
cheese dangers while Buzz sat rooted in a chair, averting his eyes,
as if the ladies in the waiting room were already naked from the
waist down. It was still early in the game and the doctor had
decided not to do an ultrasound until I had two more weeks
under my belt, but she wanted to sit down and have a conversation regardless.

I should mention here that I had a little thing for my ob. During my first appointment, a year earlier, we'd gotten into a pro-
found debate during a breast exam about Duncan Hines cake
mix versus Betty Crocker. When I learned we were on the same
side of the controversy (Duncan Hines makes the better cake
hands-down; Crocker takes it for frosting), I left knowing I was
her favorite patient and that she most probably did a little two-
step when she saw my name on the day's schedule. Had we met
in grade school, I knew we'd have had matching knee socks. In
gym, she'd have been next to me, laughing as our gym teacher
stretched out before the Presidential Fitness Awards while his
private parts spilled out of his Adidas. We would have made
crank calls, stayed home together watching *The Love Boat* when
we weren't invited to Kenny Weinstein's basement party. Sure,
we'd have lost touch when she went to med school at Columbia
but, regardless, we'd have been tight.

At one appointment she even hinted at having lunch together,
but I panicked and coughed a lot. A few weeks later, I sent her
a handwritten note, telling her I'd love to have lunch sometime,

but it was never mentioned again. The reality was she poked at my cervix and I sent in the insurance claims. We were star-crossed lovers. It just wasn't meant to be.

"Goodstein!" Buzz shouted, like they were on the football field. I'd warned him to behave himself in the office and not make too many jokes. I stressed that it was a serious appointment, but really I just didn't want her to like him better.

"How are you feeling?" she asked me from her swivel chair.

"A little nauseous," Buzz said, rubbing his stomach. "And grumpy."

Goodstein laughed. I kicked him under the desk.

"Okay, so we'll do an ultrasound in a couple of weeks," she said. "But for now, I'm just going to ask you some routine questions."

I unraveled my pack of Wint-O-Greens.

"So, we already have your health history," she said, looking my way. "What about your dad? Any health issues?"

"Just some high cholesterol," I said, swinging my feet back and forth.

"Mom?"

"Does negativity count?"

Breezy laughter all around. This was turning into a pleasant day.

"And what about their siblings?"

"What do you mean?" I said, shifting in the chair.

"Do your parents have brothers or sisters? Your aunts or uncles?"

I'd been filling out health history forms for years, and never once did they canvass the ancillary branches of the family tree. It was always a bunch of check marks in the No column, The End.

"Does your father have a sibling?"

"Yes, a sister," I said, busying myself with the roll of mints.

"Any issues?"

She was starting to bug me. "Physical or mental?"

"Either. Both."

"Is paranoid schizophrenia an issue?"

The only sound in the office was Goodstein's scratching pen.

"Uncles?" she said, head down, all business.

"One. My mother's brother."

She looked at me. "Anything?"

"He's kind of depressed," I said. Buzz's eyebrows shot up to his hairline. "Fine. He's suicidal."

"Grandparents?"

"Heart disease on both sides. Heart attacks and bypasses. High blood pressure and cholesterol. Um, skin cancer, dementia, and Alzheimer's. I think there is some legal blindness there, too. Depression. Lots of depression. Manic, I think. Or was he bipolar? No, no, it's manic. My grandfather on my mother's side takes an antipsychotic. Sometimes. I spent my entire life thinking he was just quiet. Turns out, he was wildly depressed."

No one was saying anything, so I added, just for levity, "My other grandfather was kind of a jerk, but he was an orphan so we give him a pass."

Goodstein's pen scurried across the page. She turned to Buzz, who seemed to have sprung some sort of leak, sweat globules dripping from his forehead. She looked at him, signaling that it was his turn. I could tell he didn't want to go.

"Well, my father was a paranoid schizophrenic, like her aunt," he said. "But then he died of pancreatic cancer."

He then went on to spew out a list that doubled my own. Calamitous diseases, festering conditions, and plagues. If there was a defect, syndrome, or disorder to be had, we had it. Goodstein needed extra paper.

"My aunt has terrible panic attacks," added Buzz.

"Oh!" I shouted. "We have that, too!"

We were giddy kids comparing Halloween loot. But the giddiness wore off quickly. As Goodstein transcribed our list of decay and doom, it hit me.

"Tell me the truth," I said. "Did anyone else do this bad on the test? Are we the worst?"

"It's not a test," she said, eyes still on the form.

If she were any friend at all, the correct answer would have been *No way! Of course not! You should see the Messermans!* And if I were indeed her favorite patient, she would have broken that dumb doctor oath and shared the horror stories of others, just to make me feel better. Judging from Buzz's droopy shoulders, I knew he'd be good for at least three cheeseburgers and a donut the moment we stepped out of the building.

"Did we make a lemon?" I asked.

"Oh, stop," Goodstein said, pushing her chair back and standing up. "I'm sure it's all going to be fine."

Pffft. What did she know, anyway? Of course we'd made a lemon. I was a lemon. Buzz was a lemon. We came from a long line of lemons, a whole fucking sack of lemons.

The F train was empty save for the lady at the end of the car wearing a fur coat and mittens even though it was May. She was asleep, or dead, gripping onto the handle of a Food Emporium shopping cart chock-full of stuffed animals and a hubcap. I saw the future.

"Two paranoid schizophrenics *and* a manic-depressive," I said. "You think anyone else had that on their list?"

"I'm sure we're not the only ones," Buzz said, getting up and swinging his messenger bag around to his back.

"Suicidal genes and pancreatic cancer," I said. "What could go wrong?"

He kissed the top of my head and told me not to waste the rest of the day obsessing. Or Googling. "It's all going to be fine. Just like Goodstein said." When one person in the relationship is going nuts, the other has to assume a position of sanity, but, really, I don't know which of us Buzz was trying to convince.

I wanted to ask him if he'd been actually listening to Goodstein, because she didn't say it was all going to be fine; what she said was "I'm sure it's all going to be fine," which, to the untrained ear, might *sound* like she was saying it was all going to be fine, but what she really was doing there was coming up with some sort of vague company line, a brush-off, to appear like she thought it would be fine just so we would get out of her office. Clearly, anyone who knew anything about anything would understand that nothing about any of this would be fine.

I walked down my street, kicking pebbles, head down Mitchell-style, which was code for *Leave me alone, I'm baking a crazy baby*. Once on my couch, I visited with the Cosbys, where Vanessa was having a party. With *boys*. I was almost positive that there was no mental illness in Clair's lineage. For them, it was all choreographed dance numbers and flashy sweaters. (Until Theo got caught with a joint. But it wasn't his. I swear.) The Junior Mint kicked me; she probably already had ADD.

Yes, she was a she. We opened the kraft paper envelope when we got home from the amnio but before the squirrel break-in. Buzz insisted on being the opener, which meant he would make me guess. I hated guessing. Men love this game. I am forever being forced to guess the bill at a restaurant or how many points someone scored in a game I didn't even see. My whole life is a jar of jelly beans at the county fair.

"I don't want to guess. I'm tired," I said.

"Come on. Just guess. It will be fun."

(NOTE: It is never fun when people promise you it will be fun.)

"Come on," he said, trying to tempt me by waving the envelope just out of my reach.

"Can I not guess this one? Can I just see the envelope, please?"

Buzz changed his wording. "What do you *think* it is?"

Did he think I was a turnip truck casualty? This was just regular old guessing dressed in a funny hat and glasses. Regardless, I didn't even have to guess because I'd had enough dreams about the baby to know its sex, and the oversized book insisted that I believe those dreams. I just wanted confirmation.

"Just give me the fucking envelope."

"You're no fun," he said. "What happened to you?"

I should note Buzz asks me this question weekly. And it's not because I used to be fun and now I'm not. I am not now, nor was I ever, fun. Whenever I don't do exactly what he wants me to, he questions what has happened to me. This is some version of a rhetorical question, because we both know that nothing has happened to me, that this is my setting, but sometimes Buzz insists I must have been different when we were dating.

Beleaguered, he threw the envelope.

"Ow!"

"*Ow?*"

"Yes, ow. You threw that at me."

"I didn't throw it at you."

I opened it carefully so as not to rip the sonogram hiding inside. The baby was far enough along that her outline finally made sense. Pointing southward was a thin line, and below the line was a caption: I'M A GIRL!

"It's a girl!" Buzz shouted. He hugged me, then launched into his I'm-in-control tic, sweeping the bedroom floor.

When you are pregnant, strangers feel that is some sort of invitation to be your new best friend. Straphangers touch your stomach without asking, passersby warn you not to call your child Alana because she will be mean and bulimic, or Piper because they once knew a slut in high school with that name. And they all insist they know what you're having, owing to the size of your ass. They will get too close to your face and say, "Girls are precious. They're the best!" They whisper this so as not to upset all the suckers who are saddled with boys.

But, say what they will, I knew better. Girls are harrowing. They roll their eyes a lot and scream, "No one understands me!" and "I hate your guts!" as they slam bedroom doors. Girls force you to drop them off three blocks away from school. Girls get dodgeballs to the face. And the first person a girl throws under the bus is her mother.

The Junior Mint kicked my spleen into my liver. *Great*, I thought, *already with the vitriol*. I was doomed. And while I didn't break it to Buzz, I knew he was doomed, too. Our house was just one chewed-up lime and a sack of bad lemons.

A week later, the results came in. The baby had one head, no tail or hooves. She was cleared of any genetic disorders the procedure tested for.

"Those tests are wrong all the time," I told Buzz.

He didn't say a word, just grinned and went to sweep the stairs. But, let's be honest, if the disorders didn't get the Junior Mint, something else would.

The first night at home with the baby on the outside, we sat on the couch together watching *The Cosby Show*. Well, I did most of the watching. The oversized book said she couldn't see much yet, plus she was crying so loudly I couldn't hear a damn thing. She came out with the requisite amount of appendages. She wasn't deaf, which I know because I frequently dropped stacks of books on the floor just to make sure, and she was breathing and eating and doing all that stuff thriving babies are supposed to do. She passed the tests in the hospital and wasn't even yellow anymore. I held on to her and did the math:

Nine years before the eye rolling.

Thirteen before she couldn't stand me.

Eighteen before she left for college and I was an empty nester, buying baby goats to keep me company and taking up weaving or canning or bridge.

It was quite possible Rudy wouldn't break Clair Huxtable's heart, but the jury was still out on Vanessa and Denise. And who even knew about Sondra. So far, my daughter wasn't a lemon, but she was still a daughter. It was all just a matter of time.

Be Careful Out There

. . . . . .

I once spent two hours at a craft store debating the purchase of glitter. There I stood, in the aisle, puffy down coat unzipped, smitten by a very sexy twenty-four-pack of Martha Stewart Essential Glitter. The set showcased a distinguished group of colors with fancy names listed across the vials, names like BROWNSTONE and FELDSPAR and LAPIS LAZULI. But there were other choices on the glitter shelves. Not only different colors but different species—Iridescent, Fine, Tinsel—half the aisle was dedicated to glitter.

And so it began. Should I buy the twenty-four-pack or go off the grid and make my own small collection? But how does one choose between AQUAMARINE CRYSTAL and SMOKY QUARTZ? Not to mention which glitter phylum to pick. Iridescent had a snow-in-the-moonlight quality but the Tinsel variety was old-timey, plus the thicker flakes seemed easier to get out of my hair. The world, however, would be open to me if I owned the twenty-four-pack. Plus it said *Essential* right there on the front, meaning I kind of needed to have it.

I started overheating in the glitter aisle. Noxious fake cinnamon smells coming off the pinecones in aisle 7 rendered me craft-drunk and dizzy. Could I justify spending over thirty dollars on glitter? I had walked in there to get an eraser. I didn't have a craft project in mind. I don't even do craft projects. But, oh, the glitter. I knew my life would just be better if I was the kind of person who had twenty-four bottles at the ready. I called a friend for guidance, but she wasn't home, instantly putting her on the list of who not to call in case of emergency. Clearly I was alone in the (craft) world. Still, a decision had to be made, so I placed the twenty-four-pack, plus six individual bottles, into the plastic shopping basket and then walked to the rubber-stamp aisle to decompress.

Moments later, I ran back to the glitter aisle and put all my choices back from whence they came. I did not need any glitter. Or did I? I put the twenty-four-pack back in the basket, along with three of the Tinsel variety in colors not featured in the Essential pack. But if they weren't Essential, did I really need them? I put those guys back on the shelf, then walked over to the bone folders down the aisle, which was a rookie move because seconds later I was back with the glitter.

It was then I saw the oversized bottles.

I sat on the floor, laying out all my options. After 127 minutes of deliberation, I left the store with the twenty-four-pack, a small bottle of turquoise Tinsel, and an oversized shaker of a coarse variety in the shade of CRYSTAL. And a bone folder. Totaling over fifty dollars. Two days later, I returned the twenty-four-pack. I still haven't opened the other jars.

I'd like to say the Great Glitter Incident of 2012 was an isolated event, but the truth is I have a small problem with decision making. I don't make up my mind lightly (*see* glitter), and having to choose any thing of any kind brings on a variety of deranged behaviors. It's never the size or scope of the decision that makes me mental, it's the act of decision making itself. When I do finally make a choice, there are lingering repercussions for all—often weeks of fallout. My having to make a decision is really not good for anyone. And so when Buzz suggested packing up our urban, briefly suburban, existence and moving operations to rural Vermont, I sat down in the aisle of our lives, unzipped my coat, and began to take things on and off the shelf.

I was surprised Buzz even made the suggestion, since our moves to date had not gone very well. He claims not to harbor ill will from our first relocation together, but I know he's not over it. I still contend that one was Denzel Washington's fault. We were four days away from changing our Upper West Side address to a neighborhood in Brownstone Brooklyn, when we decided to rent *Training Day* and eat red licorice. Three minutes into the picture, I began to panic. Something about Denzel's one-man–Good Cop/Bad Cop eyes Svengalied me. A switch flicked on in my brain, causing me to equate the wide front lawns of our new Brooklyn neighborhood with the mean streets of Los Angeles.

Buzz gnawed on his Twizzler, not a care in the world, but I gripped mine, foreseeing the sprays of bullets, cops gone nuts, choppers overhead. I pictured all the ways I could be in the wrong place at the wrong time and, naturally, my inevitable bloody demise. *What have I done,* I wondered, *agreeing to this move?* Why was I leaving the safety of my Manhattan fifth-floor walk-up, a place surely never to get robbed—or rats—because there were just too many stairs to climb?

I'd worked that theory out when I moved in, ten years earlier. Something to the tune of, If a bad guy were to come all the way up 128 stairs to disembowel me, it would be because he was looking for me specifically—a revenge plot of some sort—and there was nothing I could do about that. A revenge seeker could find me anywhere. I took comfort in knowing that although most people don't really like me, they certainly don't care enough to march up all those stairs and butcher me. My careful, sound, and statistical equation told me I was safe on the top floor. If someone came to my apartment building with murder in mind, he'd probably nab a victim on the first two floors, which is exactly what we'd signed on for by renting the first two levels of a brownstone in Brooklyn. We were practically asking to get slaughtered.

I was antsy on the couch for the remainder of the movie. I tried suffering in silence, really, I did. But at the end of the day I am not skilled in that arena. The second the end credits rolled, I let Buzz know the move was off, assuring him we were being irresponsible by relocating to such a sketchy neighborhood and that we were moments away from being decapitated or chained to a radiator until further notice. At first he ignored me, but I may or may not have been relentless, so before he fell asleep that night he told me we'd deal with this "nonsense" tomorrow. To me that meant we were canceling the move, to Buzz it meant I'd forget about it all by first light. When he woke the following morning, my eyes were staring at him.

"Still with this shit?" he said, putting the pillow over his face.

He will tell you that he made the call to Brooklyn's seventy-sixth precinct to assuage my fear, settle me down, but I knew better. I knew by the look in his eye and the way he punched the little phone buttons that he knew this Brooklyn place really was the epicenter of blood and guts and danger and that's why he made the call. Deep down we were in agreement that those pleasant grassy yards with trees and inviting stoops were just a ruse. Buzz recounted, word for word, what the nice officer had to say. Even the part when the cop laughed at him for making the call.

"There," Buzz said. "You feel better now?"

Not really. I was sure the policeman told Buzz the place was safe, just as he'd told all the other callers who'd asked the same question, a verbal form letter. What was he going to say? That the place was crawling with deranged psychos and daily bludgeoning? Naturally, I needed to take matters into my own hands, so I cleared my schedule the following day for research.

The computer gossiped about the glorious world of organized crime that had taken place on the very streets we were heading to. Granted, the information was from years gone by, but people don't change. Tired of mafia stories, I moved on to the big guns, something I save for when I really need soothing—the police blotter. I prefer to read my blotter stories while holding a thin, local newspaper, but in a pinch a virtual one will do. No matter its format, the content always pleases me. A blotter has everything, danger and drama and all the comings and goings of the town. Some people enjoy reading about the good restaurants a place has to offer or what there is to do after dark. I enjoy knowing who got shot.

"You see!" I said to Buzz, following him down the hallway with a fistful of printouts. "There is *too* crime!"

Buzz refused to read about the knife fights and break-ins and urged me to stop looking up all the horrible things that could happen to me. I told him he didn't even understand what the Internet was for. Unfortunately, my campaign was weak and we moved anyway. And no, we didn't get murdered or knifed on our way to buy bananas at the health food store. We did suffer some lawlessness, though, when a box of Pampers was stolen right from our front stoop. And, of course, there was the squirrel break-in. I'm sure Buzz was on some sort of ego trip because we didn't get murdered, as he'd predicted, but I didn't let that interrupt my vigilance. I remained an informed citizen, staying abreast of bank robberies and car thievery until, like with most things, I lost interest.

Seven years later, the subject of moving came up again, this time to the suburbs. It was common in our part of the world to emigrate beyond the boroughs now that we had two small school-aged children. We'd lost our will to fight with shopping bags weighing down our strollers, wanted to let our four-year-old son out to roam the yard like a family hound, and finally admitted that we never went out to museums or for Ethiopian food at 1:00 a.m. We'd stopped using New York City and were ready to move to what our Realtor called Brooklyn West.

The first order of business was finding a house. We saw fifty-one. We toured schools and talked to suburban veterans as well as the newer recruits. We did not call the precinct. Montclair, New Jersey, was home to stately trees and liberal folks and a good school system. Buzz sussed out real estate taxes and I went straight to the crime. This was not your mother's suburb. There were multiple robberies and crack busts in school zones and gun assaults and spies. Spies! Montclair had the finest police blotter I'd ever laid eyes on.

We moved into the prettiest house I'd ever live in. Buzz would return home on the train from a day of show business and I'd be at the door with news of fresh crime. He'd shuffle past me, muttering how this stuff would never happen to Don Draper.

There is something about reading the blotter that mellows me, like caffeine to an ADD-addled person. It's a form of self-medication that usually works, but, as festive as the Montclair blotter was, things were gloomy for me in New Jersey. I was able to get myself out of bed in the morning and the kids off to school, but my despondency was acting up and the crime business was no longer keeping me cheery.

I came up with another equation: decisions + action = transition and change. If decisions make me mental, then transition and change make me take to the bed. My brain was tricked into believing that moving would fix me. A different location would be the new sweater to change my life. It was the first time I understood the expression *Wherever you go, there you are*. I realized I probably should have moved to New Jersey without me.

Chin up, Jersey Girl, I told myself, all those sad sack computer-investigating hours were not feckless. As it turns out, difficulty making decisions is actually a thing. It seems to be a real issue for people who have anxious personalities, which, I am pleased to report, I do! I didn't read the whole article, mostly because it was kind of long and I noticed they started mentioning other things wrong with the uneasy and agitated crowd I run with and I didn't want to kick myself when already down and living in Jersey. I just scanned the piece to confirm that others were equally plagued and tacked this ailment to the running list of things wrong with me. It was validating.

I thought these revelations would cheer me up, but it was still all rainy days in my brain. It was then that Buzz jumped in again, to fix things, to help. Buzz is a producer by trade and by nature and I love him for it—when it works in my favor. If I need to pack for a trip or make a schedule, it's heavenly. But when he uses his powers to "get me out of my funk," as he calls it, I wish he were a plumber instead.

"Why don't we move to Vermont?" Buzz said.

We had lived in New Jersey for seven months but we had built a small house in southern Vermont five years earlier. Settling there permanently was an idea we'd flirted with for years, something we'd talk about forever but never really do. Knowing it was there if I needed it was sufficient. It was the secret money stashed inside the Chock full o'Nuts coffee can. "Now? I thought we were going to retire there."

"Well, let's go while the kids are still young. Let's try a whole new way of living. Something totally different."

I no longer recognized this character standing before me. Nor did he have any clue who stood before him. I didn't care for new things. I liked old things. I was set in my ways, a seventy-seven-year-old man. I drive only on roads I know, I always sit in the same chair. I don't want people touching my television, I think everyone steals from me when I can't find something, and I don't like advances in technology. I am old-fangled. Do not wave some electronic tablet for me to read on, I like to hold books. Do not try to force me into sharing an online calendar with you, I prefer the oversized paper one Zaida Max used. I like pens and pencils and writing stuff down. I don't want to ride in your flying car. Don't get me wrong, I'll sample a new brand of seltzer that comes on the market—I'm not insane—I just don't think I am suited to trying a completely new way of life in the middle of mine.

"So you'd rather stay in New Jersey?" Buzz said.

"Yes."

"Even if you're miserable."

"Yes."

"Really?"

"Yes, really. I hate moving. I don't ever want to move again. I hate those boxes and the sound of the ripping tape and I hate the trucks and the contractor bags I have to run out and buy for all the stuff I forgot to throw into the boxes."

"But you're so unhappy here," Buzz said, again with the fixing of things.

"I'm unhappy everywhere!"

"So, wouldn't you rather be unhappy with fresh air?"

We entered into a game I like to call *the malcontent's duel*, where he throws happy, glass-half-full scenarios at me and I block them with my half-empty glass. It was the only game I was good at.

"Let's put a pin in this conversation," Buzz said. "But let's revisit it."

"I think we should just take it off the table."

"Why?"

"I can't move to Vermont, realistically."

"And why not?"

"I'm not a farmer."

"You think only farmers live in Vermont?"

I bit my thumb. "No."

"So?"

"I don't look rural."

"What does that even mean?"

"It means I don't look rural. I don't look like I belong in Vermont."

"What do you look like?"

I shrugged and walked into the kitchen.

"You realize that this is not an argument, right?" Buzz said, following me. "Your not looking rural and not being a farmer. You understand those are not real points, right?"

"What if I don't make any friends there?"

"You make friends everywhere."

"No, I don't."

"Yes, you do."

"No, I don't."

"Oh my god, this is stupid," Buzz said.

"Exactly," I said, trying to break the orange netting on a bag of clementines. "This idea is stupid."

"Not the idea!" said Buzz. "Your excuses for not wanting to go!"

"Oh, those are not stupid," I said. "Those, my friend, are solid."

"Right," he said. "Your not looking rural is solid."

Buzz was getting on my nerves. "What would we even do there, realistically?"

"We'll just live, man," he said. "We'll figure it out."

"We'll just live, man?" I said. "You're Matthew McConaughey now?"

Buzz is the guy who gets a restaurant menu days before he is slated to eat there just so he'll know what to order once he arrives. *Now* he wanted to just walk around living?

"Are you worried you won't be unhappy in Vermont?"

"Oh, please," I said. "I can be unhappy anywhere."

"Then what's the big deal?" he said. "It's not like the other places we've lived have worked so well for you. What's the difference if you're miserable here or there? At least there we'll have a view."

I rooted around in the bag of clementines, trying to find the perfect one.

"Hello?" Buzz said.

"What if I have to go to the dentist?" I said.

"They don't have dentists in Vermont?"

"Not real ones."

"Okay, this is now officially the dumbest conversation we've ever had," Buzz said, pelting two clementines at the pantry door. "I'm going to bed."

"Fine," I said.

"You win."

"Good."

"We'll stay here because of the dentists," Buzz said, storming up the stairs, leaving me to pick up the fallen fruit.

I sat in front of our flip-the-switch fireplace for hours that night, thinking about Vermont. We'd been visiting for years, way before we were married or had kids, but I'd considered my relationship with it a superficial one, a fling. All I really knew about it was its fresh air and mountains and woodland creatures. It was a postcard, one I'd attach to the round mirror of my sit-down vanity and stare at longingly, if I'd had one of those set-ups or did that kind of staring.

I'd floated in its ponds and snowshoed on its trails and hiked up its mountains. I'd picked apples and sampled all varieties of syrup and filled up the basket I'd bought at Basketville (real name) with local kale and purple carrots and fingerling potatoes. My friends who lived there would clear their schedule when we arrived for the weekend, making us feel like we were the best and only friends on earth. I'd drive the back roads, taking in the white barns, and fall in love a little more each time, knowing deep down that every quick trip was a tryst with John Irving and Sam Shepard, who, in reality, would have no interest in me because I didn't look rural.

When it was over, we'd drive back to sludgy New York and I'd pine for Vermont and dream of living there permanently, where every day would be maple syrup and forest friends. But really I didn't know this Vermont character at all. We'd never stayed up all night talking about its dysfunctional family, compared pet peeves or stories or scars. What did it do when I went home? And what would happen when the magical attraction eventually fizzled?

It was time to call up the police blotter. If Vermont wasn't ready to share its stories just yet, it left me no choice but to snoop around. "All right," I said out loud, "let's see what you got. . . ."

Various DUIs. A bar fight. Someone's Havahart critter trap stolen from Woods Road. Ho and hum. Three entries, less than seven minutes of investigative work. Montclair's always took at least half an hour. What was Vermont hiding? Where were its secret fetishes? Its second family? I'd even settle for a weird rash. But there was nothing. A different route had to be taken with this one.

Enter the catamount.

I'd heard this name on prior visits to the Green Mountain State. It's possible I'd even seen a billboard somewhere. I thought Catamount was a ski resort, but it made little sense that a mountain would warrant gaspy noises from the locals I was dining with, no matter how many black diamonds it had. Being the victim of a mortifying no-soap-radio incident as a youth, I have made a lifetime practice of pretending I get the joke, or whatever it is people are talking about, followed by in-the-know noises so they don't think I'm daft. I was a city dweller, though—what did I know about how seriously they took their mountains? When it just didn't add up anymore, I pulled my friend aside to ask her what the hell a catamount was.

"Oh," she said, fishing around in a bag of organic chips. "It's a mountain lion."

A *what?*

This was the nugget I was searching for. Never mind the blotter, look to the great outdoors. I couldn't believe it took me so long to get there. I went to work. The wilderness websites were abuzz with news of this majestic creature prowling the countryside; there had been sightings in six towns. Great debate ensued over what to call this thing—some liked *eastern cougar*, others preferred *mountain cat* or, worse, *mountain screamer*—but no matter its name, they all seemed hopped up about it.

The catamount is a stealthy beast, able to jump seventy feet in order to pounce on deer or rabbits or, potentially, me. The mountain cat kills you by digging its hind claws into your legs, front claws into your shoulders. Then it bites your neck with these special teeth, ones with nerve endings that aid in finding the perfect spot at which to pull apart the vertebrae before snapping your spine. Finally, it drags you to a ravine and eats your organs. The catamount has been known to stalk its prey for a few days, familiarizing itself with your habits so it knows exactly when to strike. I turned off the light and closed the blinds.

Working under cover of night for the next few hours, I began to feel a kinship with this stalk-and-ambush predator, who, it turned out, is also reclusive and usually avoids people. Catamount attacks were rare but they still happened, mostly when people entered their territory. Statistically, there were maybe four attacks a year, one being a fatality—a fact I didn't dare share with Buzz, because he'd accuse me of being narcissistic for believing I'd be the one-in-four to get murdered by a puma. I had a comeback for him should the need arise. I'd tell him that although they don't attack frequently, when they do it's usually a small kid or a solitary adult. It's then that I'd remind him that for the most part I'm a solitary adult. He'd just sigh and leave the room. This was not a strong enough case to keep us in Jersey.

I needed more information about the troublemakers I'd be sharing my new neighborhood with if we moved. I started small by familiarizing myself with what the local snakes liked to eat (small rodents and toads) and where wild rats might nest (I don't want to talk about it). There were two varieties of fox that might saunter onto the property—red and gray. Both species inhabit the same territory, though they prefer not to interact with each other, so they use the land like a time-share in Florida. I'd already pegged the reds as favorites, because they were famous for being intolerant of one another.

I wondered about the moose, an animal I'd been obsessed with spotting. Apparently the most likely problem with a moose-tangling would be hitting one with your car. However, they were showing up as special guests at certain ski hills, one even recently charging a skier. Of course, there were the bears. No matter how many times I read about them, I never remembered which I was to fear, the brown or the black. One is an opportunist, eating whatever berries it finds in the forest, and the other eats the people. Studying up on nature hooligans seemed to give me the ease and pleasure I felt when reading about crime. I thought it quite adaptable of me, to switch what there was to worry about so effortlessly. I guess it is all how you choose to see things.

City people often tell you the country terrifies them, that it's too dark and quiet. They feel safer with people around. Nightfall in the middle of nowhere can be daunting, especially if you have a lush imagination. In Montclair, I'd lie in bed hearing the sigh and whine of the DeCamp bus outside my window, but rarely did it make me conjure up the Wood Chipper Murder. In Vermont, the sounds of crunchy noises outside my window brought images of fanged creatures traipsing through the brush, ready to rip me to shreds.

My Internet connection might be slower in the country but my typing skills and patience are as sharp and fierce as what lurks outside. And they need to be when, at four a.m., you hear shrill screeches belting through the trees. At first you think you are imagining things, but when the yowling pierces the air again, it all sounds a little *Jurassic Park* out there. You can't wake the husband or call friends at that hour, and you certainly can't shout out the window to keep it down! All you have left is the Internet.

So you type in things like "weird screeching noise in southern Vermont." It is then you meet the fisher cat. Yes, it sounds adorable. Conjures up stuffed toys my son might have, a soft kitty complete with rain hat and fishing pole. Inquire about the beast, however, and you'll learn it has nothing to do with fishing or cats. This thing hails from the weasel family and looks like what might ensue if a woodchuck screwed a bear. It doesn't eat people (although watch out for the family cat), but when this varmint is mating or back from a kill, you can't imagine the racket. Teeny hairs you were not familiar with make special guest appearances all over your body.

There is also another group of no-goodniks responsible for caterwauling—the coyotes. Honestly, I never would have pegged coyotes to sound so effeminate. Don't tell them I said this, but I always imagined them to be macho things. Really, they sound like a pack of teenage girls on a teen tour bus. A local vet told me that when coyotes meet up in the middle of the night, all that screaming is just their way of catching up with each other. Those freakish yelps, the ones that make you want to hide in the closet, are them having a little chitchat. Just gossip. I have no idea what stories hang off the coyote grapevine, but I can promise you I want no part of it.

I was feeling slightly jazzed about Vermont until I read that the coyote is super adaptable, able to live happily in all habitats, including the suburbs. I then took issue with the coyote, hostile toward this creature that was so mangy and yet still more well-adjusted than I was. Frankly, I took issue with the whole state of Vermont. Buzz was annoying and the country was stupid and I was not moving. Animal research did not do the trick, and now, on top of it all, I couldn't sleep. I typed in medical symptoms I'd been experiencing just to end the evening on a high note. "Crunching sound while bending knee" took me well into the wee hours.

People will tell you life is a journey. To them I say, I don't care for journeys. They're long and dusty and they make you tired. I was already fatigued from all the research and the decision-making process. I just wanted to know what would happen to me if I moved. See into the future a bit. Flip ahead. A side note about my nature: I am terribly nosy. I have participated in some diary hijinks of which I am not proud. I can't help it if I have stealthy eyes and I notice stuff. I like to think it is my job to be observant, that all this interest in other people's privacy helps me hone my craft, but really I'm just a snoop. And while I will definitely dip into your letters, I will never read a book out of order. Ever. I do not, under any circumstances, flip ahead. (I also never peek at the author photo, because if the author is peculiar looking I spend the entire reading experience focusing on the wrong thing.)

A book and its chronology demand respect. Plus there was a small incident when I was nine and accidentally opened the soft cover backwards and read the ending of *I Was a 98-Pound Duckling*, by Jean Van Leeuwen. I was assaulted by the second-to-last line of the book, which then promptly imprinted on my brain: *I now weigh 102. I now weigh 102.*

For years, the line continued to harass me. It would taunt me in math class, during a root canal, even once at my wedding. Now when I read a book I have to actually cover the last few lines of a paragraph just so I don't read ahead. I kind of think it was Jean Van Leeuwen's fault. She was probably the trigger for a lot of my special behavior. Let's go ahead and blame her for some other stuff that's wrong with me, too.

But I wanted to flip ahead. I also probably needed to, because Buzz seemed slightly annoyed with me and was throwing fruit around. Also, the act of deciding whether or not to uproot was beginning to make me mental. I tried filling up a glass halfway by stuffing it with fun animal facts, but the truth is my glass is never even close to half-full—I barely even have a glass. Sometimes, when my decision making goes poorly or gets to this point, I ask a small committee of friends to tell me what I think. Unfortunately, they tend to say stuff like, *You've got nothing to lose* or *You can always move back* or *The city will always be there* or, the very worst, *Live every day like it is your last—carpe diem!* Which, frankly, all sounds a little too pom-pomish for me.

You know what? If I found out it was my last day on earth, I can guarantee I wouldn't rummage through my desk to find some sort of bucket list. And I can also promise you it wouldn't be called a bucket list, because the only things that annoy me more than the term *bucket list* are poached chicken and com-promise. If I found out it was my last day on earth, I'd take to the bed and worry about the exact time said death would be happening.

Come to think of it, I *have* been living every day as if it were my last. There are mornings when I am drinking coffee or mois-turizing and I cook up all the gruesome ways I could go. I even hear the sound bites by neighbors and reporters recounting how my day began just like any other, with coffee and moisturizing. When I leave for an airport and foresee my fiery demise, I envi-sion the article that would begin by stating that my day began so routinely, so normally. This is how I spend every day living like it is my last. And, for a little extra credit, when I have the sniffles I don't just reach for the tissues. Instead I head to the computer to call up that article I read about that woman who *thought* she had the sniffles, only to find out that what she really had was some ghastly flesh-eating cancerous plague virus malady, and died not six hours later. If my stomach aches, it's that festering tumor I once saw on *Nova*, the one that grew so big it ended up sprouting hair and teeth.

I had to show Buzz I was taking this decision making seri-ously, so I made the family try on Vermont numerous times to see how it fit, check if the mountains made our ass look fat. Once there, I started interviewing anyone who'd talk to me. A woman at the co-op told me she breathes easier there and can hear herself think. I don't think anyone needed *that*. I've had quite enough of myself, thank you. I can hear my thoughts as loudly and as clearly as that freaky pack of coyotes. That is why I needed to flip ahead.

Will I actually start that vegetable garden, or change my mind and raise goats or cheese or hemp? Will I be lonely or bored or satisfied? Will I hit Hank, our resident woodchuck, with my car by mistake? I really do get giddy when he makes an appearance and I'd miss him if he were dead. I used to feel the same way every day in Brooklyn when I'd spot a character I knew only by face, one of the many day players in my life. Maybe exchanging hipsters for field rodents wasn't a bad thing.

But what about the family? Will the kids fall out of trees or get run over by wild turkeys? Will Buzz lose three of his fingers to the gleaming new machete he insisted on buying because he's now convinced he is G.I. Jew? Will all that silence and nature calm me down or turn me into *The Shining*? I kind of need to know.

It took me 127 minutes to buy glitter and 172,800 to settle on resettling in Vermont. *How bad could it be?* I eventually told myself. The Ingalls family were mostly happy in Walnut Grove living in their little house on the prairie, even after that street urchin Albert came along to get adopted and ruin the show. And should I ever go blind like Mary, I am told the community would absolutely rally around me. That's what small, hempy communities do. They rally. They call you by name at the post office and DMV. They make meal trees. That woman from the library assured me that if something happens to one of their own—say, they get stricken with some cancer—the whole town comes together, helping any way they can. It was a touching exchange and very reassuring. I left that conversation finally feeling like I could do it, just pack the bags and everything would be fine.

It was only later that night, after we drove all the way home to New Jersey, and I put the kids to bed, and locked the doors, and checked that I'd turned the oven off even though I'd never turned it on—it was only then that I got into bed and thought, *Wait, I'm going to get cancer?*

Sorry, Nana

. . . .

Here's what I know about Jews:

1. We don't name our houses.

2. Due to weak constitutions, propensity for nausea, and irritable bowels, we are not seaworthy.

And,

3. We don't celebrate Christmas.

Were she alive today, my nana would tell me not to feel bad and to look on the bright side (neither of which, I might add, are normal activities for the Jews). She'd *tsk*, saying we have our own customs and holidays sprinkled throughout the year, some even involving deli. If I think about it, I'm okay with my house being anonymous. Half the time I'm convinced the furnace will combust, so it is probably better that I don't humanize the place and get too attached. I feel little pull toward the ocean, because I am not a strong swimmer and am terrified of sailboats. But Christmas, with its twinkle and catchy tunes, well—that's the one I can't quite let go of. Christmas is pretty. I want to hug Christmas. I want to deck the halls and hang my stocking with care. I want trees and cookies and shiny wrapping paper with twinkly bows.

"What about a nativity scene?" Buzz says. "You want that, too?"

"Why would I want that?" I say, knowing full well the dog would eat it.

"Uh, to celebrate the birth of Christ?"

"What does Christ have to do with it?"

"Everything?" Buzz says. "You know that Christmas is the celebration of the birth of Jesus, right?"

"Oh, please," I say. "Since when does Christmas have a thing to do with religion?"

"Since always!"

I want to tell him he is misinformed, that Christmas is about those teeny precious foil-wrapped milk-chocolate balls, but he seems agitated. Anyway, what does he know, the Grinch? Perhaps I should put nothing under the tree for him. Yes, I have a giant tree dominating my living room, shedding its glorious needles, as the woodstove dries the place out. I don't even mind the constant sweeping. No matter how get-off-my-lawn Buzz gets about my obsession with Christmas, I'm not ruffled. Why? Because I embrace the holiday spirit, that's why. And he best get used to it, for I—and please forgive me, here, Nana—I am a Christmas Jew.

"I think you're kind of missing the whole point of Christmas," Buzz says under his breath.

Once again, Buzz is misguided. I have seen every Charlie Brown special ever made; I know the meaning of the holidays. Every single one. With the possible exception of the Jewish ones, because there aren't many cartoons about Yom Kippur. Growing up, we were cafeteria Jews. Sliding our tray along the line, picking and choosing which parts of the religion looked good that day. In my house, being a Jew involved a yearly family trip to temple and some after-school Hebrew lessons for my brother in order to prepare for his bar mitzvah. Ace had no choice in the matter, but I was asked if I wanted a bat mitzvah in the same way I was asked if I wanted liver on my plate. The answer to both was no. Liver was gross and the guy who came over to give my brother bar mitzvah lessons smelled like vegetable soup, plus he wore these little rain boots over his shoes no matter the weather, ones he called "rubbers." I'd peeked in a few times on their training, and, frankly, it seemed like a drag. Religion just wasn't my thing. I paid no attention during our enforced yearly visit to synagogue, just counted the myriad of overhead lights and swung my feet back and forth with enough gusto to warrant leg pinching by my mother. I took home teeny bruises under my tights but never any Talmudic lessons or Judaic nuggets. I had retention problems, anyway, unless it was for *Happy Days* episodes.

Religion seemed old-fashioned. My house was all about modern times, and modern times called for modern measures—shortcuts, really—the rearranging of dusty rules instilled thousands of years ago in some desert. If women could vote and be firemen and wear pants now, why couldn't they wear their pants while sitting next to their men at synagogue? That is why, my mother told me, we joined the reformed Temple Emanuel, the one Zaida Max said was for "idiots."

According to Zaida Max, his shul was the real deal—the only deal—plus it didn't cost "an arm and a leg" like the one his son went to. Things were as they should be at Zaida Max's house of worship. He sat up front with the men and Nana was in the back with the womenfolk. The ladies were to organize the yearly

rummage sale and talk gefilte fish in the pews, just as they'd done
throughout the ages.

The Jewish holiday dinners were Zaida Max's show, so we'd
pile into the family Jaguar and cruise across town to their split-
level. There Zaida Max would take his place at the head of the
table, telling his wife that she'd outdone herself with the trays
of desiccated chicken and various other mystery meat dishes she
swore were our favorites. I should note here that while Nana
Esther made all her food with pure love, she was in danger of
having her nana license revoked for being a rotten cook. Occasionally Zaida Max would throw my other grandparents a shank
bone by letting them host the holidays over at their apartment
where the food was edible.

As the years passed and Nana began using salt when a recipe called for sugar, my father took over the festivities. By that
time, my parents had sold our childhood home and moved into a
swanky apartment, which almost made Zaida Max blow a head
gasket, "but if that's how he wants to spend his money. . . ." Nonetheless, he'd drink the Chivas Regal he'd requested and mutter
under his breath about the latest electric knife or track lighting
my father tried to impress him with.

"The holidays are about family," my father would toast from
his new seat at the head of the table, raising a glass of cabernet
instead of the usual Manischewitz.

"What's he saying now?" Zaida Max would shout, refusing to
wear his hearing aid. "Jesus, whoever heard of half this food he's
cooked up?"

Nana Esther would smile and say it all looked delicious.

"Since when does a man take a microwave-cooking course?"

We had all been trained not to listen to Zaida Max's com-
ments. That became increasingly challenging when, at the last
Passover seder, he had one too many Chivases and regaled us

with stories of himself back in the day when the ladies loved him because of his "ten-incher."

The one Jewish holiday we celebrated without my grandparents was Hanukah. The Festival of Lights. Which, in my estimation, is not only a bitch to spell but not that much of a festival. Eight nights of gift giving and candle lighting sounds intriguing on paper, but if you've ever seen a Hanukah present, you know that they are almost always socks or a toothbrush, and eight nights of candle lighting is eight nights of panic that the house could end up in flames, which amounts to eight nights of lost sleep. Hanukah usually falls around Christmastime, so they are often lumped together as the highlight of their respective religions. But Hanukah is not the Grand Poobah of Judaism. That title goes to Yom Kippur, which is our fanciest holiday, about atonement, which is nowhere near as sexy as tinsel.

I have spent many hours going over my upbringing, trying to untangle why I love Christmas so much. As a kid, you compared yourself to others to see what they have that you don't. If there were Ding Dongs in your friend's Bee Gees lunch box, your browning pear looked sad and detestable, as did the paper sack with drawn-on smiley face it came in. If your neighbor had the full ColecoVision setup (complete with steering wheel and gas pedal), it just wasn't the same to sit in your room trying to spell *boobs* on your Little Professor calculator. You inventoried what you had—be it toys or holidays or parents—and constantly wanted something other than what you were saddled with. Even if your parents raised you right, with Walton Mountain values, you were still a kid, and kids measured life in stuff.

What other control did we have? We lived under our parents' rules, dreaming up our escape, in the same way that our own parents felt locked into the customs of their parents, searching to find their loopholes as they had families of their own. My father's parents were steeped in Jewish religion and tradition. And while they weren't true Orthodox and didn't keep kosher, they followed the rest of the religion to the letter of the law.

When it was my father's time to rule his own roost, he settled into his own comfort level. No stranger to decorations or sparkle, it seemed natural that my father felt a tug toward Christmas. He made up his own conditions that would allow him to celebrate the birth of Christ without rotting in hell, or wherever misbehaved Jews were sent. A tree would be bought, but one that lived outside on the balcony of the teeny country lake house where their best friends' nanny drowned. It was where we sardined ourselves for long weekends and the two weeks that the *shmattah* industry closed down every Christmas.

Accessorizing the tree was acceptable, but only with strands of lights and absolutely no star at the top. This was enough Christmas for my father, and I took what I could get. Inside the house there were no Yuletide signs, only recent candle wax residue stuck to the counter to remind us we were indeed Jews. However, much to my delight, space was made around our fireplace for Santa to worm his way down the chimney with care (extra care, of course, because we were Jews, and we worried about his descent).

Ace and I would watch the specials—Rudolph or the Grinch or Charlie Brown—going to bed straight after, praying to God that Santa would not mind that we were Jewish, or at least not mind *enough* to bring me a McDonald's Play Set, KerPlunk, and the much-coveted Mr. Microphone. The idea of Santa was allowed, as were his lovely gifts, but no contact was permitted— definitely no time spent together taking pictures on his lap at the mall.

"Now, this is what the holidays are all about," said my father as we ripped open our haul. It's possible, like all his other pronouncements around holiday time, that he was referring to family. I took it to mean Christmas was about presents. And getting as far away from your family as possible so you could play with your toys in peace.

When left to my own devices as an adult, I may or may not have pulled some holiday trickery. I should add a disclaimer here: Our daughter's birthday falls around Christmas, and I am in charge of all present fetching and cake baking, and I am quick to frazzle. One night, after the kids were in bed, Buzz walked into the kitchen as I was looking for my Christmas cookie-cutter collection.

"Hey, when's Hanukah this year?"

I made some extra clanking noises in the utensil drawer.

"Hello?" he said.

"Oh, hello."

"Didn't you hear me?"

"No," I said. "Sorry. It's really loud with all the spoons."

"When is Hanukah this year?"

"Um," I said, face still in the drawer, "I think it was last week."

"What?" He squinted and tilted his head.

"I skipped it."

"You what?"

"I skipped Hanukah this year."

"You skipped it?" Buzz said, like he was the religion police. "Isn't lighting candles the bare minimum we could do for the kids? It's not like we do anything else Jewish."

I regretted that speech I'd made years earlier, the one about how when we had our own family we'd let our kids decide if they were interested in religion. We would do our part by doling out the information, and they could figure out what they wanted to do with all the Jewish business. The problem being I was so focused on my award-winning speech that I might have forgotten to give them any information at all. And now Buzz was actually calling me on it. It's not like I hadn't made other sweeping speeches before the kids showed up, stuff about no television or plastic toys, and all that went out the window. I thought it only natural that the Jewish stuff would follow suit. Buzz had always ignored my soapbox in the past. Now, suddenly, he was a rabbi?

The next year, he paid closer attention. Shortly after Thanksgiving, he started in with the Hanukah reminders. In order to avoid another fight, I set out about the streets of Brooklyn to find my family something Jewish. I brought home a darling menorah in the shape of a Christmas tree. I thought it was terrific— genius, even—but have you met my husband, Moishe? He found it offensive and grumbled for the entire eight nights. It was better when we skipped the whole affair.

I solved the following year's holiday dilemma by ordering a battery-operated menorah. Turn a candle clockwise and watch it twinkle. It was better for the environment, plus there wasn't an iota of fire panic. I think the exact word Buzz used to describe my new treasure was "bullshit."

When Hanukah rolled around again, I told Buzz to get his own damn menorah. He found one in the desk drawer of his childhood room. It was ugly, and quite possibly broken, since it seemed to have only seven candleholders. Either his mother had bought it on sale at an outlet center or it was a Kwanza candelabra. Either way, when he does things his way, Buzz rarely complains, so that issue was finally laid to rest. Things were relatively smooth after that, until the year when Hanukah had the nerve to barge in on Thanksgiving. Everyone was talking about how it wouldn't happen again for another 700 years, giving it dumb names like *Thanksgivingmukah* and trying to meld latkes with mashed potatoes. People really went out of their way to spotlight the holiday I was secretly planning to skip again. Instead, off to Rite Aid I went, in search of knee socks and Band-Aids, steadying myself for eight nights of fire *shpilkes*. The good news is that Hanukah ended early enough to give me almost the entire month of December to focus on Christmas.

When Buzz and I were young marrieds, I used to buy the most Charlie Brown Christmas tree I could find. Tree sellers from the wilds of my home country would set up stations along the blocks of New York City, the scent of pine overtaking the smell of rat pee coming from our local supermarket. The tree hawkers would sell syrup and wreaths and trees, sleeping in their vans when the last purchase was made for the night. Knowing that space in Manhattan equaled wealth, they'd jack up the price of the larger trees, because one had to be well-to-do to fit an oversized spruce in their classic six. No matter. I looked for the saddest excuse for a tree, one that was slightly bald and whose weak branches drooped and looked fearful of ornament hanging.

"I'm not putting anything on this tree," Buzz said, after being wrangled to join me on my excursion. He had rules and principles for everything.

"Fine."

"Like no star at the top or angels or anything like that."

"Obviously no angels," I said. "We're Jewish."

"And none of that silver string stuff."

"Tinsel?"

"Yeah. No tinsel."

"Whatever you say."

"I just want to go on record as saying I am officially against this tree," Buzz said, securing his gloves so that he didn't get hurt by pine needles. "If the dog eats it and dies or water spills everywhere, you have to deal with it."

"Absolutely." I often agree to Buzz's terms but rarely follow them. "Can you just help me carry it home?"

He sighed. "I gotta do everything around here."

After much deliberation, I pointed toward my desired tree.

"That one?" he said. "It looks dead."

"It's not dead. It's hilarious."

"Does our Christmas tree have to be funny?"

"Kind of."

"It's a runt."

I then delivered a line Buzz was famous for giving me. "You can't be against this and also have input."

Hoist by his own stupid petard, he helped me rescue the challenged sapling and bring it home.

Once settled in by the window, the tree looked naked. And dejected. I felt sort of bad for it. I knew it had spent its life unpopular and friendless in the Canadian forest. And every time I walked by it, a sense of malaise and loneliness came over me. I thought I was being a do-gooder, rescuing a loser tree no one else wanted, but all it made me do was think about all the other losers out in the world. All the people who were alone on the holidays, eating French bread pizza in their basement apartments, considering asphyxiation. My tree made me sad for all the sad people out there. People with nowhere to go. People who hid in their dark rooms until the second of January, when all the merriment and sparkly shit was over. My people. There were tons of us in towns all over America, probably even Canada. The morale sappers, the downbeat, the petulant—we were everywhere. And then it finally hit me why I love Christmas so much.

Despondency is traditionally a solitary event. Feeling kind-of-bad a lot of the time, like I do, is barely an event at all. If you bother to explain constant malaise, people roll their eyes, thinking you're just trying to get attention or that you're a hypochondriac or jealous that you don't have celiac. But at Christmastime we have brethren. There are legions of sad sacks all over the nation, hunkered down alone or, worse, with family, who tell them to snap out of it and remind them of people out there with real problems.

People say the Christmas spirit is about kindness and giving—maybe so. But the unsung part of Christmas is having really low, terrible spirits. These days, however, mental health has an excellent PR machine behind it. Especially in December. If you tell someone you find the world a sad and lonely place on a Tuesday, they smile and back away and go talk to someone else at the bank. But if you share that the holidays make you blue, it's become perfectly acceptable. At Christmas, you are not alone in your aloneness. You don't even have to fake it till you make it or whatever nonsense your therapist or Page-A-Day calendar tells you. You can go ahead and feel bad all you want. You can listen to "I'll Be Home for Christmas" and weep, you can not show up to parties, you can stuff down Santa's cookies to try filling the void. It's a mental-health all-you-can-eat buffet. With presents. It makes me positively giddy.

Understanding that the uncheery had their very own season gave me a whole new reason to buy a tree. The year after our loser tree, I went a different route, purchasing one from Urban Outfitters—white-and-silver, acrylic, with poseable arms. It never required sweeping or watering, which, if you're in the doldrums, can really take great effort. Plus with no heavy lifting or potential water spillage, there was little for Buzz to complain about.

"Oh, you're still doing this," he said, when he saw me dragging the delivery box into the brownstone.

He told me that if the tree fell over, I had to pick it up.

"I thought you liked tradition," I said. "Christmas is like the tradition of all traditions."

"Not for Jews!"

He still didn't get it.

And then came the kids. If Christmas wasn't for the darn children, then who was it for?

"The Gentiles," said Buzz, packing up the car for Vermont. We would only be up there for a week, so I boxed up our acrylic tree and Buzz couldn't grouse because we had a basement in which to store it. That year I had a penchant for all things turquoise and bought some Christmas balls to match my obsession. I spent hours arranging the arms and balls to look just the way I'd seen Martha Stewart do it.

"Looks good," said Buzz.

"You think?" I said, tilting my head. "I dunno. Looks too Jewish."

"What?"

"All the blue and white. It's like a Hanukah tree at the bank."

When we moved to Vermont permanently, and Christmas rolled around, we were finally in a real house with real room for a real tree. It was time to begin with the ornaments. With themes. Every year each family member would choose (or, in the case of Buzz, have chosen for him) an ornament representing him- or herself over that past year. The tree is covered in Matchbox cars and lip balm and key chains from different places we've lived. Finally my tree had personality and lights and enough nostalgia to really make me morose.

When everyone went to bed, I could sit in front of it and feel weepy about how everything was going by so fast and how even though the kids were still in footie pajamas it would only be a matter of minutes before they were off to college and not wanting to come home for the tradition I'd spent their entire lives trying to create for them. Alone with my tree, I could eat cookies and cry and feel as bad as I wanted. It was a Christmas wish come true. Hanukah candles burn fast and bright. It's fleeting. But the tree sits there for weeks, allowing me to nurture my pit of despair. I can feel thankful for what I have and awful that I don't have the tools to appreciate it. I can admire my handiwork on the tree and also suffer guilt for potentially being a bad Jew. A tree can do all that for me, and then some.

When the kids rip into their Hanukah socks or Christmas Batman Castle, I want to give them the spiel about how the holidays are not just about presents. But then they'd ask me what they *were* all about and I'd have to change the subject because I only have vague information about oil and the desert but not enough to make a point. I don't think they even know who Jesus is, unless it's to use his name in vain, and I don't even know how to begin explaining that guy. And I certainly don't want to spark the idea in them that the holidays are about bad feelings. They can figure that one out on their own.

Buzz often says we are cultural Jews. I take that to mean I am Jewish because I am nervous and also prefer dry, overcooked chicken. But when I think about how I really enjoy wallowing in a vat of despair around the holidays and then also feel guilty about it, I think maybe that's how I bring my Jewishness into the mix. I make a mental note to do better, to locate some matzo, to write a treatment for a television special called *It Would Have Been Enough for Us, Charlie Brown*. I would watch it with my kids every year.

In the meantime, I continue to increase my Christmas tradition by embracing a new trapping every year. Ornaments, handmade advent calendars. This year, I want stockings. I can't help myself. Mingling my grim attitude with decking the halls feels like home to me. Feeling miserable and enjoying it, that's who I am. For I—sorry, Nana—I am a Christmas Jew.

In No Particular Order

· · · · · ·

In the movie version of my life, the role of me is played by Catherine Keener. As for who portrays my husband, there is hubbub in the casting office. I am adamant about wanting Don Draper but they tell me Jon Hamm is busy, and I say I have no interest in Jon Hamm, I only want Don Draper. They speak slowly when they tell me he is a fictional character on a television program, which, I mutter, is no excuse. Some headshot shuffling ensues until an assistant suddenly remembers that Don Draper is currently on location. She then shares that he is about to be indefinitely tied up because—and here she lowers her voice, signaling we are in quiet cahoots—he is strongly being considered to be the new James Bond. I wink, just to let her know her secret is safe with me.

I ask for Mark Ruffalo but they say he's hard to work with. Paul Rudd is at an eating disorder camp. No one will believe Johnny Depp is a Jew. Eventually we settle on Robert Downey Jr., who, at the time of production, will be on his eighteenth valiant comeback. Now, since this is my fantasy, I make up all kinds of things about myself. For starters, I play piano. I can pull off wearing '70s-style dance wear in my daily life. I can drive a stick, stay up past nine p.m., and I like people. I am also a type A personality.

In my real life, I am a type F personality. My dearest friend, the Shirley to my Laverne, she is type A. Shirley (not her real name) is enviable for other reasons, too. She wears a size zero, thinks it's fun to vacuum, and alphabetizes her spices. She is lovely and charismatic and ridiculously well liked. I wear regular-sized-person clothes. My vacuum is heavy. And, frankly, I'm more of an acquired taste—acquired by a scant few. I am the Good & Plenty of people.

When I am with Shirley, I feel inspired to leave my F status behind and sprint up the type alphabet. And so, in an effort to be more A-ish, I decide to run a controlled experiment. Perhaps if I borrow some of Shirley's customs, osmosis will occur. Lists are what immediately come to mind. Shirley is forever making them, so I decide to try my hand at a nice, crisp list.

First up, the To-Do. This is a beginner's list. Simple in nature, pretty hard to mess up. Nonetheless, I am an F, so this list proves complicated. I spend way too much time trying to find the ideal pad, the sublime pen. I stare at a blank page for half the day, laboring over what to write. Should I jot down things like *make doctor's appointment*, or is it more of a grander To-Do, something along the lines of *learn Spanish* and *knit poncho*? This takes up most of my day, and before I know it I am asleep on the couch as *House Hunters* drones in the background.

The next day, I outsmart the list. I go about my business, and as soon as I do anything short of breathing, I write it down and at once cross it off. I include all daily tasks, even *brush teeth,* so as to have a fat list. I walk around the house (a lot), then write down *exercise* and tick it off.

A few days in, I tire of the To-Do. My fetching notepad gets pushed under the bed, where it will remain for the year, like a second grader's recorder. This kind of list-making seems like too much pressure for someone with follow-through issues. Here I could easily abandon ship, but no, I am dedicated to change.

Part of what makes Shirley so organized involves lists, yes, but who's to say what kind of list? Isn't a list a list? Lucky for me, I have spent much of my life trying to find loopholes. This is energy I am comfortable expending and a place where I can blossom. I do not forgo the experiment—I tweak it.

Let's begin with . . .

WORDS I DON'T CARE FOR

1. panties

2. playdate

3. moist

4. gubernatorial

5. blog

6. mound

7. poached

8. hash tag

9. mixologist

10. Croissan'wich

11. pubes

12. barista

13. luncheon

14. whiff

This type of list gets me jazzed. I come up with its cousin.

SAYINGS/EXPRESSIONS THAT ANNOY ME

1. Cool beans.

2. Keep calm and carry on.

3. Brain fart.

4. We're not worthy. (Extra credit for the dumb bowing hand gesture.)

5. Do me a solid.

6. Put on your big-girl panties.

7. My bad.

8. Date night. (*Playdate* could easily fit here.)

9. That being said. (I prefer simply *that said* or *having said that*.)

10. Kick it up a notch.

11. The whole fan damily.

12. Hot mess.

I soon discover this list has a nascent little sister.

**WORDS OR PHRASES I DON'T ACTUALLY MIND,
JUST CAN'T GET AWAY WITH SAYING**

1. No worries.

2. Buddy.

3. Man. (As in *Hey, man*, not *Did you see that bearded man?*)

4. Fabulous.

Things are looking up. I get a jittery sensation in my gut, the same one I felt in the eighth grade during the only four-minute chunk of math I ever understood. I should note here that this is usually the point in any undertaking when I decamp. A modicum of achievement is usually my cue to exit stage left. But, if you were paying attention, I am not being myself, I am being Shirley. So I challenge myself with . . .

THINGS I TRY REALLY HARD NOT TO DO

1. overuse the exclamation mark

2. talk about the weather (Unless it's snowy/icy/could-have-an-accident-while-driving weather. I'm a little interested in this kind of talk, more doomsday, less pressure systems.)

3. use song lyrics as a status update on Facebook (*It's just another manic Monday, people!!* Also, this style of update can generate overuse of the exclamation mark.)

4. eat popcorn or other movie snacks before picture commences

5a. use emoticons (Happy to report I have never employed a smiley or winky or pissy guy. Ever.)

5b. or worse: LOL, ROFL, SMH, LMAO, FML (However, the occasional BTW or old-school FYI are okay and therefore grandfathered in.)

I do have a list that never sees the light of day, but in the spirit of the experiment I will share it.

REASONS I WISH I WERE AN OLD LADY

1. Always acceptable to go to bed at 7:30.

2. Okay to sit in chair at social gatherings and stare into space.

3. Can wear heavy woolen cardigans year round.

4. Don't have to participate in impromptu football or Frisbee tosses.

5. Appropriate to notice and discuss weird and potentially life-threatening ailments or symptoms.

6. On beautiful and sunny days, no pressure to go outside and have fun.

I suddenly feel weak from all this list making and need to sit down. From the couch, I survey my bookshelf, which not only helps to restore my energy but gives me an idea for another list.

**BOOK JACKET SUMMARIES FROM NOVELS
YOU WILL NEVER CATCH ME READING**

(and the exact point in the summary-reading where I reject book and put it back on shelf)

1. Major General Edwin Twiggs knew it would be an enduring, dusty walk home from the battle of Chicka-hominy, but he tightened his canvas gaiters and commenced his journey . . .

2. Beautiful Rose Eldridge and fiery Olivia Stickley have been the best of friends since third grade. But when one of them is diagnosed with a rare, inoperable cancer . . .

3. For fourteen thousand years, the planet Kreegon has had one leader . . .

4. Newlyweds Jennifer and Jason Jones thought their lives were perfect—and then they brought home Mr. Scruffers.

5. England. The 1520s . . .

I am now buzzing with just enough vim to continue my work. Shirley is never lazy, so, in an effort to also seem not lazy, I eke out one more. It's a bit of a hodgepodge—the junk drawer of lists; my blood sugar is low. At any rate . . .

RANDOM THINGS THAT MAKE ME HOSTILE

1. sudoku

2. Napa Valley (or any talk of trips to wine country)

3. jogging

4. gluten intolerance

5. zucchini

6. up-speak

7. footnotes

At this point, I'm quite pleased with myself and am just about to call it a day, when I remember that I almost forgot the best list of all. This is a primo list. *And* it is one that Shirley and I have joined forces on. Known simply as the List, all either of us has to say is, "It's on the list," and all is immediately understood. Because Shirley is an avid participant in this list, it fits in with my original goal and feels like the extra-credit take-home work I never once in my life took home. Having spent my entire school career being the She Has So Much Potential/If Only She Applied Herself type, I've never once gotten a gold star. Shirley, however, practically bleeds gold stars. I visualize our list with the shiny emblem on the top right-hand corner. I present you with . . .

THINGS THE ENTIRE WORLD THINKS ARE TERRIFIC AND/OR FUN BUT I DON'T

1. convertibles

2. New Year's Eve

3. Monopoly

4. eating at the beach

5. champagne, roses, and chocolate-dipped strawberries

6. traveling

7. *Mamma Mia!*

8. parades

9. fancy chocolate desserts (mousse and flourless tortes and anything with "Death by Chocolate" in the title)

10. Cirque du Soleil

11. Shirley says "pancakes" (I can't get behind this).

12. I say "college" (Shirley says I am on my own here).

I'm completely athrill; I'm actually doing it! Two days ago I was sitting in my car trying to remember what errand I had set out to do, and, just like that, I've become a mad list maker, quite possibly easing myself up the alphabet. A few more successful days like this and Shirley and I will be having sweater depilling parties, vacuum-offs, filing relays. I feel like jumping on my coffee table and acting out the old-school York Peppermint Pattie commercial. It's all happening.

It doesn't take long before the excitement wanes. Eventually, as with most of my endeavors, I decide I am doing it wrong. Who am I kidding? I am not accomplishing anything by making lists. I haven't moved up a station. I am my regular old F self, wasting my days enumerating stuff I hate. Don't get me wrong, it's a hell of a time. Now that I'm a Vermonter, I spend my time differently than when I lurked in the city. I still pace around outside instead of writing, but there are fewer people watching me do this. If I was parked on my front stoop for too long, the neighbors might start to talk about or, worse, to me. But in this fresh new setting I can enjoy hours sizing up nature-type things from a chair on the porch and no one is the wiser.

I have to hand it to myself: I have an unusual capacity for reclusiveness. I can clock hours alone in my house in the woods, getting lathered about what bugs me. I am good at this. However, I don't get full of myself or go on some big ego trip about my deftness and personal gifts. Instead I use it for good and come up with more big life ideas.

Buzz has made fun of me, more than once, about how I could very well be the Unabomber. This idea might have legs. I live in the middle of nowhere now. I look slightly disheveled most of the time. Granted, I wasn't that great in school, but I do love the mail. I have all kinds of thoughts and ideas and umbrage—why couldn't I write a manifesto? Why couldn't I be a neighborly, likes-to-bake type of Unabomber? A Jewnabomber.

This idea excites me. I pace the front porch, waiting for Buzz to get home so I can fill him in on the new plan. After a few minutes of this, I run upstairs and put on my red plaid cotton flannel from Old Navy to really hit the whole Jewnabomber thing hard, so that it's a no-brainer when he pulls up the driveway and sees me. We used to live on a congested street with speedy cars and smoking teenagers, but now our house sits atop a grassy hill and the only things that pass are intermittent UPS trucks and tick-dropping deer.

There is not even an inkling of a car approaching our dirt road, but I can wait. I have mountains of patience. My porch is twenty-four feet long, excellent for pacing and getting fired up, which I now am. Being solo, I can say "manifesto," out loud, just to hear what it sounds like. Sounds pretty good. This could very well change my life. This might even be the very thing I was meant to do, *the* reason to get off the couch. Change is afoot.

I sit on the ugly wicker loveseat I insisted on buying from Basketville. I begin to recognize that the only thing I know about a manifesto is that thing Tom Cruise wrote in *Jerry Maguire*. (Note to self: Add *Show me the money* to the Expressions That Annoy Me list.) And just as with most of the inspired ideas that wake me up in the night—starting a vintage Smurf figurine collection, homeschooling the kids—I abort plan. I go back inside, hang up my red plaid from Old Navy, and eat crackers. It is clearly time to call Shirley.

Shirley is not home. Shirley is probably out accomplishing stuff. I hate Shirley.

I want to take to my bed, but I feel bad for Catherine Keener. She's so groovy, and I owe her a stellar role—more character development, a better wardrobe, actual stuff to do. I just don't see her as the kind of broad who slouches in dreadful wicker seating wanting to call it quits because her short-lived dreams of being a list-making Unabomber are prematurely dashed. No one will believe it of her, no matter how talented and plucky she is. I need to do better for Catherine Keener. Plus I also have to consider Robert Downey Jr., since for most of this picture so far he's been MIA.

I give myself a pep talk. Usually this is where I'd get in a fight with myself, so I consider my snappy life coaching a step in a different direction, maybe even something Shirley would do. I am back to finding my Shirleyness. Listing is not all that makes Shirley Shirley. Lots of things make her a lifelong A. It's just that I can't seem to think of one of them at this moment. This is strange, because Shirley and I have been tangled in each other's lives since we were mini Type As and Fs.

We met when we were thirteen years old at a theater camp in small-town New Hampshire. We lived not in bunks or cabins but in seventeen grizzled rooms that were part of an inactive L-shaped motel. There was one picnic table outside room 12 and a chain-link fence surrounding the heart of the operation, the pool. Down a dirt road stood a rustic barn of a theater where we did a bunch of children's plays and some standard musicals like *Annie*, *The Sound of Music,* and *The Best Little Whorehouse in Texas*.

The program was based on some 1970s est training, which was supposed to help us campers achieve a sense of *compelling transformation* and *enhanced power*. On the first day of camp, the thirty of us were shuttled into a basement under the motel. It was a dank room, which didn't do my *Flashdance* hairdo any favors. There were bridge chairs set up in rows, and I took my usual seat of choice: the one in the very back. Naturally, in the very front sat Shirley, eager and freckled, like Laura Ingalls in a Benetton rugby. I wasn't paying any attention to the questions being tossed over our heads, but Shirley's twiggy arm shot up many times at rapid speeds. I put on my *get a load of this one* look, but nobody was interested. Everyone wanted to be around her. Well, everyone *else* wanted to be around her.

I wanted to throw stuff at her. All that pep and optimism, it was just gross.

On the third day of camp, we were ferried to a dance class held off the motel property. We assembled in the back of a pickup truck that transported us to a rickety church. Our dance teacher, let's call him Baryshnikov, was foxy and muscled and more feminine than all of the Rockettes combined. I was glad I'd picked out my best shiny Capezio leotard, because I knew deep down that even though I was maladroit and inelegant and couldn't *pas de bourrée* to save my life, there was no doubt Baryshnikov would fall in love with me the second I adjusted my leg warmers.

We were sitting in a semicircle to have a chat about the finer points of dance when I noticed Baryshnikov was wearing some pretty threadbare black tights and just might have forgotten to put on his underwear that morning. I had already read *Hollywood Wives* and *The Thorn Birds*, so I was well-versed in the sex department. However, sitting in plain sight of Baryshnikov's real live Members Only, I panicked. It was a dead-animal-on-the-road situation. I knew to look away, but couldn't, but had to, but couldn't, but had to. No clue how to calm my eyes, I scanned the room to give them something to do so my fellow campers wouldn't think I was having a seizure. And then my gaze landed upon Shirley. Our eyes locked like Legos.

We kick-ball-changed around the church together all morning after that and then were glued for the rest of what would become my most cherished summer. We borrowed each other's bathing suits, snooped through our motel mates' bags together; we even made out with the same dashing Jake-from-*Sixteen-Candles*–looking guy, though not at the same time. (I should note that years later I read that he was found executed in a burning

Mercedes SUV in an upscale North Hollywood neighborhood.
Something to do with twin *Playboy* Playmates, a Ponzi scheme,
and a replica of the diamond-and-ruby necklace Richard Gere
gave to Julia Roberts in *Pretty Woman*.)

We've kept this coalition going for almost thirty years, which
means if anyone can come up with the arcane leisure activities
that make Shirley Shirley, you can be goddamn sure it's me. I
decide to make a list. I call it . . .

SHIRLEY DIVERSIONS

1. vacuuming

2. alphabetizing

3. putting things that don't have specific homes in bowls

4. thinking positive

I think maybe that if I take any of these up, or all of them, they
could serve as the montage commonly seen in romantic come-
dies. I have spent many moments in the car listening to songs
on the radio, making mental notes about which ones would be
appropriate to underscore my film. I always imagine that I would
be driving as the opening credits rolled, like Albert Brooks in
Defending Your Life, minus the part where he gets hit by a truck
and dies.

Attempting to follow this new list, I (1) walk to the guest bathroom shower, which is where I store my vacuum, but notice that in
order to take out said vacuum I'd have to move the used ice skates
and box of photographs that share shower space with the vacuum,
so I leave the bathroom and head to the kitchen, where I (2) will
begin my grand alphabetizing enterprise, but upon the opening of
the cabinet I notice that it holds at least 390 jars of spices, and who

in their right mind wants to deal with that, so I move on to where I (3) keep a collection of bowls and fetch a broken hair clip, a pot of lip balm, an unclaimed watch, and a mini Etch A Sketch and throw them in, all the while (4) thinking positively.

I stand in the middle of the kitchen and wait for some sort of game show–style alarms to go off. Who the hell am I kidding? I don't have the time to put homeless things in bowls or think positively. And, even if I did, I couldn't keep up with the pace. I am a yo-yo get-things-doner at best. What will I get out of this besides overflowing bowls and the security of knowing that chili powder will forever sit beside cinnamon?

Plus, if we're being honest, this is a movie. And although I am certain no one will pay one clam to see Catherine Keener do the regular stuff I do, I am even more certain they wouldn't pay to see her vacuuming and putting stuff away after she uses it either. There is the slightest chance that if I went down that whole manifesto route once more, I'd have slightly more luck with my film, but we all know I'm not writing that any time soon.

What if the movie of my life was some sort of action adventure instead? I could wear the red plaid Old Navy and get into it with a bear. This could also go documentary, I guess, if I'm feeling brave. Suddenly, none of it feels right anymore. Staring out on the mountains, I imagine myself driving a tractor, sporting a formfitting gingham dress and pigtails, when all of a sudden the tractor breaks down right in front of a veterinarian's office, and since this veterinarian just happens to be a doctor of oversized animals, he is working outside assessing an ailing cow, *and*, as luck would have it, he is very rugged and handsome (the vet, not the cow), so I nimbly dismount my John Deere and, coquettishly, ask for help. This is a movie someone might pay to see. But then I realize this is a porno movie and I couldn't do that to Catherine Keener.

That's it. Screw *Jerry Maguire* and the Jewnabomber and the hot oversized-animal vet. And fuck you, Shirley. I hate everyone.

I wouldn't pay seven cents to see the movie of my life. The movie of my life sucks. It is neither a popcorn flick nor a Sundance biopic. It's not even a Lifetime event. This would be a great time to sit down at a piano and play something motivating to inspire my life. But I don't have a stupid piano or know how to play. Shirley is out doing things. Where the hell is Robert Downey Jr.? I decide to officially give Catherine Keener an out. I cancel the project. I no longer am supervising the Untitled Type A Jewnabomber Project, Spring 2013.

I do feel a lot less pressure now that the movie is off. I don't have to deal with my wardrobe or work on my new walk. I don't have to clean my house or change my personality or bowl things. No one will be moving to Vermont for six months to observe me in action just to make sure they are accurately portraying a living character. I won't have to pay a dime for the rights to the original cast recording of *Pippin* for the montage.

Life will return to normal up on the hill. I call Shirley again to inform her that the movie is off and that, for now, she can be the Type A in the friendship. Shirley is not home. I put the phone in the bowl.

Good Grief

......

Buzz did not have a breezy childhood. He was, like many '70s kids, the product of a mangled home. When things fell apart, his mother put on her smartest cardigan and marched herself over to a Jewish singles mixer at the synagogue with the intention of fixing what broke. There, by the tray of noodle kugel, she met a young widower—a benign accountant with two boys of his own. It wasn't long before the two families merged. A gift, as Buzz's mother saw it. And although this gift was sheathed in bargain wrapping paper and none-too-sticky tape, at least, she thought, at least there's a gift at all.

If you meet Buzz at a barbecue, he will ask you umpteen questions about yourself. He'll hang on your words and you will relish feeling you are that night's guest on *Charlie Rose*. Secretly, you'll marvel at how interesting you are and leave the party chock-full of potato salad, and yourself. You will, however, have learned nothing about Buzz. An armchair Freud might diagnose Buzz's parlor tricks as deflection. Claim that he is using the old switcheroo so he doesn't have to give up much of his own history. This would be a fair interpretation. However, if you stick around long enough like I have, eventually a few childhood nuggets will surface. The ones he remembers, anyway.

Like many of us casualties of lackadaisical parenting, Buzz has great plans to do things differently. Traditions and celebrations were not big players in Buzz's young life, so they feature heavily in his adult one. *Taco Tuesday! Family Hike! Let's Make a (Dessert) Deal!* Our life together is a series of bar mitzvah parties, complete with omelet bar and fajita station. You can't get in his way, though, and you'd be a pill to try.

Buzz suffers from a bad case of emotional pica, an insatiable craving to fill himself up with the sand and dirt of childhood he missed out on. It's draining but (on my compassionate days) I understand it. I roll my eyes while rolling out pizza dough or ordering the piñata because I know what it feels like to be slightly defective. And so when Buzz said to me, "Kim, we're going to Disney World," I wanted to politely decline and say there was no way in hell I was making that trip, but I smiled and nodded, then took to the bed, and secretly thought, *Good grief*.

Mention the word *Disney* out in public and you'll get two different reactions. One person hearing it will develop little Mickey Mouse silhouettes in place of his pupils, Saturday-morning-cartoon–style, complete with sprays of hearts and fireworks shooting from his scalp and ears. The other will rant, letting you know her daughter does indeed *not* need a prince to live happily ever after, thank you very much. If you go further and mention Disney World, you will witness a conniption or be forced to relive someone's memory of Mr. Toad's Wild Ride or how they almost barfed on Dumbo.

It seems like everyone has a Disney chronicle to recount. Even Buzz. I learned that his blended family made the trip via Chevy Impala wagon. Not enough seats in the car forced Buzz to be stuffed, alongside his stepbrother and all the luggage, into the trunk section of the wagon. Buzz's strongest memory was begging his stepfather to hit the Wet 'n Wild water park, the one you encounter a mile before the entrance to Disney World itself. His request was denied. The only other thing Buzz recalled was hearing his stepfather mutter to his wife on the long drive home, "Well, we are never doing *that* again."

My own revisionist Disney history lives in Tomorrowland, when no one in my family could handle a ride speedier than the Hall of Presidents. And although I begged for any of them to ride Space Mountain with my nine-year-old self, I was met with three *absolutely not*s. My father held on to his Gucci belt and suggested I ride by myself because he'd probably barf. My brother told me to forget it, too fast and scary and also the barfing. My mother, sensing my indecision, insisted I make up my mind already because she thought she heard thunder and also she wasn't feeling well. An imaginary chalk line was drawn at that very moment, separating me from them. They had become a band of lame superheroes—the Non-Avengers. Together they fought nothing, setting out to actively not save the world, because they were worried, nauseous, and chicken. I studied their side of the line and thought, *Fine, maybe I will ride alone. Maybe someone will steal me. Maybe I'll fall out and die and then they'd see.* Which is precisely what I did (ride alone, not get stolen or die). I recall nothing else.

A trip to Disney World, like parenting, is a giant do-over. Some return to the park with their young families to relive the magic. Others go back to patch up well-worn holes. Buzz and I handle our childhood fix-it kits with different techniques. He plans fiestas and Best Day Evers and I make sure no one rides alone. But, even with all the wrongs I wanted to make right, I still had no interest in taking the trip. I pulled a signature move of mine. I tried getting out of it.

"You know, I was thinking. Disney is kind of expensive," I said one night, while loading the dishwasher. This defense usually gives Buzz pause.

"Well, you only live once," he said. "They'll remember this forever."

"Isn't it hurricane season?"

"There won't be a hurricane," Buzz said. He was on the couch, deep into researching the best memory-making pool in the greater Orlando area. "Do you care if we don't stay on campus?"

Campus. Already using the argot. I was in trouble.

"What if something happens while we're there?" I said. "Something bad."

"Like what?"

"Like, you know." I widened my eyes as a clue but he didn't even look up from his iDevice.

"Do you think a four-acre pool is big enough? It has a water-slide."

"Because it could happen, you know."

"Come check out this hotel."

"You're not listening to me."

"What are you even talking about? What could happen? Someone gets sick? We'll go to a doctor. It's Florida, not Siberia."

"I'm not talking about getting sick."

"Well, then, what are you talking about?"

I shut the dishwasher door, wiped my hands on a bar mop. "What if someone blows the place up while we're there?"

Buzz looked up. "What?"

"Like a terrorist or something."

Buzz sighed. "Really?"

"Yes, really."

"You are so narcissistic," he said. "Why would something bad happen when *you* are there?"

"Why wouldn't it happen when I was there?"

Buzz squinted at me. "Kim, no one is going to blow it up."

"How do you know?"

"Because I know."

"You don't know. You don't know there won't be a hurricane and you don't know there won't be an incident. It's actually kinda arrogant to think you do."

His head was back down again, focusing on his research, which was code for *I am done with this chicanery*.

"If I were a terrorist," I said, "I'd totally blow up Disney."

"Okay," he said, shaking his head. "Noted."

"I just want to know how you know no one will blow it up."

"Because people don't just go around blowing stuff up!"

This was a popular defense for Buzz, one I find very aggravating. When buying a front door for our house in (isolated) Vermont, Buzz wanted one made entirely of glass. I vetoed this door, for obvious reasons.

"If a serial killer comes to the door," I said, looking for a steel option in the catalog, "he could see right in."

"If a serial killer comes to the door," Buzz said, "and it was a solid door, couldn't he just look in through the window next to the door?"

"Maybe we shouldn't get windows."

"This is ridiculous," said Buzz. "People don't just go around being serial killers."

We bickered about the door for a week, eventually compromising on a one-pane-of-glass situation. But I keep the porch lights off when it gets dark so Ted Bundy can't find his way in.

As usual, I had to talk my own self off the terrorist ledge by deciding that if there were to be nefarious happenings at the Kingdom, they would most likely take place on an auspicious date like July Fourth or Christmas. We were only going on June 12. This thought assuaged my fear but still didn't address why I had no interest in taking the trip. Sometimes, when I don't know how I feel, I consult friends and strangers so they can tell me what I think.

I took an informal poll. My findings showed that people have some real gripes with Disney World. There are six factions:

Occupy Disney: Veins bubble on foreheads when spitting out what they believe to be wrong with that world. *Consumerism! Commercialization! Corporate capitalization!* This hostile group has no problem telling you what's what, reminding you also that Walt was an anti-Semite, along with various and sundry other issues. If you brought these politicos to the park, they would pack (along with their sunscreen and rain ponchos) buckets of blood with which to soak Goofy along the parade route. They might be heard shouting "Racist!" or "Nazi!" at Gaston.

The Mickey Moderates: These guys don't get as riled but that doesn't mean they are happy with the place. These are more of your middle-of-the-road haters. They feel it's overpriced, the crowds are annoying, the food is processed and terrible, and the whole thing is a giant waste of money. They take issue with paying seventeen dollars for a plastic spray bottle with fan attached. Many of this group will end up at the park, at least once in their lifetime, but they will grumble about it while getting soaked on Splash Mountain.

The Wanderlusters: These traveler types wonder, Why pick Disney when there are so many other places in the world to see? There are ruins and mountains and pyramids out there. Shouldn't we explore a legitimate castle in Bavaria, instead of being forced to just stand outside one because the only way to actually gain entry is to call up 180 days in advance to make a reservation at Cinderella's table or pay an obscene amount of money to get a royal makeover at the Bibbidi Bobbidi Boutique?

The "I Hate Florida" Fan Club: Pretty self-explanatory, but these people don't even want to set foot in the state, let alone Orlando. Be it the politics or the climate or the belief that they'd feel too Middle America–ish, this group steers clear of the place.

The Odd (Donald) Ducks: This is a hodgepodge of a group, a sprinkling of people with disparate concerns. I have subsetted them into three categories: (a) believe they will have to wear a fanny pack to enter the state, (b) do not want to be told they have to have fun, (c) can't stand tourists.

And finally, my all-time favorite group, the excuse I enjoyed most and refer to every time I need a quick mental pick-me-up:

Rage Against the Machine: This group is anti–Disney World because—well, because the place has too many kids.

Now, don't get me wrong, I love ire and a group of complainers as much as the next guy. I just couldn't get as worked up as my test groups, try as I might, because (a) lines and consumerism don't really get my dander up, (b) I'm not that political (Canadian), (c) I don't usually get worked up over things that actually matter, and (d) at the end of the day, being part of a group stresses me out. It was only a couple of days later, when a friend called after hearing we were Orlando-bound, that it all started to make sense.

"Have fun," she said, laughing at her own joke. This friend takes great delight in my grumpy nature and malcontentish personality. She called to share the secret tips Magic Kingdomers like to dole out upon their return. But insider information and guidebooks were not all she was interested in sending along. She had one more chestnut to impart before she hung up.

"I cannot wait to hear how *you* handle the Happiest Place on Earth."

(1. denial)

Our black rent-a-Prius was directed to the Heroes lot, Simba section, spot 111. I noticed the other parking option, the Villains lot, and immediately wanted to switch, but since we got there early, like the Book insisted, we were stuck with all the other goody-two-shoes and corporate-capitalist-loving rule followers. Apparently the Villains lot was closed and would open later when the cool kids showed up. Buzz and I each took a kid's hand (let's call them Minnie and Pluto) and marched with the other Heroes to the shuttle, which took us to the monorail, which took us to the entrance of the Magic Kingdom, which was already swarming but not yet officially open.

My backpack was heavy with sunscreen and rain ponchos and healthful snacks and water and printouts and tear sheets from the (heavy) guidebook (although I also brought the heavy guidebook) and Ziploc bags, lest anything get wet on a ride. Stuck in a holding pattern, waiting to get our bags inspected for weapons, I noticed that a good portion of the early-birders came dressed in Mickey attire. The getups ranged from garden-variety Ts to intricate headgear and even a few full-on costumes. There was no shortage of grown men in Goofy caps, with which I quickly became obsessed. A baseball-style hat showcasing black and white vacant eyes, a flesh-colored brim with a nose at the tip, and requisite long black dangly ears.

"Is it at all weird to you," I said to Buzz, "that so many people are wearing Disney clothes here?"

He shrugged his shoulders and said, "Where else are they gonna wear it?"

There is no situation where I feel at ease in a crowd. I get frazzled knowing that if need be, I cannot make a swift egress. One of the first things I do when I get into a place is plan how I might get out. In order to escape Disney, I'd have to take down hundreds of autograph book–wielding children, packs of families in matching clothes, and a number of girthy people on Rascal scooters. This idea did not relax me. As we waited to get our bags checked so that we could gain entry to the entry of the park (which was *still* closed), I kept my eye on the security man and his line, just like I do at the airport, to determine which guests were up to no good and whom to avoid on the Pirates of the Caribbean. Finally, our turn, and a happy fellow rifled through my bag, returning it unzipped but cleared for entry. He looked at me with his cheerful face and said, "Have a good day, Princess!"

Fuck you, I thought.

"Ladies and gentlemen, girls and boys!" said a voice from an undisclosed location. "Welcome to the Magic Kingdom!"

Music pumped in, people cheered. We were now just outside the main entrance, all staring at the railroad station above our heads, waiting for someone to let us in. A man appeared, shouted "Good morning!," and the crowd parroted greetings back. This was the Mayor of Main Street. Dressed in a straw boater and old-timey shirtsleeves, he could have been moonlighting as the fourth in a barbershop quartet or a hipster barkeep from Brooklyn. The mayor was sent in as a warm-up act to get the crowd good and buttered before they were let loose into the wilds of the park.

In case we needed more, he unleashed some citizens of Main Street on us, out-of-work actors forced to dance a jig in some old-fangled costumery. As they hopped around, I felt a rumble under my feet. *This is it*, I thought, *terrorist activity*. Something had exploded in those underground tunnels they didn't want us to know about, resulting in Sleeping Beauty guts on walls and ceiling.

I was just about to alert Buzz, when a train pulled into the station and a smattering of characters jumped off—Snow White and Cinderella and her Fairy Godmother, Tiana and Tangled. Some old-school folks also showed up. Donald and Honest John and the sexy white cat from *The Aristocats*. I thought that was it until the very last two scurried off the train: Chip 'n' Dale! The life-sized rodents of my youth! I gasped. Audibly. I loved those guys.

"Who's they?" said Pluto. "Those two bears near the talking guy."

Who are those guys? Only two of my all-time favorite guys. "Chip 'n' Dale!" I screamed in his little ear. "They're chipmunks. What is that weird thing with the giant eyes and ears?" I asked.

"Which thing?" said Minnie.

"The gray thing on the end," I said. "What *is* that?"

"That's Lilo & Stitch," she said. "Do not go on that ride, Mom. It's all dark and they poke your neck and then someone spits on you."

Even Minnie had secret tips and information.

The mayor began a group countdown. The citizens of Main Street were sweating glee.

Ten . . . nine . . . eight . . .

Minnie balled up her fists. Pluto hugged me. And, just like that, I wanted in.

. . . seven . . . six . . . five . . .

No, I didn't. How is it I'm here? I am not here.

. . . four . . . three . . . two . . .

Listen here, Disney, just so we're clear: You don't get me, okay, I get *you*.

. . . one!

Fireworks! Music! Applause! The mayor shouted, "Let the memories begin!"

I closed my eyes and thought of England.

(2. anger)

"Who is this elephant again?" Pluto asked.

I adjusted my backpack straps. "Dumbo."

"Is this ride scary?" he said. "What is this ride? His ears are too big. The music in here is making me a little bit sad. Like when I saw *E.T.*, remember?"

"Do we have snacks in the bag?" Minnie said. "I have to pee."

We'd left our parked car at least an hour ago and had yet to board a ride. Was Dumbo the best choice? You never forget your first ride. Was a flying elephant the way to go?

"Do we even want to go on this thing?" I said.

Buzz sighed.

"Well," said Minnie, "it doesn't look *that* great."

"Who is this elephant, again?" Pluto said.

"I kinda have to pee."

Buzz closed his eyes.

"Maybe we shouldn't start with this one," I said.

When Buzz is set on a plan, he does not like to veer. "Don't even give them the option," he said.

I examined the serpentine line crammed under the big top. An hour wasted there was an hour we could be doing something else.

"Let's go," I said. "We can do better. They don't even know who Dumbo is."

We were let out of line, single file, escorted through the back of the tent.

The digital clock above Peter Pan's Flight let us know there was a thirty-minute wait. I squinted, debated, weighed, wavered, and looked around. Buzz, on the other hand, went rogue, fleeing the group to push the button at the FastPass kiosk. Out slid a ticket, allowing us to return to the ride and board, via a special no-line entrance, but not until 12:50 p.m.

It was 9:30 a.m.

"What have you done?" I said, narrowing my eyes.

"What?" he said, an innocent all of a sudden.

"We didn't discuss the FastPass."

"No big deal," Buzz said, putting the four tickets in his wallet. "The kids wanted Peter Pan and now we can go on it."

"In three hours!" I said.

"So? We'll just walk around, do other stuff and whatever, then come back."

I wanted to shove Buzz and his new laissez-faire attitude over. This is a man who always requires, and adheres to, a plan. This is a man who, while eating breakfast, needs to know what's for dinner, so he can plan lunch.

"You can't just wander and *do stuff and whatever*," I said. "Otherwise we won't maximize our time at the park."

"Now you care about maximizing your time?" he said, keeping an eye on the kids as they window-shopped. "I thought you were all *get in, get out, and nobody gets hurt*."

"Why is it," I said in a growlish whisper, "that when you have a plan we all need to snap to it, but when I have one you do whatever the hell you want?"

"Whoa, whoa, whoa," Buzz said. "What's the matter with you right now? It's just a freaking FastPass."

"It's not just a freaking FastPass! It's a prison sentence. Now we have to stay in Fantasyland for like three hours. Even if we don't want to!"

"We can go wherever we want!" Buzz said. "We just have to be back by 12:50."

I took a cleansing breath. "First of all, we now can't get another FastPass until this one expires. Second, the Book says we should never get a FastPass if the line is thirty minutes or less. Peter Pan said thirty! And now we have to run around like lunatics and be back here at the exact time I wanted to go back to the hotel to rest so no one starts freaking out! That's what the Book says!"

"Dude, you need to relax."

I should note here that being told to relax is the gateway to having an aneurism; don't even get me started on when your husband calls you *dude*.

"Let's go on Pooh," said Pluto, returning from his walkabout and pointing to the ride.

"Fine," I said. "Let's go on Pooh."

The LED numbers over the Hundred Acre Wood read forty-five minutes. Had Buzz not been an overzealous *Press Your Luck* contestant earlier, slamming buzzers before he knew answers, we could have FastPassed Pooh. Instead, we joined the line.

The Imagineers had built interactive stops along the queue to keep kids busy as they waited. What these Imagineers failed to create was a separate line for dueling spouses or a penalty box for freewheelers with itchy FastPass fingers who went around jamming buttons like it was nothing. I gripped the straps of my backpack, eyebrows scrunched together. But I wasn't alone. If I scanned the line or the stores or walkways or streets, it seemed like I had all sorts of pissy company. Husbands everywhere were sparring with wives, mothers were shouting and grabbing at children, children were whining and crying and melting down. Sure was a lot of discord at the Happiest Place on Earth.

I made a mental note for my friend back home, the one who couldn't wait to hear how I'd fare in this happy place, to let her know I was just fine, actually kind of among my people. We, the disgruntled, together under one fake roof, breathing in the phony vanilla–scented air. The place seemed riddled with turmoil and anguish, and for that I was thankful. I uncurled my shoulders. The line moved swiftly. We were locked into our honey pots in under thirty.

"You see?" Buzz said. "Those times are bullshit. We're gonna sail through this thing no problem."

It's a Small World is a musical boat ride, originally built for the UNICEF pavilion at the World's Fair (sponsored by Pepsi) as a tribute to the children of the world. When the attraction was conceived, it was decided that each country would be represented not only by a creepy doll in traditional dress but by its respective national anthem as well. Walt, however, found the whole thing cacophonous, so he plucked a team of brothers from his staff to create one catchy, easy, translatable tune to worm its way into the ears of millions.

The Sherman Brothers presented a song that had legs but ultimately was too slow and sad and Cuban Missile Crisisy. They were asked to pep it up. And while no one is truly against world peace and unity, the iconic song could quite possibly land you in a mental institution, and the sluggish ten-minute-and-thirty-second boat ride is enough to make you want to stick a fork in your eye, but it was a time-honored tradition (said the Book), one you felt obligated to embark on if you'd bothered to get yourself all the way to the Kingdom.

We entered the grand doors of what appeared to be the Inter-national House of Salt Water Taffy—after no wait at all—and sat four across in a boat. As we set sail and I began to hear the song, I forced myself to have a good attitude for my children and the children of the world. Plus, it was the least I could do for the

UNICEF kids, a payback of sorts for the Halloween I dressed as Fonzie's chick and collected change in the orange box, promptly spending it all on Dubble Bubble instead of turning it in to Mr. Bowker.

It seemed that the bottom of the fake lake was covered in coins. Rummaging through my wallet, I produced two quarters and a plastic dinosaur. I handed over the money for chucking, figuring it might give Minnie and Pluto bigger ticket wishes.

"Here, you guys," I said.

"Why are you giving us dimes?" said Pluto.

"Throw it in," I said, pointing to the water. "Make a wish."

They peeked overboard to see the glint of coins for themselves.

"Whoa," said Pluto. "There's like a thousand hundred forty-eight dollars down there."

The kids spent most of India and part of China thinking up a wish. Minnie finally plinked hers in. Pluto said he was no way telling his wish but that it was to have another "light saver—a bad one this time" and to spend more good time like this with his family, except next time bring the dog.

We were three minutes and fifty-seven seconds in when it happened. I was sitting in the boat, minding my own business, when I noticed I was not feeling hostile. I immediately began making excuses for all light and airy feelings I may or may have not been experiencing: Those dolls are only trying to get my attention, they're so damn proud of their heritage and clearly spent a great deal of time getting dressed; the frosty air is undeniably pleasant; the kids are pointing and shiny-eyed. It all came to a head when I realized that the song was not only not eating my brain but causing me to sing along—toe-tap in the boat, even. And, somewhere around the South American rain forest, there were tears. My own. Right there in the stupid boat, my eye sockets filled up and I had to look to the pseudo sky to keep them from spilling out all over the jungles of the world.

I turned my back on the family and faced the dolls, knowing full well that if Buzz caught on he'd never let me live it down. I'd be in for a good ten years of how I broke down in phony Uganda. The guy is a pit bull with jokes and mockery. I chewed the inside of my lip until I tasted blood, hoping to jar my nervous system. Was this how Linda Blair felt before she turned green? Do you get signs first, or is it an immediate transformation to pea soup and salty talk? I tried to hide it, but there was a hideous truth lurking in the Small World boat: I was not hating it.

Get it together, I said to my pulled strings. *This here is not* Sophie's Choice *or* Schindler's List, *it's not even* Rudy. *You didn't cry at* The Champ, *so you don't cry here. This is simply a Benetton ad underscored by a song that would make anyone in their right mind lose their will to live. Yes, the air conditioning is a boon and the kids seem to have that stupid magic in their eyes the commercials swear by, but come on, man, remember who you are! Stop making eye contact with the dolls. Don't look at the kids. And, for God's sake, turn a deaf ear to that music. Yes, it's a small world—no one said it wasn't.*

I don't want to blame Minnie for what happened next, but really, who else in the world had such a puny bladder? And what was with Pluto, peacemaker all of a sudden, giving me the business about how you can't help it if you have to go? Why bother studying the Book and mapping out a day if all members of your group have to step off your plan every twenty-eight seconds to find a bathroom? Why even make an itinerary the night before, if this is how everyone is going to treat it? This is exactly why I never studied in school.

Also, wasn't Buzz constantly yammering about having a crackerjack sense of direction? Well then, how was it that the bathroom search he took the lead on veered us so off course? I didn't just blame Minnie, I blamed the whole lot of them. If they hadn't been so cavalier about the plan, then we would have been standing in line for Ariel's Grotto instead of Keystone Copping through super dull Liberty Square, ending up exactly where the day started—on Main Street, USA, where the fake sidewalks were suddenly jammed with camera-ready guests. And then, the music piped in.

Fuck me, I thought. *Here comes a parade.*

It started, as all parades do, with the low-hanging fruit. A bunch of wannabe summer stockers, dressed in head-to-toe turquoise or red or yellow polyester outfits topped off by shiny white vests, waving and sashaying and smiling like freaks, mostly following the Dr Pepper–commercial choreography. I stood on my tippy toes to see what was coming next and also to note how long we'd be stuck there, because good luck escaping a parade in those parts. The Book said not to even try. I leaned against a pretend mailbox to wait the thing out like a bad storm.

I hate a parade. I don't even understand what a parade is. Who needs all that waving? The world gets all hostile when you admit to hating a parade, like there is something wrong with you if you don't see the charm. People scrunch up their faces and tell you to take off your cranky pants. These are the same types who yell, "Smile! It's not that bad!" if you walk down the street with a plain face. I could see Mickey in the distance, high atop his float, again with the waving, but there was no end in sight. Meanwhile, my kids were waving like maniacs, too, in the hopes of getting character attention. They could not have been more pleased about our whole life-is-what-happens-when-you're-busy-making-plans moment. *Kids are dumb*, I thought.

I was so focused on trying to see the end of the procession, I almost missed what was right in front of me: Chip 'n' Dale! My guys. They waved and danced their rodential hearts out, swinging their short arms and tapping their feet. They were pretty graceful for chipmunks. Chip, as always, was the brains of the operation—you could just tell from his dancing and the way he could connect with the crowd. And Dale? Well, he was a moron, but man, did he love a good time.

They still possessed a strong work ethic, not only as rodents but also as showmen. Unlike a certain princess, who shall remain nameless, totally phoning it in with a limp wave and, if we're being honest, kind of a grumpy face. Stitch, meanwhile, must have sensed the sheer professionalism of Chip 'n' Dale, because there he was with my boys, really trying to put it on with maniacal waving. He had a bad walk, if you could even call it that. It really was closer to something between a waddle and a lumber. And when he waved, he did this whole rotate-his-arm-over-his-head maneuver, but without any verve. Like he was stretching. Plus he was wearing three ties. He didn't even make any sense.

Settle down, Stitch, I thought. *No one cares about your slick fur and oversized eyes. No one even knows who you are! Like anyone is even here to see you—good luck with the whole autograph thing. Look around, asshole, you're not even on a backpack or a shirt. You are not etched in the hearts of any. And we all know about your ride. So ease up with that wave and move along. And why don't you watch how the real critters do it? Three ties, give me a break—you're only embarrassing yourself.*

My nature is tricky, my attitude rarely good. I am not a joiner or a gamer or a person who knows much about fun. Even as a kid I was uncomfortable in my skin. Hating things and sitting in the back row of math was often bait to lure other struggling kids. I wasn't mean or anything (except for a brief spell from '78 to '80), just sad and kind of weird.

When situations get the better of me, I seek out a like mind. Just like in high school, I locate the person in the room with the worst attitude and hitch my curmudgeon wagon to their dispirited horse. Safety in numbers and all that (although the numbers are rarely high, and I can promise you we are not the group you want to invite to your costume party). Waiting outside (another) bathroom for Minnie (again), I spotted none other than Gaston himself, positioned outside Gaston's Tavern. He was all hopped up, flexing and preening and jaw jutting. Bunches of small girls and large women lined up in the hopes of a second with this miscreant, who had his own restaurant and a prime spot in the Villains parking lot.

Lurking around Gaston was a man, sixty years old if he was a day, wearing shortish brown pants with a ragged hem, and a butterscotch-colored shirt. Rounding out the outfit was a rectangular nameplate pinned to his chest, letting us know his name was John. Observing this man on the melting sidewalk, dressed like a Lost Boy in pants he'd most probably had in his closet when he was a kick-the-can–playing kid decades earlier, I knew he showed promise. I wasn't sure what his official job was, be it restaurant greeter or Gaston-wrangler, but he had a fabricated smile and an aura of droop. This was my guy.

The sun was a blazing spotlight on us all, but at least we had armor in hats and sunglasses and Mickey umbrellas. John was defenseless on the streets of Fantasyland, squinting and wiping the sweaty droplets pooling in the crags of his face. I tried getting his attention with eye contact but he wasn't noticing. Probably had trouble focusing, what with the sweaty eyes and all, so I did something I rarely do.

"You look hot, John."

I should note here that I never call a waiter by his or her name. That's a move reserved for dads and people who say "pardon my French." But the man refused to see me, so I was left with no choice.

"Excuse me?" he said.

It hit me that my wording might not have suggested casual conversation but more of a pickup situation, insinuating that John looked hot/sexy in his peasant shirt and Tom Sawyerish pants.

"Warm," I said. "You look like you're kind of warm out here."

"Me? Oh, no," said John, turning on the cast member smile. "Not at all!"

"Sure is hot out here," I said, switching to a more folksy tone.

"Much better than yesterday!"

"I guess. But, come on, it's pretty hot out."

"Can't get mad at sunshine!"

"Well, you *can*," I said.

"It's better than the alternative!"

"Really? You wouldn't love a little rain or snow right now?"

The ring of sweat spread under the arms of his flouncy shirt. "Come now. It's a beautiful day!"

"Is it?"

"Sure is!"

"Okay, fine," I said. *Well played, John.*

"Have a magical day!"

Settle down, John. You won.

No matter how many lemons I pelted at John, he made a delightful and refreshing pitcher of lemonade. I was off my game. I blamed the park. John probably had been required to take some sort of malcontent's defense course in order to get the job. *Can't wear the shipwreck pants until you pass. They must never break you*, the teacher would say. *Never let on anything is wrong here. Ever. If cats start getting out of bags, the guests will see that deep down, you are sad.*

"Look! There's Smee!" I said to Pluto as our galleon flew over the London sky, dipping in and out of mountains and volcanoes and Neverland and the Darling household. I wasn't clear why our boat was flying any more than I understood why I was at it again with the crying. It's also unclear why, upon disembarking, I was pissed at the kids for exiting through the gift shop (as you are forced to do on every ride) and breezing through without asking for so much as a stuffed crocodile or, at the very least, an eye patch.

"Let's go on it again!"

You know who said that? Me. I said that. I wanted to ride again. And again and again. And it wasn't just Peter Pan's Flight. It was the Many Adventures of Winnie-the-Pooh and Under the Sea: Journey of the Little Mermaid and Mickey's PhilharMagic (where I wore 3-D glasses over my regular glasses and wept under both pairs). It was the clean fake streets you could eat entire meals off of, and those calm, reassuring voices that came out of magical speakers when rides broke down at scary moments. The kids were happy and Buzz was enjoying himself, all right, but me? When I wasn't paying attention, someone put something in my twenty-seven-dollar water— possibly a Disney roofie—because I was one minute shy of pushing down my own children to secure a closer place in line to hear some Enchanted Tales with Belle. I was in the middle of a Best Day Ever.

Uh-oh, I thought. *What the fuck is happening to me?*

(3. bargaining)

Dear God,

Please help me.

In the spirit of honesty, which I'm guessing is a big deal for you, I just wanted to put out there that I don't believe in you (no offense). But, on the small chance that I'm wrong (like when I insisted the Internet was a harebrained scheme no one would cotton to), I thought I'd try, just in case. If this helps, I'm not against the idea of you, or the potential collective energy thing, but I felt dopey entitling this letter Dear Universe, even though I now live in Vermont and am fine with the whole *Kumbaya*-and-kale business. Let me also take this opportunity to apologize for making the rabbi remove your name, in its entirety, from our wedding ceremony twelve years ago. And also for saying *Oh, my God* so much, or worse, *OMG*, which really I just do in that annoying teenager voice to make fun of others.

I'm writing to you from Adventureland. It's an odd sort of place, a mix of jungle and desert and tropical island. To get here, you have to cross this wooden plank of a bridge, which is pretty congested and actually kind of dangerous, because people are driving their Rascal scooters at high speeds and they have no problem running over feet. Anyway, to the matter at hand . . .

I'm pretty sure I'm just dehydrated, nothing this forty-five-dollar icy Dole pineapple Whip won't fix. I'm almost positive this treat and break is all I need to be shocked back to my regular self, but on the slim chance it's not, this is where you come in. Lord, I seem to be one minute shy of buying a full-on Snow White costume and a Goofy hat.

Please, God, if I promise to never yell at my kids again, will you help bring back my cranky hate-everything self? What if I promise to call my mother—will you do something about all this crying on the rides? If I promise to teach Minnie and Pluto about you and all your stuff, or at the very least play them the original cast recording of *Godspell*, will you lend a hand? I'll devote my life to whales and hungry people. I'll stop judging others. I'll do whatever it takes if you just ease me back into my comfort zone. I'm open to making a deal, too. You don't have to bring me all the way back, just give me a slight push to the place where I snicker at my mother-in-law's love of the fanny pack and not secretly wonder if they sell them here. Can you even hear me?

I'm all turned around here, God. At one point today, Minnie needed a break, wanted to sit out a ride. You know what I did? I told her to *man up*. I basically used force to have her ride Splash Mountain with me. I don't even want to go back to the hotel to rest like the Book said. When we got our Dole Whips, Minnie got the orange to my pineapple (both of which were dreamy, but hers tasted like the best Creamsicle you've ever had), and I said that I'd definitely be getting the orange kind next time we came to Disney. Buzz stopped drinking his gargantuan pineapple float and said, "Next time?!" Come on, God, this is retarded.

This is all Buzz's fault. If he'd had a less tortured upbringing or one sleepover party at his house growing up, or even dealt with any of the above, I wouldn't be sitting here across from the Swiss Family Treehouse, devouring this bewitching pineapple Whip (no, seriously, you have to try one). Between me and you, I can't handle this. I'm all smiles and light and I want to participate in everything. Even parades. *Parades!* I don't even care that I'm dripping to death (although if there is something you can do to turn the temperature down, I think everyone would appreciate it).

Do you have some sort of suggestion box? Because I have some ideas. Simple stuff like forcing me and Buzz to get in a

fight or making me wait forever in a line, only to close the ride
for repairs as soon as it's our turn. I'd even settle for vomiting up
this exquisite toxic yellow confection. If you do this for me, in
return I'll send Mickey and Pluto to a Jewy Sunday school (or is
that Saturday school? Maybe an online thing? Do you do that?).
I'll go out right now and buy a seder plate and throw salty waters
on a shank bone. I'll do unto others. Just please, God, make me
feel bad again before I have a full-on nervous breakdown. But
first let me just see how long a wait it is to get back onto Peter
Pan's Flight.

Thank you.

Amen.

(4. depression)

I felt pretty jazzed about my talk with God.

Minnie and I barely had to wait in line for Splash Mountain,
and when it broke down right at the top of the drop, in the dark
before a rapid descent, instead of needing to breathe into my popcorn bag I enjoyed the cool air and the soothing voice assuring us
that life, as we knew it, would resume shortly. Not the sign I was
hoping for. When someone offered us two FastPass tickets to Big
Thunder Mountain (Pluto's favorite ride, one we'd already been
on four times), causing a mirth flare-up, my belief began to waver.
And when the four of us sat in the saloon-style theater, watching
life-sized bear puppets singing folksy songs about country life
and child abuse, and the slutty bear was lowered from the ceiling
and I laughed harder than the rest of the audience, maybe even
clapped, I lost the faith completely. God hadn't heard a word I'd
said. I was still happy. How depressing.

"I think Minnie and I are done," said Buzz. "We're hungry."

Fine, I thought. *Whatever.*

Pluto wanted to ride the roller coaster for the fifth and final time.

"We'll be in Tomorrowland, eating," Buzz said. "Just text me when you're off and we'll meet up and go home."

Minnie perked up at the idea of food and bed. Pluto was grabbing at my hand to get back to the haunted gold-mining town. Moments ago, I would have knocked over a few wheelchairs to board that runaway train, but now? Well, it was all I could do to get off the bench. *Who cares?* I thought. *You go up, you go down, big deal.*

"If you want," Buzz said, before heading into Tomorrowland, "you could do Space Mountain before we go."

"Maybe," I said.

"I think I'm too tired, Mom," said Minnie. "Is that okay?"

It was fine. I was used to navigating the dark alone anyway. Happy, sad, alone, together—what's the point? Weren't we all on a giant roller coaster in the dark, alone, anyway? I mean, really.

Pluto ran down the ramp into the phony abandoned mine shaft. "Don't forget to hold me with your arm again. Like last time."

I knew the drill: once safety bar is secured, use arm as extra seat belt. Wait for Pluto to test by pushing arm, hard, because otherwise Pluto is convinced he'll fall out. I'd already done it four times.

The sun hovered above the Magic Kingdom. Using its last moments up in the sky in a show-off move, it turned orange, casting an enchanting golden-hour light across the (frontier) land. Beautiful. Naturally, I wept.

Clickety-click up the rickety track. Pluto pushed my arm repeatedly, testing my strength. We moseyed up, a mix of dread and thrill taking over. Finally, our mine shaft car was at the top. Perched. Balanced. Paused.

I surveyed the Magic Kingdom.

I seat belted my son.

I wondered how much it would cost for a time-share.

Fuck.

And we plunged.

Whoosh down the tracks, our bodies jerked and heaved, faces peeled back with the wind.

"Tighter!"

I got you, I thought. His body wouldn't fit this perfectly in my arm forever, so I tightened my grip. *Don't worry, I got you.*

"Is it over?" He'd asked me this question, on the hour, since we entered the park that morning. I held Pluto's small hand as we exited the haunted mine. "Are we going home?"

I nodded.

"I'm a little bit sad," he said.

(5a. acceptance)

People ooze from every spoke and hub. The Electrical Parade looms and a *Lord of the Flies* situation is brewing, as sweaty and frazzled guests try securing plum spots. I'd read a hundred times over to avoid parade routes, but this humdinger seems to cross every part of the Kingdom. We are surrounded.

The sky is moonless, and all around me voices sound underwatery. My scalp tingles, my skin's damp, and I am abruptly overwhelmed with a hunger I believe is plotting to take me down. Pluto and I continue through the masses. We are pieces of well-done meat in the corporate capitalist soup. I feel all my personalities of the day seeping out of me. My mental skin is disintegrating. I am Cinderella at midnight. I need to get out.

Buzz texts me.

Buzz: Eating by the castle. Near Tomorrowland. Where are you?

In a typical Buzz move, he calls right after texting. Tells me he is at a place called Cosmic Ray's. I vaguely recall seeing a *Jetsons*-style eatery earlier and head in what I think is its general direction. I yank Pluto, pretend it's a game.

I text Buzz back.

Kim: In the restaurant. Where are u. (I have a brief fight with myself for spelling you with a u, but quickly let myself off the hook because the situation is dire.)
Buzz: On castle side.

I don't know what he means. That damn castle is on every side. Except in the restaurant I am in. I see no castle. *I see no castle.*

Kim: I am freaking out. Don't know where you are!
Buzz: Relax. At Cosmic Ray's. Bay 3.
Kim: I don't know where that is!
Buzz: Where are i.
Buzz: U.
Buzz: it's at the my race of Tomorrowland.

(What is he even saying?)

I find my way to the *Jetsons* place and stand by the ordering counter.

Kim: at ordering counter of Jetsons place.
Buzz: entrance of Tomorrowland. Go to nay 3.
Buzz: bay 3.

I smile at Pluto, and probably look like an insane clown. I don't know what the hell Buzz is talking about with the bays. I am helpless all of a sudden. In the paper bag people can't find their way out of.

Kim: I don't understand the bays!!!!

(*Four* exclamation marks. I despise the overuse of these things. Officially losing it.)

The phone rings. I am in one of those kidnapping movies all of a sudden and have been up for six nights drinking coffee with Ray Liotta waiting for a call from some creep who stole a kid. I don't even say hello when I answer. I am Harrison Ford gone mental, awaiting instruction.

Buzz speaks loud and slow into the receiver. "Ask someone where Cosmic Ray's is. We are in bay three."

I don't want to ask anyone for directions, but if I don't, Pluto will have to scrape me off the floor when parade-goers trample me. Lady in hairnet tells me where to go, and I grab Pluto's hand for the last time. Power through.

Minnie sees me first. I am pale and clammy. She hugs me. "I. Need. A. Coke."

"Ew, Mom, really? Soda?"

I want to knock her down but I let her lead me to the table instead. I stare into nothingness until Buzz returns with a red sticky tray. On it sits a large Coke, a basket of undercooked fries, and a gorgeous thirty-seven-dollar hot dog.

(5b. acceptance)(ish)

On the monorail, to the shuttle, to the Heroes parking lot, Buzz was back on his iPhone, Minnie reminded me that she was exhausted and how long until we were at the hotel because she had to go to the bathroom, and Pluto cried because he wasn't allowed to open his Buzz Lightyear Space Ranger Ion Pulse Cannon and Target Set to save the Galactic Alliance from the Evil Emperor Zurg until we got in the car. Not yet at Simba 111, and the Disney tingle was wearing off. I didn't feel well. I got into a small fight with myself.

Knock it off, I thought. *It's not like you had the best time in the world or anything. Disney tested your malcontent mettle—it was a fierce opponent. Chalk it up to a brief lapse in personality, a chink in the armor and all that. Anyway, it's not like you have to tell anyone what happened. Just go home and take a* Silkwood *shower and scrub off all the pixie dust the park threw at you. No one has to know. Ooooh! Look! Fireworks! Awwwww, so pretty. No! No, no, no! Look away. Be gone, Magic Kingdom. We don't need your kind around here. You, Disney, are a big bully. You, Disney, are a date rapist.*

I walked off that monorail with my head (sort of) held high. I never did end up riding Space Mountain. I couldn't go around fixing all my broken baggage. Plus it soothed me knowing many handles and zippers were still busted. And, in my quiet moments, I still contend that at least, at the *very* least, I didn't buy that darling tiara.

I Don't Have a Happy Place

......

Sometimes I feel bad my mother isn't an alcoholic. Equally troubling is how my brother never killed anyone and that my father only likes me as a friend. If any of the above were my reality, my attitude and daily mood would be appropriate, standard behavior for someone in my situation. People would nod as I shuffled past, whispering how they'd be the exact same way were they forced to live under such conditions. They might even cheer me on when I ventured out to the supermarket, but still keep their distance lest they catch what I was plagued with.

The problem is I wasn't born into brothels, nor did I fight for survival in a concentration camp; I was raised in a regular old Canadian suburban town in the 1970s. And while my mother was nauseous a lot and my father wore makeup, I really never had any legitimate, solid excuse for being unhappy. Which, if we're being honest, kind of stinks.

I come from a long line of malcontents. A small tribe of depressants, neurotics, and mental patients. We run the gamut from garden-variety depression all the way up to paranoid schizophrenia, covering most of the *DSM-V* in between. The pessimism in my family is Olympic. Unhappiness and negativity course through our (probably diseased) veins. And, in a cruel trick of nature, we tend to live a long, long time.

We do die eventually, though. A few years back, I lost three out of four grandparents in the span of one year. We huddled up at the shiva call, mildly joking how often we'd put on our black clothes that year, sharing deli meat and repeating how we wished we were seeing each other under different circumstances. My uncle ambled over, potato knish in hand, in an attempt to avoid participating in other conversations by joining ours. Ace told the group that we could take a collective breath, rest easy for a spell, because bad things always happened in threes.

"Uh, don't say *that*," my uncle said.

"Why not?" said Ace, confused.

My uncle shook his head. "Because then it starts all over again . . ."

Later that night in our hotel bed, Buzz repeated my uncle's line a hundred times over. "How do you ever win with that outlook?"

My sad sack uncle is right. Eventually, three more bad things will plague each of us. I imagine, for regular people, once the trauma quota is filled, they take a break. Maybe even enjoy some time off, go fishing, or take in a game. In theory, I'd like to be one of those fishing game–watchers, I really would, but my setting is a little bit too gloomy for recreational activities, or living. People say happiness is a choice, but I think that's just what happy people say when they go out together to be happy. I don't really care for going out.

At this point in my story, I'm used to my setting. It's a defect really, an emotional limp. On the days I leave the house, I can joke about the foundation of my personality, which I have to because I live in a small town now and run into people all the time. And although they still don't know what to make of me, I can promise they'd way rather think I'm the love child of Larry David and Woody Allen than listen to the Sylvia Plath–itudes that often sneak out of my mouth when I'm asked, casually, how I'm doing.

It's taken me almost my entire life to understand my wiring. I've spent most of my years thinking I was just in a bad mood. I was actually in a bad mood for twenty-nine years before it occurred to me that was an awful long time to be cranky. It was then I finally called for backup.

Let me note that this was not my first trip to a therapist. I was sent at nine years old due to a very bad case of what my parents dubbed "behavioral problems." Buckled into my mother's silver 1976 Corvette T-top, I had no clue where we were headed, as the Bee Gees quietly insisted that we should be dancing. My mother wore smart navy slacks, worrying her cuticles while gripping the top of the steering wheel. She wasn't a chitchatterer, minus occasional mentions of hazardous weather or recent death, so when we pulled into the parking lot she turned off the car and stared out the windshield.

"Okay," she eventually said, sounding annoyed. "Let's go."

The car abutted a sign suggesting we park for only one hour. I read the words backwards in my head—my latest obsession. After a few rounds, I asked my mother where we were.

"When we're done," she said, "you can have a bag of chips."

Dr. Ingrid Kalisky was the first grownup I'd met who had a bowl haircut. I imagined her walking into the salon armed with a photo of Dorothy Hamill, asking for the faddish wedge she'd seen all over the television, and later trudging out, swearing under her breath never to return to *that* place again. Dr. Kalisky had also boarded the feminist bandwagon, evidenced by her dark trousers, but one-upped my mother by adding a three-button vest and maroon necktie to her getup.

I slouched and Dr. Kalisky talked about herself. I paid less attention to her credentials, fixating on more intriguing matters—her chair. It was squat, swivelly, exactly like the ones on *The Mike Douglas Show*. And since Dr. Kalisky was already sporting a tie and making introductions, I took it upon myself to pretend I was a guest on the program, like Adrienne Barbeau or Wayland Flowers & Madame.

Having recently exchanged my desire to be a diner waitress for an imagined career in ventriloquism, I was ready. My allowance afforded me a slim volume on the craft, which I'd flipped through once but didn't understand. However, I'd seen enough talk shows to know you could lose your audience if you didn't have a charming story at the ready. I plotted mine, organizing an amusing chestnut about how, not having a ventriloquist dummy, I was left to my own devices, forced to hone my burgeoning artistry by draping our Yorkshire terrier's yellow plastic raincoat and bonnet over my arm to practice. The sounds of laughter and swelling applause bounced around my head, assuring me I was killing.

Kalisky, on the other hand, didn't seem as enthused, and her raisin eyes sent poisonous darts deep into my soul. But really, what good was being a nine-year-old ventriloquist with behavioral problems if you didn't gum up the works every now and again? First, I entertained the idea of answering her questions using my fist as a puppet but worried she'd send me straight to a mental institution, so I created a private challenge instead, just to bug her. The rules were thus: Scan the bookshelves, and if I recognized a single title, then, and only then, would I be able to answer any of her mental health probings.

"So," said Kalisky, "why are you here?"

Swinging of the boots. Eyes fluttering. Shrug.

"Well, why do you think?"

The top shelf had all the fat, important-looking textbooks. Below those were volumes like *The Drama of the Gifted Child* and *On Becoming a Person*, things I'd never seen out in the real world. I stayed mum.

"I'm fine to sit here until you are ready," Kalisky said, gripping her Bic. "I have all day."

I was scanning the lower shelves when I saw it: *Passages: Predictable Crises of Adult Life*. I knew that book well: the wine-colored cover, the way the rainbow-hued bubble letters seemed to be walking up stairs. My mother owned two copies. It was now my move. I could advance on the game board, say something insightful.

"I don't know," I said.

"Bullshit!"

"Excuse me?"

"Ab-so-lu-te bullll-shit," she said, stretching her words like taffy. "You, my dear, know very well why you are here. To pretend that you don't is complete and utter bull crap."

My ears tingled. I didn't offer up any facts about myself.

"Mmmmhmmm," Kalisky said. "Keep it up. Keep up the bullshit."

She seemed kind of hostile. By the third outcry of *bullshit*, she lost me. The first one, I'll admit, kicked up some dirt. It was not common practice in the Marlo Thomas era for adults to swear at kids. It's not that I'd never heard that kind of talk before. I'd used it myself, on occasion. But I didn't expect it to be hurled my way by an adult, especially a professional one. As the session progressed, no matter my answer, Kalisky called *bullshit*. You could tell she found this technique revolutionary and cutting edge, like it gave her a sense of badassness not usually reserved for the macramé belt–wearing set. It was a tedious hour.

When time ran out, Kalisky sent me home with some nonsense on poster board, suggesting that if I cleaned my room and stopped throwing things at my mother, I would get a sticker. Once enough stickers were amassed, a prize would be mine. If we're being honest, the only thing I ever threw at my mother was a pair of those brightly colored sun goggles we wore back then, the ones with the little cutouts that made you look like a bug. I, for one, didn't believe a single tossing incident necessitated a Magic Markered chart and six weeks of smutty language. It was a drag to sit there. Plus it really cut into my after-school crank-calling hours. The good news was that follow-through was not a strong family trait. Eventually my mother tired of the chart and its scratch-and-sniff fruit stickers. I never threw anything at her again. I was cured.

The next time I visited a therapist happened three months before my thirtieth birthday. Not a ventriloquist but a talent agent's assistant in Manhattan, I was very busy being terrible at my job, feeling consistently under the weather, and weeping. Some other ways to describe me at that time:

1. cynical

2. negative

3. dejected

4. skeptical

5. hermetic

6. introverted

I am not trying to be a wisenheimer when I say I truly didn't think there was anything out of the ordinary in that depiction.

It was just a list of words, a flawless one, to describe my personality.

One of my coworkers didn't agree with my assessment and slipped me a business card on her way out to fetch a roasted vegetable salad for lunch. She was a literary agent and she intrigued me. Not only was she a dead ringer for Wonder Woman and at least six feet tall, but she managed to pull off wearing this voguish salmon-colored suit. I wanted her to like me. I assured her I'd promptly call when I got home.

Did I promptly call? No. I promptly took umbrage. I hailed from a long line of crabby people, none of whom got help, so why should I? *What nerve,* I thought, *looking like Wonder Woman and pretending to use her superpowers for good, like I needed some kind of saving. Just because you got away with being a maypole and somehow still looking classy in a suit that could have doubled as a platter of lox at a bris, does not mean you are the authority on all things mental health.* I spent the next three days giving her dirty looks from afar. I made sure to *tsk* and *pffft* a few times when she breezed by my desk. I made fun of her unwieldy hair. Her dumb suit. And *then* I made the call.

The waiting room rendered me a day player in a Woody Allen picture. The Upper West Side address, the faded terra-cotta Oriental rug—I almost expected Diane Keaton (or Wiest) to walk out of the office with crumpled tissues and an oversized hat. Should I knock on the door or wait to be collected? I coughed, shuffling the *New Yorkers* around to signal my arrival. There was a small round noise machine, placed right outside the door, that was supposed to drown out the sobbing coming from inside, but that apparatus wasn't fooling anyone with its gentle whirring. It wasn't a barricade, it was one of those giant shells you put to your ear, convinced you hear the ocean. I made a mental note to not raise my voice above a whisper when it was my turn.

The door opened, at long last, and out popped the Lorax's mother. After taking in her pencil skirt, complete with purple and chartreuse felted swirly appliqués, and an updo so unnaturally red it brought to mind Atomic Fireballs, I wanted to go home. What would this character know about the likes of me—clearly I wasn't wearing a Bar-ba-loot suit, so where would we go with this? She motioned me in, showing me to a black leather chair. She hadn't even uttered a sound yet and already I deemed her a complete idiot and this whole exercise a colossal waste of time.

"Why don't you tell me why you are here?" Mama Lorax said.

I didn't say a thing—I hated audience participation of any kind, plus I wanted her to intuit what was wrong with me, figure it out, if she was such a hotshot. Shifting on her couch, she breathed evenly and stared, therapist code for *You have rented me for the hour. I can wait.*

"Why do I sit in a chair and you on the couch?" I said. "Isn't the patient supposed to sit on the couch? Or lie on the couch?"

"Client."

"What?"

"I prefer to call them clients. Not patients."

There was little sunlight filtering in. The ficus in the corner hung on for its life.

"Would you like to sit on the couch?" she said. "Would that make you feel more comfortable?"

"No." I tried settling, to have good posture, but the chair was slippery and hissed when you moved. "It's just this chair makes all kinds of weird and awkward noises."

"Do you feel weird and awkward being here? Is that how sitting in that chair makes you feel?"

And there it was. The quintessential *How does it make you feel* question. Cardigan-wearing shrinks all over town were asking their patient-clients how everything made them feel. Bad, Lady Lorax, it makes me feel bad. That is why I am here, because I feel bad. I feel bad all the time and apparently, according to Wonder Woman, it is bad to feel bad all the time. I made a mental note to quit my job.

"Look," I said, throwing her some chum. "I'm about to turn thirty. And don't ask me how that makes me feel because it makes me feel like I'm in *Ordinary People*."

"It bothers you when I ask you how you feel?"

"Kind of."

"Why?"

"I don't know." I crossed and recrossed my legs. We stared at each other in silence, like the cowboys on those old Sunday afternoon westerns Zaida Max used to watch on TV.

"Because it's dumb."

"Dumb?"

"Yes. It feels dumb. It's so clichéd, that question. Can't you do better?"

I was agitated and surly and wanted to get out of there. I didn't feel like sharing anything with her. Also, I seemed to not recall one thing I'd wanted to talk about before I got there. Mama Lorax could sense my urge to flee.

"How about I promise to refrain from asking that question for the rest of our time together?"

She was waving a white Thneed at me, so I gave her a break. Don't get me wrong, I was still going to continue hating her, but, regardless, I would participate, because I needed her to like me. I needed everyone to like me, no matter how I felt about them. It was a problem.

So out came the dogs and ponies and organ grinder monkeys. I wanted her to enjoy me so much, be so entertained, that when she was filling up her Ball jar with water at the cooler she'd feel

compelled to tell my stories to the other crackpots in the building. Gold star, favorite, teacher's pet—I wanted her to like me
best. I pelted my best material at her and before I knew it the
time was up. I stood, but to my surprise she put her hand up
to signal that I remain in that rambunctious chair. I guessed it
was time for the awkward exchange of money or a check, but
instead she had some final remarks. Mama Lorax did more staring, which I believed to be some sort of shrink voodoo, retrieving
a pencil from her updo, until she felt she had my full attention.
She opened her mouth, and in a voice just north of a whisper she
asked me this:

"Can't. Kim. Be. Happy?"

Well, now she'd gone and done it. Her psychobabble barely
settled in the air before *Can't Kim be happy* became the punch line
to every joke for the next ten years. It started slow. If I recounted
a bad day to a friend, we'd end the story with the facetious *Can't
Kim be happy?* When choosing an outfit or a movie or what to
order at Bagel World, I'd use the sentence as fodder. Eventually
I became expert at it, able to even shuffle the words around. If a
friend had a long day: Can't said friend be tired? If they wanted
a certain food: Can't so-and-so eat potatoes? Can't phones ring?
Can't syrup be sticky? Can't winter be cold? It was the bumper
sticker of my life.

The joke wore thin as I entered my fortieth year. Okay, it
didn't really lose its punch at all, it still makes me laugh as I write
it, but I was pretending to be a responsible and mature member of society because I now had children. At a less-than-mature
forty-something, the tagline was still very much in my repertoire,
continuing to delight me. Problem was, little else did. A bit of
mockery does go a long way, but just not long enough. I was still
in a bad mood.

• • •

My favorite thing about therapists is how they never answer the phone. This allows the unhinged to leave weird, rambling messages without having to tangle with actual people who can see through them. It also gives the shrink time to judge your level of crazy on their own time, and, in turn, you can screen your calls to do the same. When this new therapist returned my message on a day when I was feeling particularly moody, I picked up the line and struggled to find a time in my schedule that worked for both of us. I hadn't even set foot in her office and already there was verbal judo and Wiccan trickery—and that was just setting up a time to meet. It was as if she could sense all my disorders through the phone lines, like she was already on to something. Not since my Ouija board spelled out the name of our dead family dog had I been so spooked. I still fear that if I even whisper anything resembling the therapist's name in the privacy of my own home, she'll know. Her wolf eyes and psychological superpowers will activate. She scares me a little bit. Let's not use her real name.

Dr. X was scrappy, might have beaten up a few MSWs in her day. We spent our first forty-five minutes together verbally sparring. This was no Dr. Kalisky saying the word *bullshit*, this was plunging an open fist into my innards and pulling out a bloody, mangled liver. I left her office (liverless) to walk from University Place down toward the very bottom of the city, dazed and unsure of what had just taken place. Part of me didn't want to return the following week but the other part was terrified she'd telepathically kill me in my sleep if I didn't. Dr. X had some Svengali maneuvers, and also possibly put some sort of addictive pharmaceutical in the tissue box, because I ended up returning to her chair, week after week, until I ran out of blood-drenched organs to carry home in my messenger bag.

Toward the end of session 2, Dr. X presented me with a small token. If not feeling well brings you to the doctor a few times yearly or forces you to spend much time with the trusty search engine and medical websites of your choice, you hope to leave with a parting gift—a diagnosis. I'm not talking pancreatic cancer or type 2 diabetes, but would it kill someone to hand over a minor condition? Something that simply required a mushroom tincture or prescribed sleep? And could they be so kind as to label it, preferably with a fancy title, allowing you to opt out of social engagements at your leisure? Naturally one doesn't want to hear they need a kidney transplant, just a cute disease to make all your mentions of feeling unwell not be in vain. Validation comes in all shapes and sizes, and wraps beautifully.

"I don't know what's happened in your life," said Dr. X, with seven minutes left to go. "But being dysthymic might have clouded some things for you."

Wait, wait, wait. Hold the phone. What did she say right there? *Dys*-something or other. I didn't hear a word she said after that big one, nor did I even bother to ask what it meant. I had something! I actually had something. A bona fide, official disorder. The gift was just my size, with a catchy title but seemingly casual enough to handle with talk and not heavy medication or a room at Bellevue. I was positively giddy. When Dr. X mentioned my malady, I nodded, which was my way of letting Dr. X know that I knew about the affliction so we wouldn't have to actually explore it. I certainly didn't want to do anything about it, I just wanted to have it. Plus I hated opening presents in front of others. I ran home to research.

How many hours had I spent at a computer, foraging for ailments and answers and relief? I'd finally moved up a station in life. No longer was I just a type-in-a-symptom sort, I had something real to look up. I hit those computer keys with relish, eager to see what my search would yield. There were many results, so that was good. Greek roots. A few descriptions. But the hope that had puffed me up not three minutes earlier dissipated. They tried to make the disorder seem fancy by translating it from the Greek, but it all just amounted to four words.

1. *ill* and *bad*

2. *mind* and *emotion*

Turned out that dysthymia (dys-*thigh*-me-ugh) was just low-level depression. I know, I know, I begged for something lightweight to call my own, but this didn't even seem like a real ailment. It was the gluten intolerance of mental disorders. I started making throaty noises at my desk. Buzz wandered over to see what the hubbub was all about.

"It just means 'mild depression,'" I said, hangdog.

"Isn't that a good thing?" he said.

"No, it's not a good thing." I wanted to throw my keyboard at him. "It's not even a *real* thing. It's just crummy old chronic mild depression. Big deal."

"Well," Buzz said. "It's chronic. Isn't that something?"

"No, it's not something. It's nothing! It's lame. *Uch*, even my depression is lame."

Buzz shook his head, wandering out of the room. "You're insane."

"Clearly I am not insane!" I said, following him into the kitchen. "If anything, I'm just low-level insane! Mild insane!"

"Look, you wanted a diagnosis and you got one. There's just no winning with you."

"Yes, there is," I said. "There is *too* winning."

"When? When is there winning?"

"Oh, there is winning," I said. "There is a lot of winning. Anyway, why are you so obsessed with winning? Do we all have to be winners? Winning is so stupid."

Buzz was agitated as he rummaged through the pantry. He shook a bag of chocolate granola in my face. "There is just no joy with you. You got exactly what you wanted and you're still unhappy. When are you *not* unhappy? Can't you just go lie in a field somewhere and call up your goddamn happy place?"

"I don't have a happy place!"

Buzz slowly put the granola on the counter. He gave me the once-over, taking in my flailing arms and tear-stained sweat-pants. And then he laughed. Buzz laughed, alone, for a good seven minutes.

"What a catch," he said, kissing my head. "What. A. Catch."

Mild depression. *Mild.* What did that even mean? Temperate? Gentle? Bland? If we're being honest, I found the diagnosis kind of insulting. *Mild.* Did people get mild leukemia? Did my depres-sion not have a good personality? Did it lack sizzle? Why was I being penalized for being able to get out of bed in the morning and not feeling sad and hopeless and lonely *enough*? My depres-sion didn't seem to be trying hard, it wasn't living up to its poten-tial—my depression was me in high school. Maybe I should have considered killing myself more often. Why couldn't I suffer from blinding depression instead of mild unrest? I imagined that in the olden days, at the very least they'd send people like me to the country, to lie down. Nowadays they leave you to your own devices, roaming free, and call you lame names. What about the gold standard, *depression* depression, the one where you wear your what's-the-point sweatshirt for seven weeks and can't even bring yourself to shower anymore? I wished I had that one instead.

I started cataloging all the other problems I'd had over the years, to see if they were equally bland. There was that spell after college where I felt uncomfortable leaving the house sometimes, but I still went out occasionally. I didn't start peeing in Ragu jars or eating the furniture. Probably just *mild* agoraphobia. I was always very scared to fly, imagining my fiery demise at least three days before I was slated to get on that oversized cigar tube. And even though I cry during takeoff and keep my eyes glued to the stews to make sure they look casual, I still get on the plane. *Mild* fear of flying. What was wrong with me? Who knew my deficiencies were so meek?

Surely I had problems that were out of the ordinary. What about my hypochondria? Because I don't feel well, you know. I never feel well. If I am not listless or feverish, then I am definitely coming down with cancer. That small red mark on my arm is probably mange. I know I once had SIDS. Remind me again what side the appendix is on? I spend countless hours on the computer researching the intricacies of lupus and taking "Are You Normal?" quizzes in magazines. My hypochondria spans both physical and psychological ailments. Not only am I dying but I am dying mental. I'll see your mild hypochondria and raise you one hamster-wheel brain whose incessant squeak reminds me hourly that I have little time left alive.

What about my negative attitude? Surely that would get me some sort of non-mild badge. I'm incredibly negative. I don't even think my brain has a side that accepts positive thinking. When receiving a compliment, I wonder what the person is *really* saying. If they tell me I am doing *this* well, aren't they just finding a creative way to say I can't do *that*? When I changed my daughter's first diapers, I wept because she'd be heading off to college. When I signed my book deal, the very first thing that came to mind was how I couldn't go on any sort of book tour because

I'm a terrible packer. And really, I didn't have that author reading voice, that one you hear on NPR or at those readings at the 92nd Street Y, that lilt and cadence of serious writers like Russell Banks, who write stuff about dead children and sound all smart and serious doing it. My head won't even entertain processing good news. It can't. It doesn't know how. I wouldn't call that mild. I'd actually call that super not mild.

I needed to consult someone about this pathetic diagnosis. Obviously I couldn't talk to Buzz, because he'd launch into some sports jargon about winning and then force me to guess how many grapes were in a bag. Lord knows my dear friend Shirley would be of no help. She'd come over to my house with her perspective in her organized purse, flinging her positive outlook in my face. "Why not look at it another way?" she'd say. "Why not think of it as *good-natured* depression, or *warm*, or *soft* depression?" *Uch*. She'd come to my own living room and say this stuff. I wanted Shirley to go home.

I wondered if Dr. X had even heard a word I'd said in that chair. How my body literally rejects happiness, kicks it to the curb. Or how I felt the day I saw that ad on TLC for a new reality show starring these conjoined twins, Abby and Brittany. There they were, coiffed and painted, as cameras documented their every labored move. These sisters would graduate and try to find jobs and go off to Europe with the biggest shit-eating grins on their faces, all the while having two heads on one body. One of them had a third arm removed, one that was growing out of her back. They shared a bladder. And still they looked like they'd won the lottery. I had regular old limbs sprouting out of me, mild limbs, and couldn't seem to find joy anywhere. Wasn't *that* depressing?

We moved to Vermont shortly after my nondiagnosis. Here, nestled into a small, lovely community, complete with fresh air and biblical morning skies, I notice that, on occasion, while still my regular old self, for some very brief pockets of time, I am feeling okay. Mildly so. Buzz has even mentioned that I seem happy. I tilt my head in confusion.

"Well, as happy as you get," he says. "Happy for *you*."

And then, like at the end of "a very special episode," I figure something out. (Can't Kim figure something out?) Sure, most days, my brain is a cluttered studio apartment I'd like to move out of. But occasionally, *occasionally*, I am now able to take a break from despondency or dying to allow something to sneak in that presents itself as a good feeling. It might occur when I am taking my despondency out for a three-hour walk. It could surface when my six-year-old son requests that I stop making dinner so we can snuggle or when my nine-year-old daughter asks to borrow a scarf so she can look like me or when Buzz laughs at something dumb I've said. It's fleeting. I've learned that about myself. But isn't all happiness fleeting? Even regular people's? Mine is just a little bit more fleeting, like a quick little tornado that sweeps into town, swirling out as fast as it came in. And, Dr. X, if you are reading this, I wouldn't call a tornado *mild*.

The characters implicated in my world should win a lifetime supply of Rice-A-Roni. I am exhausting and draining and something to be managed, like diabetes. Mind you, I am also a decent baker. Can't Kim be happy? Meh. Not really. My dear friend Shirley believes that your glass is as full as you let yourself pour. She's adorable that way. When it comes down to it, I really and truly do not have a happy place. But, on an off day, I might have a happy *moment*. It will leave me the second it gets here, but it gets here. Sometimes. And sometimes I can even see it. But don't think I've learned some big lesson or anything, and understand that for the most part, even if happiness does pester its way in, I feel uncomfortable letting it.

We live in a new, everyone's-a-winner era. They don't keep score at my son's T-ball game. When my daughter tries out for shows at our local youth theater, they all get the part. Everyone is celebrated all the time, even if they don't do anything. And the world's life wish for us is to be happy. Do we all *have* to be happy? What if one gets crampy walking in the meadow of bubbles and unicorns? What about the muddy field of unhappiness and constant discomfort? How come there aren't ribbons or trophies for sadness or searing despondency? Don't even get me started on if your despondency is lukewarm—or mild—and not even recognized by the pharmaceutical companies or the advertising world or the general public. We are not even considered an official group. Looks like everyone's a winner these days, except the dysthymics. We don't even rate. Which, I believe, makes us—makes me—a complete failure at depression. But at least I'm a failure. I couldn't be happier.

Acknowledgments

......

I often say the people in my life should win a lifetime supply of Rice-A-Roni. Or, at the very least, a reward or token for dealing with me. Baked goods are nice. . . .

For Jen Bergstrom, a plate of macaroons—sophisticated and styley like you, cookies-about-town. Please enjoy these treats in France, without me, because I don't like to travel. I hope they are life-changing, because that's what your initial call about my weird blog was for me.

For Tricia Boczkowski: a pineapple upside-down cake just like Rhoda Morgenstern would bring over to Mary's apartment when things weren't going so well at the window dressing gig. We'll polish off the cake while making fun of Phyllis, and you'll sharpen my words and sentences as beautifully as you do. I bet we share head scarves.

For Kate Dresser: lemon squares, neatly cut on a white plate, with just a touch of powdered sugar. I'd tell you when they'd be arriving, and you'd be one minute early to receive them. I'll email to make sure they got there; you'll respond immediately. You'll notice every single detail about said squares, and have the wherewithal and patience and sincerity and just enough OCD (the good kind) to discuss every last crumb. I will want to hug you.

For Meagan Brown and the rest of the folks at Gallery: I'm not sending one of those oversized tins of tri-flavored popcorn you get assaulted with at holiday time, but rather a giant assortment of cookies because, really, what says thank you for so much hard work better than cookies? I'll even throw in some sandwich varieties. That's how much I appreciate all you do.

Elana Stokes and Tanya Ferrell: For you, Wunderkinds, I will break out the candy thermometer (which I don't actually own yet, but will purchase when you force me out of my house). To you super-cool ladies, I will hand-deliver (see? I told you I'd leave the house) a box of freshly made caramels. Goat's milk caramels. Ones you can keep in gorgeous glass jars in your office or loose in your purses—little bursts of smooth, buttery energy you'll need in order to deal with me. Consider the scattered plastic wrappers around your lives reminders of how grateful I am for you.

For Hannah Brown Gordon: I once promised you a loaf cake—lemon, I believe—which I'm happy to send along. They're simple to make and slice, and they freeze well. But after thinking about it, I should probably send you a croquembouche: it's unusual and complicated and it looks kinda high maintenance and no one's really heard of it—it's the me of desserts. I'd put in the hours building it, making sure it never toppled over, and pluck it from obscurity, just for you—because that's what you've done so elegantly for me. And then some. But after rethinking my thinking, I realize I don't want to send you a dessert that signifies me. We've had enough of me—I need something just for you. I'll go back to my original loaf cake but make it in twenty-seven different varieties, with all kinds of icings and frostings and glazings, because I am awed at how many different hats you wear. And let me just say, you wear a hell of a hat. I'll also package up some peanut butter cookies, ones I make for special friends who stick their necks out and take chances on me. Thank you, Hannah. You deserve all these desserts. And the lifetime supply of Rice-A-Roni. Or maybe just my promise to lay low for a spell so you can eat all this stuff in peace.

To my shiny new Vermont community: You know who you are, mostly because I refer to you by your last name, probably shouting it in a field or across a parking lot. You are so nice to me and truly good friends. For you fantastic, welcoming, and supportive people, I will learn to bake pie. And I will personally hand-deliver each one to your respective homes so you don't have to attend another potluck.

To authors I don't actually know but who inspire me time and again—Tom Perrotta, Maria Semple, Judy Blume, David Sedaris, Jonathan Tropper, Meg Wolitzer, A.M. Homes (and so many more): I will just imagine sending you a crumb cake because I don't know where you live. Plus, if I did show up there, well, that's creepy.

To my parents and brother, I send those dumb oat bran muffins because it's a family joke that will never die and maybe it will make you laugh, since I'm not sure much else in the book will. How about I throw in some Nana Ella brownies for good measure—for your love and support and, of course, all that material.

For the mighty Louise Rozett, who is such a supportive friend and generous reader, I will create some Death By Chocolate business (even if it is on my list of things I don't care for).

For my fake-Cousin Lou, who is also a darn good reader, I will attempt to re-create the Lorna Doone because they're weird and so is he. (He's also really funny and talented and looks hilarious in a skeet-shooting vest.)

For Barry Waxman, or Bups, I will make some chocolate pudding with skin. But I will go beyond my baking duties and invent some sort of spray that instantly makes licorice and gummy bears stale. Yup, I'd do that for him. He's done so much for me.

For Elsa Waxman, I would come to your house so we could bake together. Of course neither of us would be showered. You'd take out that old recipe tin and find the card with your grandmother's mandel breit recipe and you'd teach me once and for all how to make it properly—just like you've taught me almost everything else in my life. We'd eat them at the counter, talking and laughing and each fighting over who did the worse job. And I'd feel like I was home.

I know, I know, Rebecca Waxman, you're a savory. Your baked goods will be to the tune of some sort of weird cheese-and-chive scone inside a croissant thing with grits, but I'll also be sure to whip up a batch oatmeal raisins (soft-baked) and stick a handful of Twix and a box of Mike and Ike's and some potato product in my capacious bag—we're going to need a lot of sustenance to discuss all that soup. But no matter what I'd bring, you'd find something lovely to say about it, because that's just how you are. The Shirley to my Laverne. Punch in the arm, Dude. I love you, Man. I swear I'd be dead without you.

Yes, Adeline Rose Waxman Bateman, I know you, too, prefer French fries to sweets, but still I'm sending over some banana pudding for you. But only if you don't read this. If you read the book, even though I've told you not to, I'm returning my Godmother crown. And you'll be returning the pudding. Look! Here you are, finally, in the book. Just because I love you.

For Rich, I will bake a banana cake with chocolate frosting AND a coconut cake with cream cheese frosting and snowy coconut flakes. Not because I can't make a decision (which I can't) but because you deserve both (although I will give them to you secretly because if our daughter sees you eating two cakes at once, there's gonna be trouble). I bake you two because that is so above and beyond and you are so above and beyond. If not for you, none of us would ever stop to take in the view, laugh as hard, or probably ever leave the house. Thank you, Buzz, for being the marrying kind. I absolutely adore you. And yes, the dishwasher is clean.

For Ella I will try my hand at an unfussy vanilla cheesecake, not only because it's your favorite but also because it seems like a mature dessert and you're the most mature member of our household. For Oscar I will bake up the most delicious chocolate cake with chocolate frosting and stick some chewy candies on top because that's kind of gross and you like that stuff. I will also make red velvet cupcakes and cookie pie and ice cream and brownies and smush them all together because I love you both so much I don't know what else to do sometimes but squish stuff together and make a big mess (one I will absolutely make you help me clean up). You are truly the joys of my life. Every moment I get with each of you makes my heart explode (no, Ella, not literally, I'm fine). I love you clowns more than anything. Thank you for making me a mom.

Obviously, I can't bake something for myself, because it's just weird to thank yourself, which, if I'm being honest, kind of stinks because I just found a recipe for Depression Cake, which sounds pretty good.